Meditation Expertise

Yoga Sūtras Analysis and Application

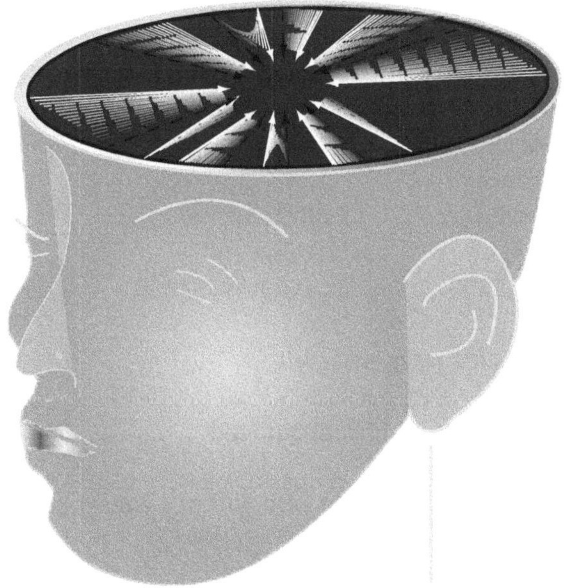

Michael Beloved

(Madhvācārya dās)

Original Sanskrit verse – downloaded from Sanskrit-Sanscrito

Devanagari script: Sanskrit 2003 Font
Transliteration: URW Palladio ITU font/ ITranslator
Word-for-Word typeset: Bernard Adjodha/Michael Beloved
Shiva Art: Sir Paul Castagna
Illustrations: Author

Correspondence:

Michael Beloved
3703 Foster Ave
Brooklyn NY 11203
USA

Paul Castagna
P.O. Box 150
Iron Belt WI 54536
USA

Email: axisnexus@gmail.com

ISBN
978-0-9819332-5-2
LCCN
2010907496

Sanskrit Text

ENGLISH
Transliteration Word-for-Word Meaning
TRANSLATION
Analysis
Application

Table of Contents

Meditation Expertise 1

Table of Contents 4

Scheme of Pronunciation 5

How to use this book: 6

A note on the diacritical marks and pronounciation: 6

Introduction 7

Chapter 1 Samādhi Pāda: Transcendence Accomplishment 9

Chapter 2 Sādhana Pāda: Practice Accomplishment 85

Chapter 3 Vibhūti Pāda: Glory Displayed 162

Chapter 4 Kaivalya Pāda: Segregation Accomplishment 226

Glossary of Sanskrit Terms 251

Index to Verses: Selected Sanskrit Words 262

Index to Verses: Selected English Words 265

Index to Analysis and Application 270

About the Author 284

Scheme of Pronunciation

Consonants

Gutturals:	क	ख	ग	घ	ङ
	ka	kha	ga	gha	ṅa
Palatals:	च	छ	ज	झ	ञ
	ca	cha	ja	jha	ña
Cerebrals:	ट	ठ	ड	ढ	ण
	ṭa	ṭha	ḍa	ḍha	ṇa
Dentals:	त	थ	द	ध	न
	ta	tha	da	dha	na
Labials:	प	फ	ब	भ	म
	pa	pha	ba	bha	ma

Semivowels:

य	र	ल	व
ya	ra	la	va

Numbers:

०	१	२	३	४	५	६	७	८	९
0	1	2	3	4	5	6	7	8	9

Sibilants:	श	ष	स
	śa	ṣa	sa

Aspirate: ह

ha

Vowels:

अ	आ	इ	ई	उ	ऊ	ऋ	ॠ
a	ā	i	ī	u	ū	ṛ	ṝ
ए	औ	ओ	औ	ळ	लॄ		:
e	ai	o	au	lṛ	lṝ	ṁ	ḥ

Apostrophe ऽ

How to use this book:

Make a casual reading page for page without becoming stressed about the concepts and ideas. Read to become familiar with the language style and presentation. If you read something of particular interest make a mental note of it and read on to get through the entire book.

Make a second reading pausing at areas of interest, where you feel you can grasp the material. Here and there, you may not follow the meanings but read on nevertheless.

Make a third reading with intent to grasp the concepts and methods given.

Finally, make an indepth study of this information.

A note on the diacritical marks and pronounciation:

A name like Krishna is accepted in common English usage. Its English spelling has no diacritical marks.

Sanskrit letters with a ***dot*** *under them, should be pronounced while the tongue touches and is released curling slightly at the top of palate.*

The **s** *sound for* ***ś*** *carries an* ***h*** *with it and is said as the* ***sh*** *sound in* ***she****.*

The **s** *sound for* ***ṣ*** *carries an* ***h*** *with it and is said as the* ***sh*** *sound in* ***shun****.*

The ***h*** *sound for* ***ḥ*** *carries an echoing sound of the vowel before it, such that* ***oḥ*** *is actually* ***oho*** *and* ***aḥ*** *is actually* ***aha****.*

In many Sanskrit words the ***y*** *sound is said as an* ***i*** *sound, especially when the* ***y*** *sound preceeds an* ***ā****. For instance,* ***prāṇāyāma*** *should be* ***praa-nai-aa-muh****, rather than* ***praa-naa-yaa-muh****.*

The ***a*** *sound is more like* ***uh*** *in English, while the* ***ā*** *sound is like the* ***a*** *sound in* ***far****.*

The ***ṛ*** *sound is like the* ***ri*** *sound in* ***ridge****.*

The ***ph*** *sound is never reduced to an* ***f*** *sound as in English. The* ***p*** *sound is maintained.*

Whenever ***h*** *occurs after a consonant, its integrity is maintained as an air forced sound.*

If the ***h*** *sound occurs after a vowel and a consonant, one should let the consonant remain with the vowel which preceeds it and allow the* ***h*** *sound to carry with the vowel after it, such that Duryodhana is pronounced with the* ***d*** *consonant allied to the* ***o*** *before it and the* ***h*** *sound manages the* ***a*** *after it. Say* ***Dur-yod-ha-na*** *or* ***Dur-yod-han****. Do not say* ***Dur-yo-dha-na****. Separate the* ***d*** *and* ***h*** *sounds to make them distinct. In words where you have no choice and must combine the* ***d*** *and* ***h*** *sound, as in the word* ***dharma****. Make sure that the* ***h*** *sound is heard as an air sound pushed out from the throat. Dharma should never be mistaken for darma. But* ***adharma*** *should be* ***ad-har-ma****.*

The **c** *sound is* ***ch****, and the* ***ch*** *sound is* ***ch-h****.*

Introduction

This Meditation Expertise is the full course for yoga as it was defined by Sri Patañjali Maharshi. All details are given but the practice itself must be instituted in the life of a yogin. Initially this translation with commentary was published under the title of *Yoga Sutras of Patañjali*. That book is still in print. This goes to complete that work by giving the application.

There are mind diagrams which give some idea of what a yogin or yogini should feel and perceive during meditative states. There are many definitions for yoga but this follows the meaning and expertise illustrated by Patañjali in the sutras. Yoga as a practice requires persistence and correct application. Yoga is not a beauty aid. It is not a remedy for bad health. Patañjali defines it as a practice for segregating the core-self from its perception equipment and for purifying the equipment and using the same while restraining the system from again becoming infused with impure energies.

This yoga has eight stages of development. Thus it is called ashtanga yoga. Should you practice it? Should you accept Patañjali as the authority of it?

Fortunately yoga is not a religion and it does not rescue its practitioners with a belief system. It challenges for practice and resulting experiences.

Chapter 1
Samādhi Pāda:
Transcendence Accomplishment

Verse 1

अथ योगानुशासनम्॥ १ ॥

atha yogānuśāsanam

atha – now; yogānuśāsanam = yoga – yoga and its practice + ānuśāsanam – explanation

This is the explanation of yoga and its practice.

Analysis:

Śrī Patañjali began with the term *atha* which means now or at this time, I will do something. He undertook the explanation of yoga and its practice, because before his time such an explanation was not presented in an academic way. He gave the syllabus for yoga, thus breaking the monopoly of the teachers who mastered yoga and taught it to their students bit by bit over the years.

Patañjali established a standard that could not be changed merely by a difference in philosophy. Just as a gasoline combustion engine manufactured in one country will be quite similar to one manufactured in another, so yoga practice will be the same everywhere, because the human body is similar in each case, and the means of changing the subtle form which produced that gross one also stays the same.

Application:

Śrī Patañjali *gave the explanation of yoga and its practice. To use this one has to be open-minded. Trust in* Patañjali *can be invoked on the basis of his being accepted by many ancient and modern yogis. He expounded the layout of yoga and gave a definitive reference.*

One legend describes Patañjali as an incarnation of Ādiśeṣa, a serpentine divinity.

Verse 2

योगश्चित्तवृत्तिनिरोधः ॥ २ ॥

yogaḥcittavṛtti nirodhaḥ

yogaḥ – the skill of yoga; cittavṛtti = citta – mento-emotional energy + vṛtti – vibrational mode; nirodhaḥ – cessation, restraint, non-operation.

The skill of yoga is demonstrated by the conscious non-operation of the vibrational modes of the mento-emotional energy.

Analysis:

Yoga is both personal and practical. It is not a group effort. Each student of yoga has to achieve higher states by himself or herself. Ultimately, yoga is an isolated and lonely course. This explains the reluctance of the public to learn advanced techniques. People like company but yoga requires the company of the self only. One must work exclusively with the psyche to be successful.

Many attempts were made to translate the word *citta*. Some say it is the mind. Some say it is the energy in the mind. Some say it is the consciousness. These terms, though accurate to a degree, bring with them a certain vagueness which further veils the meaning.

To understand *citta* we should consider two aspects, thinking and feeling. Whatever energy is used for thinking is *citta*, and whatever is used for feeling is *citta*. It is *citta* through which we think and feel. Where does your thinking take place? When a thought arises, in which energy is it illustrated? When you have an emotional response to something real or imaginary, in which part of your psyche does that take place? What sort of energy is used to develop and transmit emotion? Whatever correct answer one would give to any of these questions would identify the *citta* energy. *Citta* is the mento-emotional energy in which thoughts are formed and dissolved. It is the energy in which feelings are formed and in which the same feelings dissolve.

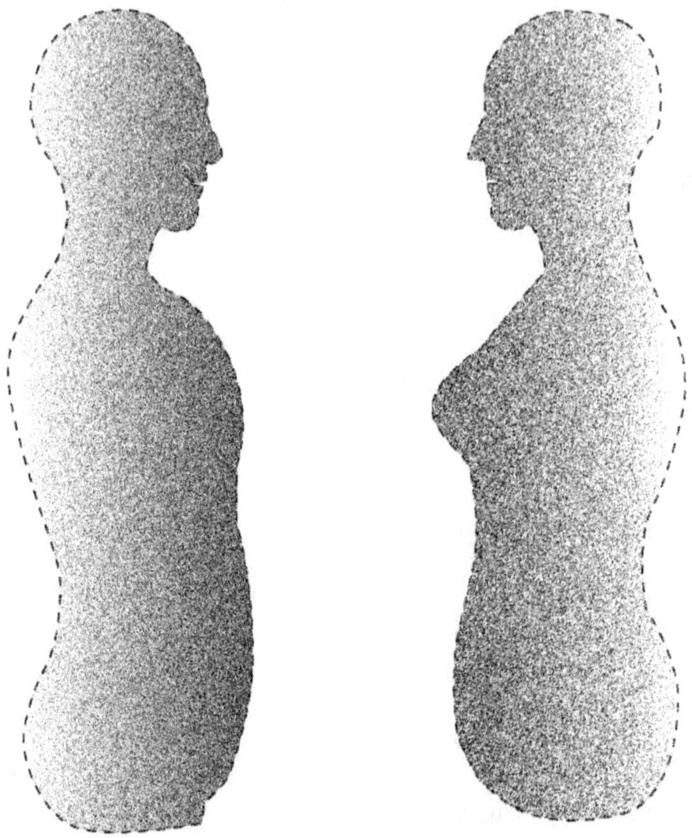

By convention the vibrational energy of the mind always keeps moving. Thus some spiritual masters believe it impossible to comply with this suggestion by *Patañjali* for non-operation of the mento-emotional force. They dismissed *Patañjali* as being an impractical theorist. The solution, they say, is to engage the mind in spiritual topics, never giving it the chance to dwell on ordinary subjects. However, human convention is not everything. When a yogin gets experience beyond the dimension of this world, he can afford to heed *Patañjali* and strive for the non-operation of the mento-emotional force in this dimension of consciousness. By endeavor and divine grace, a yogin's mento-emotional force becomes stilled. It stalls for a time and turns into a divine vision which perceives the *cit ākāśa*, the sky of consciousness, the world known otherwise as *akṣaradhāma*, *brahma* and *vaikuṇṭha*. When this happens, the yogi understands what *Patañjali* explained in this verse.

Śrīla Yogeśvarānanda Yogirāja indicated that *Patañjali* should not have suggested the possibility of completely quieting the mento-emotional force. For indeed, it is not possible to stop the vibrations altogether; rather, one may quiet it in one dimension while it shifts to operate in another. It cannot be quieted in all phases because even after the dissolution of the universe, the *prāṇa* or subtle mundane energy keeps shifting quietly for many billions of years. This slight movement might, in reference, be considered to be static but it does have a vibrational constancy.

Application:

Yoga is accomplished when as a yogin, one can stop the creative urges of the mind and emotions. At first this is impossible. One should begin by isolating the core-self which is in the head of the human body. This is done by a mental retraction of subtle energy as if one withdraws the energy spherically.

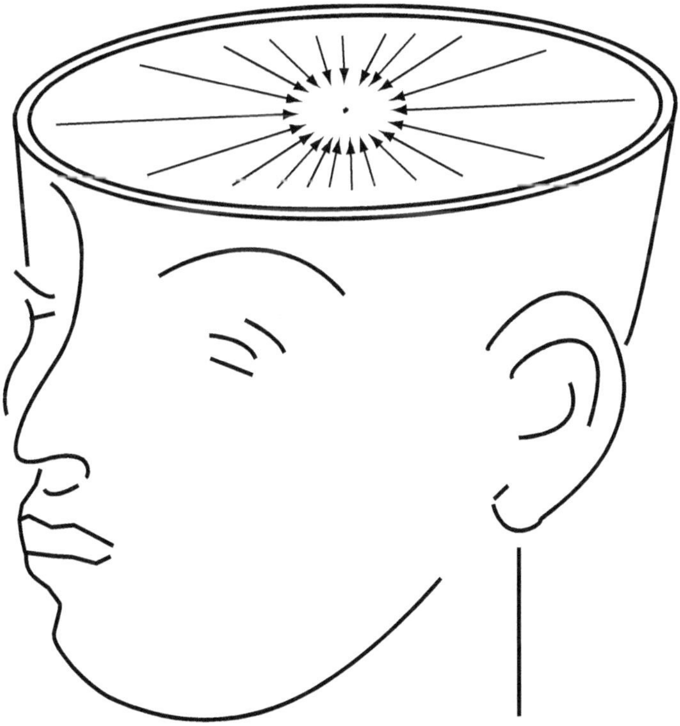

Begin by pulling the energy which flows through the eyes for optic perception.

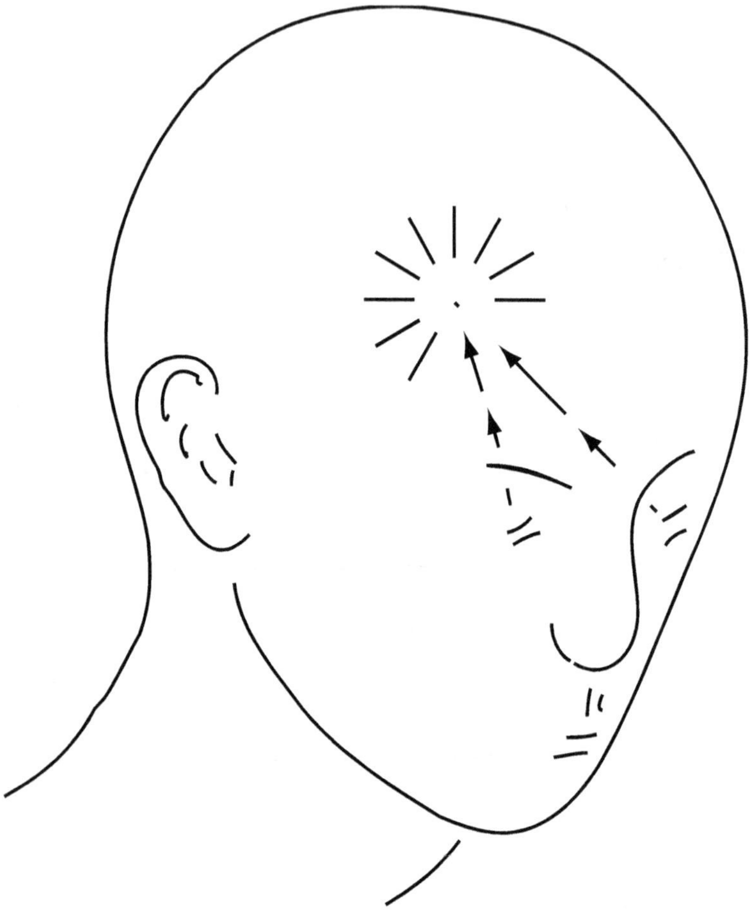

When this is mastered and you feel you are familiar with the energy which usually flows through the optic nerves, begin to pull energy in all directions from the facial area as in this diagram.

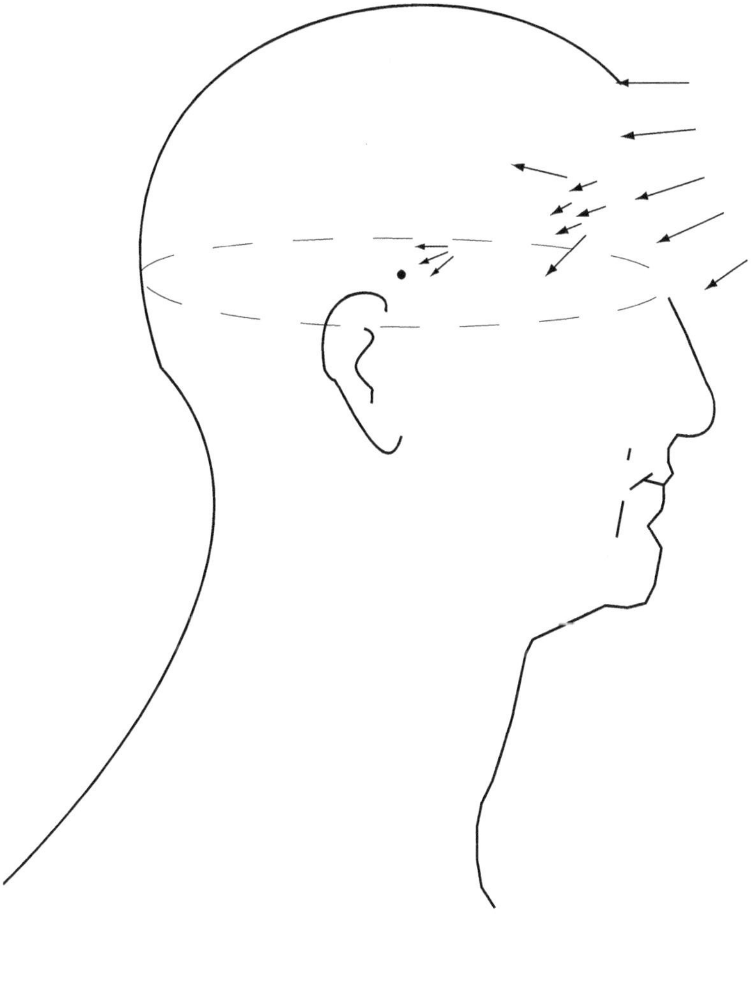

When the facial pull is mastered, practice pulling energy from the back of the head.

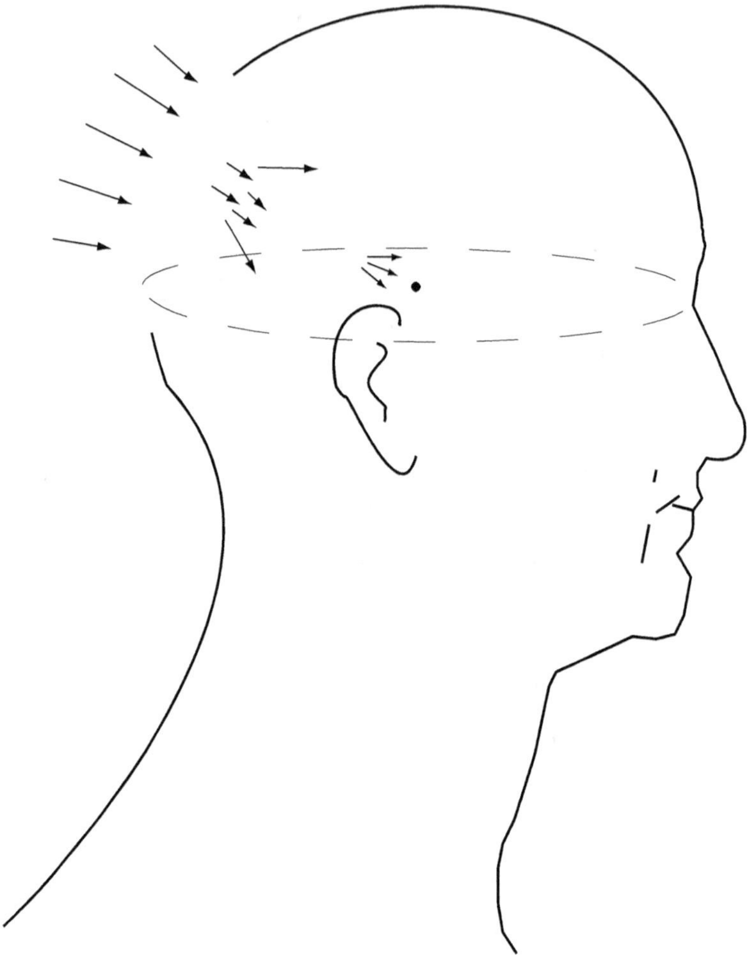

One should practice this for some time, until it can be done effortlessly. After a time, one will reach a state of quiescence where the energy takes a still feature, which is very close to the non-vibrational state required by Patañjali.

Verse 3

तदा द्रष्टुः स्वरूपेऽवस्थानम्॥ २॥

tadā draṣṭuḥ svarūpe avasthānam

tadā – then; draṣṭuḥ – the perceiver; svarūpe – in his own form; avasthānam – is situated.

Then the perceiver is situated in his own form.

Analysis:

When the mento-emotional energy reaches the state of quiescence, the perceiver within that energy, experiences himself alone without those influences. This is the state of *svarūpa*, or his own form.

So long as that mento-emotional energy vibrates actively, the perceiver is not allowed to reflect on himself. He is instead, drawn into concerns other than the core-self. Thus he responds carelessly since his sense of identity is diverted to something else. *Patañjali* gave this statement about the situation in the spiritual self, *swarūpe*, to give encouragement and to generate interest in self-realization. After all, if one does not realize the essential self, one remains preoccupied with diverse objects or energies.

Application:

By this retraction of the energies which pour out of the psyche, you can become familiar with the bare self. There is a core-self which consists of concentrated spiritual energy. It can be realized in isolation from other psychic forces; hence the necessity to extract one's interest from diverse psychological concerns.

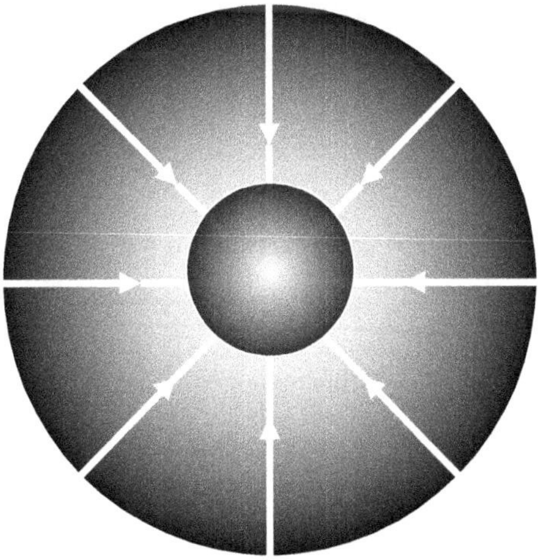

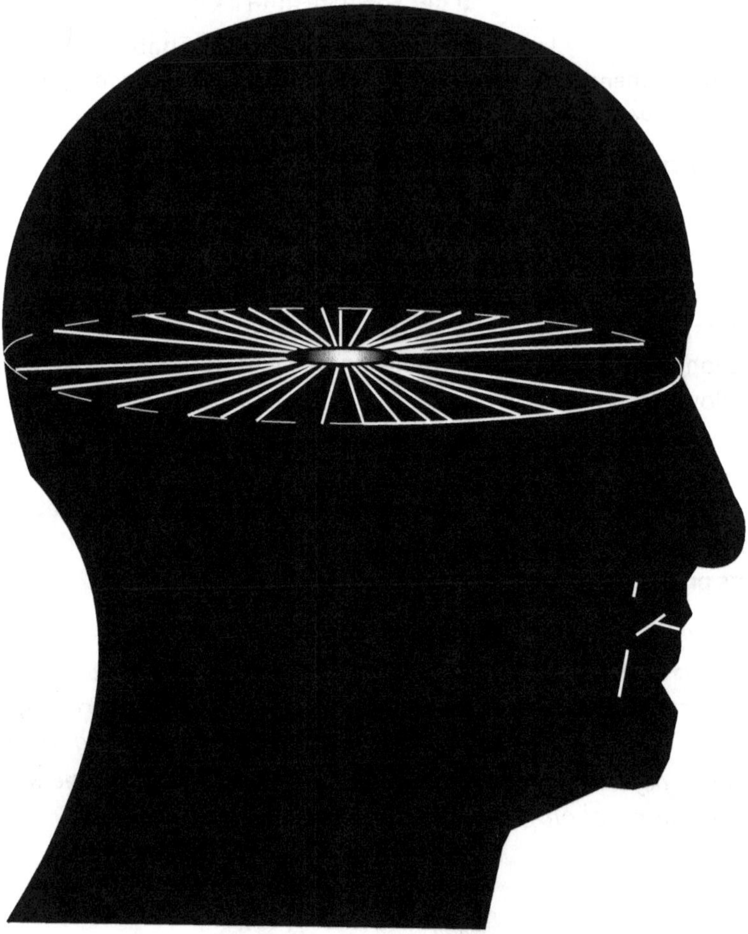

Verse 4

वृत्तिसारूप्यमितरत्र ॥४॥

vṛtti sārūpyam itaratra

vṛtti – the mento-emotional energy; sārūpyam – with the same format, conformity; itaratra – at other times.

At other times, there is conformity with the mento-emotional energy.

Analysis:

The perceiver, although he is different to the mento-emotional energy, is not allowed to show autonomy or independence when that energy is active in its concern for things in this dimension. The perceiver is forced to conform to the dictates of the mento-emotional force. He or she is forced to use the same format as the energy irrespective of a deliberate or non-deliberate interest in this dimension and its corresponding higher or lower locales. The perceiver is forced to identify with that ideation energy. It is only when the vibrations cease of their own accord or are suppressed by him or by another force, that he may realize the self.

Application:

Otherwise, whatever one does is regulated by creative urges. Self-realization, though advertised as a grand accomplishment, begins with an understanding that the core-self is basically insecure. This insecurity is offset by its fusion into sub-realities. If the self is seperated from these sub-energies, it will again seek them out to resume its integrity. To abandon these supports, the core-self has to spend many hours in isolation. It has to re-orient itself to that. This takes deliberate practice.

Expect loneliness in the first stages of this practice. If you persevere through the lonely phase, success will be yours; otherwise you will find yourself resuming the supported identity again and again and you may lose faith in meditation practice.

Verse 5

वृत्तयः पञ्चतय्यः क्लिष्टा अक्लिष्टाः ॥५॥

vṛttayaḥ pañcatayyaḥ kliṣṭā akliṣṭāḥ

vṛttayaḥ – the vibrations in mento-emotional energy; pañcatayyaḥ – fivefold; kliṣṭākliṣṭāḥ = kliṣṭā – agonizing + akliṣṭāḥ – non-troublesome.

The vibrations in the mento-emotional energy are five-fold, being agonizing or non-troublesome.

Analysis:

Śrī Patañjali has not given a middle designation or a mixed status for the mento-emotional vibrations. He simply referred to five types of these vibrations, some causing agony and some which are not troublesome. This realization in mystic yoga practice allows the yogi to become expert at recognizing the various moods of the mind and emotions. An ignorance of the operations of the mental and emotional energy will cause the self to trail behind the moods. Ignorance of one's psychology, and of how it operates, is costly to the living entity. This will invariably lead to haphazard rebirths and a tendency towards reckless acts.

As stated in the second verse, the skill of yoga is demonstrated by non-vibration of the mento-emotional energies. When the yogi ceases the vibrations, the energy converts into a supernatural vision with which he sees into the *cit ākāśa*, the sky of consciousness, the spiritual environment. The yogin inherently possesses the *citta* energy for that purpose but due to ineptness he does not use it appropriately. Instead it serves him for imagining and analyzing mundane energy.

Application:

There are five types of those creative urges. Each type has troublesome and non-troublesome interactions. Even though there are five expressions of this psychological force, it is usually recognized by its enjoying and discouraging features. These aspects cause bewilderment. They disguise the five expressions as subjective experiences. In meditation one has to bypass the enjoying or depressing energy under which the expressions are formed.

Nature endows us with a sense mechanism which parcels enjoyable or disgusting experiences. This system of prejudices distracts and prevents the discovery of the five expressions of the mento-emotional force.

Verse 6

प्रमाणविपर्ययविकल्पनिद्रास्मृतयः ॥ ६ ॥

pramāṇa viparyaya vikalpa nidrā smṛtayaḥ

pramāṇa – correct perception; viparyaya – incorrect perception; vikalpa – imagination; nidrā – sleep; smṛtayaḥ – memory.

They are correct perception, incorrect perception, imagination, sleep and memory.

Analysis:

According to *Śrī Patañjali,* whatever occurs in the mental and emotional energy must be some combination of the five vibrations. A yogin should know these thoroughly. If one does not understand the workings of his mind and feelings, one cannot become liberated.

We are endowed with a mento-emotional energy which is restricted to those five kinds of vibrations which produce either correct perception, false perception, imagination, sleep or memory. All these psychological functions occur in the *citta* energy. The problem is that the living entity cannot always know what is taking place within its mind and emotions. In most persons, the operations occur faster than the entity is able to perceive. Thus the entity sees the conclusions or feels such conclusions and does not understand what took place until after it occurred or until after he or she reacted beneficially or unbeneficially.

Let us take for example the operation of sleep. One may fall asleep and not know it until after the sleep mode has terminated. A man for instance, who drives a car in a tired state, would realize that he fell asleep at the wheel after his car crashed and he awoke in a badly damaged body. The operations are impulsively performed in the mind and emotions.

Now consider the five operations:

Correct Perception:

The most interesting feature of this operation is our dependence upon it. The question arises as to why we need a psychological tool for correct perception. Why is it that we could not perceive reality without having to use the mento-emotional energy? If as this *sūtra* indicates, we are dependent on the correct perception vibrational mode of the mind, then how can we restrict the energy so that it does not shift into the mode which gives incorrect perception or unrealistic imagination?

The only thing we know for certain is that the mento-emotional energy is capable of five modes of operation. Furthermore, normally we do not control the operations, but rather it happens reflexively. What yoga process gives us the ability to control this either partially or absolutely?

Incorrect Perception:

The problem with false perception is that within the energy itself, there is a tendency not to recognize the vibrations which cause false perception. Instead one tries to correct such perception by various haphazard applications. Therefore we must train the psychology in a different and totally new way, so that it becomes concerned only with recognizing the vibrational state from which false perceptions are derived. This means that we have to advance to higher yoga in *dhāraṇā*, linkage of the mind to higher concentration forces.

It is not false perceptions that are the problem but rather the vibrations in the energy which cause the wrong views in the first place. We must strive to recognize these vibrations and stop them, so that the mind may function only with the vibrations which produce correct or true perceptions. This will take repeated practice, because the vibrations which produce false perceptions are naturally occurring. It is not a matter of suppressing these undesirable vibrations, even though a yogi does suppress them from time to time. It is rather a feat for the yogi to cause the mind and feelings not to vibrate in that way. This requires mastership of *prāṇāyāma* breath infusement techniques and a strong development of vigilance and acute dispassion.

SPECIAL NOTE:

Two persons in particular requested that I write this translation and commentary of Śrī Patañjali Muni's Yoga Sūtras. They are Śrīla Yogeshwaranand Yogirāja who has departed from his physical body and Sir Paul Castagna who, to the date of this publication, still uses a physical form. Śrīla Yogeshwarananda thought that I was duty-bound to write such a translation and commentary and that it would benefit me. Sir Paul Castagna thought that I would further break open the meaning of the sūtras. In any case I now thank these two individuals for their pushing and tugging.

Śrī Patañjali Maharshi is not an ordinary person. And though I was reluctant to translate and comment on this classic work on Yoga and its practice, still I benefited from this task which my teacher Śrīla Yogeshwarananda and my colleague Sir Paul Castagna motivated me to begin and complete.

Imagination:

The curbing of the imagination faculty is the key to a successful *dhāraṇā* practice. This *dhāraṇā* is the sixth stage of yoga, that of linking the attention to a higher concentration force. The process of willful non-operation of the vibrational capacity of mento-emotional energy deals with curbing the impulsive nature of the imagination faculty of the intellect in the head of the subtle body. Hence, checking the impulsive operation of this faculty is the key to mastering the *dhāraṇā* practice.

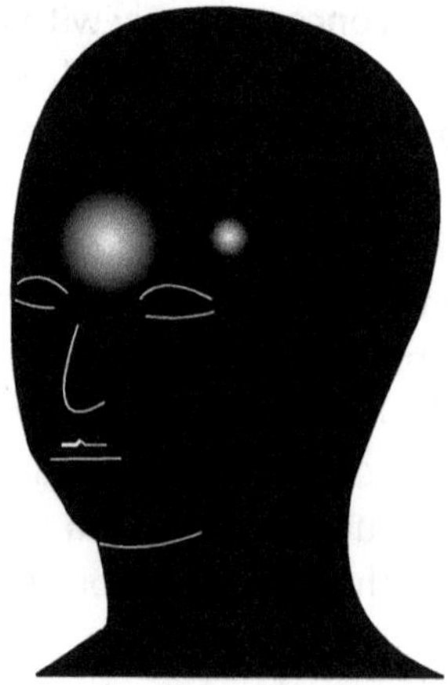

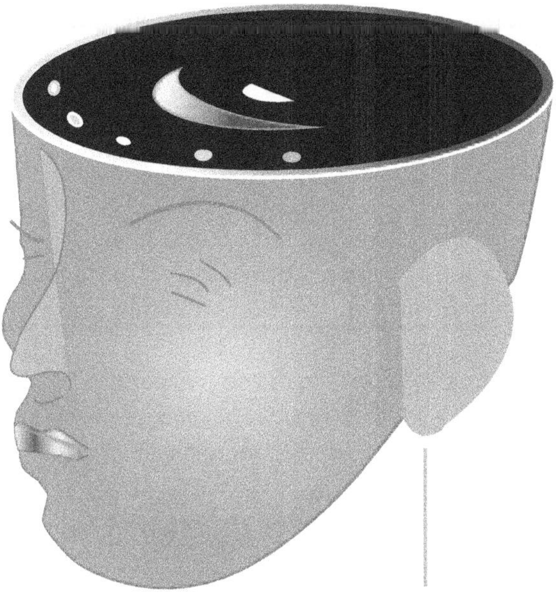

Śrī Krishna told Arjuna that for those living entities who are embodied, this technique is hard to attain:

kleśo 'dhikataras teṣām avyaktāsakta-cetasām
avyaktā hi gatir duḥkhaṃ dehavadbhir avāpyate

The mental exertion of those whose minds are attached to the invisible existence is greater. The goal of reaching that invisible reality is attained with difficulty by the human beings. (*Bhagavad Gītā* 12.5)

For a person who is accustomed to gross and subtle mundane objects and who is sensually inclined to enjoying such objects, a preliminary procedure is given by the yogi masters. That is the process of focusing on sanctified objects in this world. After some time when the student develops detachment from this world, he is introduced to the method of directly shifting his attention from this world to the *cit ākāśa*, the sky of consciousness. This begins with the naad sound *kriyā* which was given to Uddhava in the eleventh canto of Śrīmad Bhāgavatam:

hṛdy avicchinnam oṁkāram ghaṇṭā-nādaṁ bisorṇa-vat
prāṇenodīrya tatrātha punaḥ samveśayet svaram

In the heart chakra, the Oṁ sound which is like the continuous peal of a bell, resonates continually, like a fibre in a lotus stalk. Raising it by using the vitalizing energy, one should blend that sound with the musical tones. *(Śrīmad Bhāgavatam 11.14.34, Uddhava Gītā 9.34)*

When the imagination faculty is fully curbed, it develops into the eye of consciousness, which is called *jñāna-chakṣuṣ* or *jñāna-dīpah*. When this eye opens one sees into the *cit ākāśa*, the sky of consciousness. When one is steady in using this eye, one's spiritual life is sealed. That is an objective of the practice.

Sleep:

The vibration of sleep cannot be eliminated altogether but its negative aspects may be curtailed by a yogin through mastery of *prāṇāyāma* and expertise in the *dhāraṇā* linkage of the attention to higher concentration forces. According to *Śrīla* Yogeshwarananda, sleep is a permanent requirement for the subtle and causal forms. These bodies require sleep for rejuvenation. Even the cosmic god, the *Hiraṇyagarbha* personality, must sleep from time to time, thus shutting down his energies which flow into this material world.

However, a yogin should curtail the negative aspects of sleep by learning how to keep his subtle body fully charged with fresh energy.

Memory:

The vibration of memory is ever-active and functions automatically on the basis of promptings which come to it from the mento-emotional chamber. Memory circuits are triggered by impressions which arise in the imagination, as well as from the other three vibrational powers of true perception, false perception and sleep. A yogin has to learn how to shut off the automatic switch which causes the memory to be activated. If he fails to do this, he will be unable to reach the stage of *samādhi*, the highest level of practice.

Application:

The five types of expression are experienced when you gage external things correctly, when you gage them incorrectly, when you imagine anything, when you sleep and when you experience memory.

These five expressions are experienced by the core-self through its contact with the analytical orb. The five operations function in and through the orb. They are curbed by regulating the core-self's contact with the orb.

In meditation, one should find the location of the five activations or vrittis. *See the previous diagram. Suppose this diagram is incorrect. Then, what does that matter? Try to correct it. Once you find the location, you can begin the observation of how the activations operate and interact. This knowledge would lead to mastership of the psyche.*

Try to transcend the enjoying and depressing aspects of psychological expression. Then you can penetrate the charade, locate each of the five activations and curb their influences progressively.

Verse 7

प्रत्यक्षानुमानागमाः प्रमाणानि ॥ ७ ॥

pratyakṣa anumāna āgamāḥ pramāṇāni

pratyakṣanumānāgamāḥ = pratyakṣa – direct but correct perception + anumāna – correct analysis + āgamāḥ – correct reference; pramāṇāni – true perception, correct perception.

Correct perception may be acquired directly, by correct analysis or by correct reference.

Analysis:

Even though obvious, *Patañjali* alerted that we should learn how to recognize when the intellect functions in the correct mode. Everyone understands that when false information is used there will be incorrect conclusions. Analysis, when applied to false information, results in false conclusion, which leads to incorrect insight. Likewise, a reference may be the wrong one, or it may be inaccurate, hence the use of it will lead to false conclusions. Direct perception may be incorrect. *Pratyakṣa* is a combination of *prati* and *akṣa*, but *akṣa* means perception. When that perception is correct, it is *prati-akṣa, pratyakṣa*. For true perception, a yogin must have both an accurate intellect and accurate information from outside the intellect. It is not just reliant on the intellect.

If one's intellect is sufficiently surcharged with higher concentration forces, one will recognize the incorrect and unreliable information. One will not use such information to produce wrong conclusions. A yogi must be in the right position to get the right information. This is achieved by mystic maneuvers. This means that more is required for accurate perception besides purity of the psyche of the yogi. He must position himself so that he can use an accurate intellect (*buddhi*) to perceive correctly.

An astronomer may have an accurate telescope but still he cannot take an accurate reading on a cloudy night. He must put himself in the proper position to use the accurate instrument. Correct perception may be acquired directly only if the yogin has a reality-perceiving intellect and is in the proper position to use it.

Correct perception can be acquired directly through insight developed by correct analysis after getting some facts but this is solidified only after the yogin can take that analysis to the point of getting the direct sight of it.

Furthermore, by correct reference, a yogin may form an correct conclusion but that is incomplete because it is not direct sensual observation. He will have to develop himself further to reach the stage of true direct sensual perception of the supernatural and spiritual realities.

Finally, a yogin should develop the ability to identify the various true and erroneous perceptions of the intellect. Then he may suppress and gradually eliminate the faulty parts and the motivations which support defective perception.

Application:

Correct assessments occur by accurate sense perception, by efficient analysis or by using a reliable reference. One should carefully craft these by two means, namely, getting information from reliable sources such as Patañjali *and by direct perception through advanced meditation.*

Verse 8

विपर्ययो मिथ्याज्ञानमतद्रूपप्रतिष्ठम्॥८॥

viparyayaḥ mithyājñānam atadrūpa pratiṣṭham

viparyayaḥ – incorrect perception; mithyājñānam = mithyā – false + jñānam – information; atadrūpa = atad – not this + rūpa – form; pratiṣṭham – positioned, based.

Incorrect perception is based on false information and on perception of what is not the true form.

Analysis:

The vibrational mode which produces a firm conviction about something incorrect is caused by the perception of false information and what is not the true form *(atadrūpa).*

The root of this problem lies in the willingness of the intellect to accept the information given to it by the senses. The reliance of the intellect on the sensual energies must be broken by the yogin. This can be achieved by perfecting the *pratyāhār* 5th stage of yoga practice, where the sensual energies are withdrawn from their interest in the subtle and gross mundane world. The strong ability of the senses to keep the intellect under subjugation springs from the extrovert tendency of the organ. Thus if that habit is squelched, the senses lose authority over the intellect and it becomes independent. This is mastered by *pratyāhār* practice.

The perception of the sensual energies is fueled by *prāṇa* which is subtle air. When the yogi practices *prāṇāyāma* and is able to take in a higher grade of energy, the senses become purified. They no longer make as many erroneous judgments.

Application:

When one gages something incorrectly, that occurs because of false information or by mistaking one factor for another. Thus, a study of the mind is tantamount. Each yogi is required to observe the mental process. It is not sufficient to get information from a reliable authority like Krishna or Patañjali. *The information should be used like a map or a manual, for guidance to direct experience.*

Verse 9

शब्दज्ञानानुपाती वस्तुशून्यो विकल्पः ॥९॥

śabdajñāna anupātī vastuśūnyaḥ vikalpaḥ

śabdajñāna – written or spoken information; anupātī – followed by; vastuśūnyaḥ – devoid of reality, without reality; vikalpaḥ – imagination.

Verbal or written information, which is followed by concepts which are devoid of reality, is imagination.

Analysis:

It is important to understand that the same imagination faculty which can mislead the living entity and cause him to come to the wrong conclusion is the very same psychic organ which he must use to see into the super-physical world. Even though *Patañjali* listed only five modes of operation for this organ, still, when it is shifted from this world it can be used for super-physical perceptions. Indeed, it can be used in the mode of correct perceptions for spiritual insights.

When used as motivated by false verbal or written information, it develops ideas, conceptions and the like, which cause an imagination with no basis in reality. Since the living entity is dependent on it, its image creations, sounds and impressions are accepted as if such notions were reality. Thus, one makes mistakes. One should learn to recognize when the intellect becomes submissive to incorrect information.

Application:

When you hear or read of something, ideas concerning it usually form. When these concepts misrepresent the actual thing, that misconception is imagination. Control of this imagination comes by detachment from mental symbolization and reorientation to a blank mind. Nature endows one with an addiction to mental imaging but one must abandon the fascination and accustom the self to a blank mental state.

Verse 10

अभावप्रत्ययालम्बना वृत्तिर्निद्रा ॥ १० ॥

abhāva pratyayaḥ ālambanā vṛttiḥ nidrā

abhāva – absence of awareness; pratyayaḥ – conviction or belief as mental content; ālambanā – support, prop, means of conversion; vṛttiḥ – vibrational mode; nidrā – sleep.

Sleep is the vibrational mode which is supported by the absence of objective awareness.

Analysis:

There are various states of sleep but true sleep occurs when the mind has no content, such that one feels as if one barely existed. This is realized not during that state but after it. During such sleep the living entity becomes disconnected from the intellect. When the self is connected again, it realizes that it was barely connected to its discrimination and sense of objectivity during sleep.

We may consider that the *vṛttis* or vibrational modes of the mental and emotional energy are fivefold in normal consciousness. It is like a car with one reverse and four forward gears. The reverse gear is comparable to the operational mode of memory. Memory deals with recalling something from the past. The other modes or gears are all forward vibrations, which *Śrī Patañjali* gave as correct perception, false perception, imagination, and sleep.

Application:

Sleep is the creative urge which operates without self-awareness, but it can be realized by minute observation using consciousness, silence and sensitivity. The self's grip on objective awareness is inversely related to its addiction to excitement. If the need for excitement is reduced, the self develops more capacity for observing subtle and super subtle states.

There is a corridor between the conscious and unconscious. The self can learn the location of that place. From there it can watch the shift from objectivity to subjectivity. This requires mastership of deep meditation.

Verse 11

अनुभूतविषयासम्प्रमोषः स्मृतिः ॥ ११ ॥

anubhūta viṣaya asaṁpramoṣaḥ smṛtiḥ

anubhūta – the experience; viṣaya – the object; asaṁpramoṣaḥ – retention; smṛtiḥ – memory.

Memory is the retained impression of experienced objects.

Analysis:

Memory has to do with the past and therefore it might be compared to the reverse gear in an automobile. In reverse, the driver travels on the path traversed before. Memory must be curbed by a yogin, because otherwise he would never be free from the mental impressions which formed in his conscious and subconscious mind. These impressions vent themselves into the conscious mind and are appropriated by the intellect for usage in further imaginations, which lead to actions of interference in the material world. This interference produces liabilities for which the yogin is held responsible. If one does not quell the memory and disconnect from it, one cannot become liberated. Thus a yogin should find a method for neutralizing this function in the mento-emotional energy.

Application:

Memory operates anytime one visualizes something previously experienced. The control of one's response to memory comes about by weaning the self from associative thinking. Yet, even if that is mastered one has to review the advantage of recall. Recall of the past gives one both superiority and instinctual orientation, features which are required in the struggle for existence. Hence one should not underestimate the reliance on memory. Without it, one would be relegated to the position of a primitive being.

Since it is so important, one has to develop another means of experiential reference, before one can give it up. This is done by retreating to the causal plane. In that supernatural place, all seed impressions of all future states are present. That contact is the fulfillment which cancels out the need for memory.

Verse 12

अभ्यासवैराग्याभ्यां तन्निरोधः ॥ १२ ॥

abhyāsa vairāgyābhyāṁ tannirodhaḥ

abhyāsa – effective yoga practice; vairāgyābhyāṁ = non-interest, a total lack of concern, non-interference; tan = tat – that; nirodhaḥ – cessation, restraint, non-operation.

That non-operation of the vibrational modes is achieved by effective practice in not having an interest in the very same operations.

Analysis:

Śrī Patañjali Mahāmuni Yogirāja gave me a hint regarding this verse. By telepathy he sent this clarification:

> *"Those who are advanced should continue practicing with firm faith so that the connection with lower operational modes of the mental and emotional energies decreases daily. They need not read any more of these sūtras which I wrote down so long ago.*
>
> *"However those who are not so advanced should read further and take hints according to their particular progressions. In this verse twelve, these sūtras are concluded, but novices need to hear more from the teacher. This book ends in this verse twelve for those who are advanced, but others should read on for more hints on practice."*

To remove one's connection with the *vṛttis* or the operational modes, one needs to be detached from the very same operations or modes. However, for those who are not so advanced we need to hear more. Generally speaking we have to enter into the neutral mode and from there into higher concentration energies which cause sensual perception into the *cit ākāśa*, the sky of consciousness.

Vairāgya has come to be translated as detachment or non-attachment. However it is more than that. It is a total lack of interest and an attitude of non-interference in cultural activities. One gets hints about this as one progresses in yoga and gains insight from great yogins like *Patañjali.*

Application:

By not having an interest in the mental ideas and emotional feelings, one may develop the power to stop their influence. There is a magnetic pull between one's interest energy and the operations of the mind. One has to gage the strength of that attraction by practicing sensual energy withdrawal. Hours upon hours of meditation are required to master this. When the core self becomes familiar with this information conduit between itself and the senses, it can make an effort to shut down the communication and orient itself to itself.

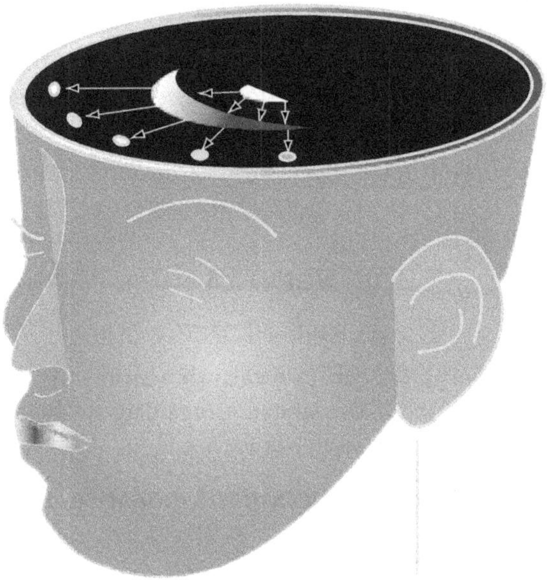

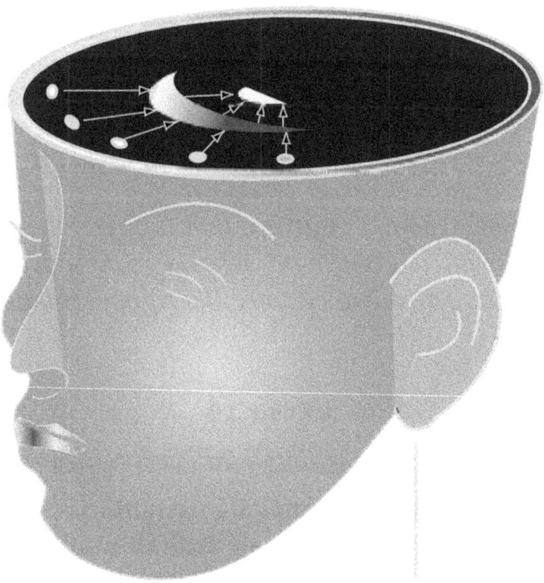

To develop a non-interest in the activities of the mind, one must first develop an interest in it with a motive to understand the details of how

it functions. If one is lazy in this matter and if one does not make the effort, then success will be elusive.

All the same, the development of an interest in the mind's operations is risky, since if one is not properly prepared, one will fall deeper in the sway of the mind. The interest should be developed with suspicion that the mind may increase its influence over the self during the observations.

Verse 13

तत्र स्थितौ यत्नोऽभ्यासः ॥ १३ ॥

tatra sthitau yatnaḥ abhyāsaḥ

tatra – there, in that case; sthitau – regarding steadiness or persistence; yatnaḥ – endeavor; abhyāsaḥ – practice.

In that case, practice is the persistent endeavor (to cultivate that lack of interest).

Analysis:

The related practice is hereby defined. It must be persistent and requires endeavor *(yatnaḥ).* One has to cultivate that lack of interest because by nature, the mind and emotions are extroverted and have a self-conceited mentality. The self-conceited mentality is for acquiring private enjoyment by the psyche in a perverted and harmful way. All this must be curbed effectively.

Application:

One should persistently cultivate that lack of interest. Persistence and association with a great soul who is more advanced and who explains the path as one advances, are the signposts leading to success of this path.

Verse 14

स तु दीर्घकालनैरन्तर्यसत्कारासेवितो दृढभूमिः ॥ १४ ॥

sa tu dīrghakāla nairantarya
satkāra āsevitaḥ dṛḍhabhūmiḥ

sa = sah – that; tu – but; dīrgha – long; kāla – time; nairantarya – uninterrupted, continuous; satkāra – reverence, care, attention; āsevitaḥ – sustained practice, aggressive interest; dṛḍha – firm; bhūmiḥ – ground, foundation, basis.

But that is attained on the firm basis of a continuous reverential sustained practice which is executed for a long time.

Analysis:

What was acquired over millions and millions of births will take some time to remove from the psyche. It will not go away overnight. Thus this yoga course is not the same as other easy promises of salvation.

Application:

Additionally, one should be reverential in the practice. It must be sustained for a long time. The reverence is directed both to the practice itself and to teachers who describe their experiences and transmit inspirations which sponsor advancement.

Verse 15

दृष्टानुश्रविकविषयवितृष्णस्य वशीकारसञ्ज्ञा वैराग्यम्॥ १५॥

dṛṣṭa ānuśravika viṣaya vitṛṣṇasya
vaśīkārasaṁjñā vairāgyam

dṛṣṭa – what is seen or perceived directly; ānuśravika – what is conjectured on the basis of scripture or valid testimony; viṣaya – an attractive object; vitṛṣṇasya – of one who does not crave; vaśīkāra – through control; saṁjñā – consciousness, demeanor, mind-set; vairāgyam – non-interest.

The non-interest in the operations of the mento-emotional energy is achieved by one who has perfect mastery in consciousness and who does not crave for what is perceived or what is heard of in the mundane existence.

Analysis:

To silence the mento-emotional energy one has to stop craving the subtle and gross existence. Any craving triggers a renewed interest in this world and its activities, which in turn, activates the five vibrational operations of correct perception, incorrect perception, imagination, memory and sleep.

Application:

Note that the lack of interest in ideas and emotions is achieved only by one who has mastery over the psychological nature. Such a person would not crave things mundane which are perceived through any of the senses.

To reach this stage, one should realize the sensual attractions and their means for influencing the self. Then one has to undermine their power over the self. So long as the self requires fulfillments through the senses, their dominance will continue. The self must find a way to forego those needs.

Verse 16

तत्परं पुरुषख्यातेर्गुणवैतृष्ण्यम्॥ १६॥

tatparaṁ puruṣakhyāteḥ guṇavaitṛṣṇyam

tat – that; paraṁ – highest (non-interest); puruṣa – of the spiritual person; khyāteḥ – of a thorough awareness; guṇa – features of material nature; vaitṛṣṇyam – freedom from desire.

That highest non-interest occurs when there is freedom from desire for the features of material nature and thorough awareness of the spiritual person.

Analysis:

This pure state of non-interest is not easily achieved. *Śrī Patañjali* alerted the student yogis that it will take a long time *(dīrgha kāla)* for them to attain success. This cultivation of non-interest is said to be part of contemplative practice *(rāja* yoga*)*, but that does not mean that one can get it by avoiding *āsana* and *prāṇāyāma* practice.

Puruṣa, the spiritual personality, and *prakṛti*, the gross and subtle material nature, display a liking for one another. It is not an easy task for anyone to nullify this affinity. A complete transformation in the psychology would be required for one to develop the full non-interest in the subtle or gross mundane energy.

Application:

The required lack of interest is exhibited when one attains a resistance to urges which usually compel one to fulfill mundane desires. That lack of interest results in the development of a thorough awareness of the spiritual self. This is the ultimate goal but for the short term one must deal with this step by step, by realizing, fighting against and effectively defeating small portions of this objective as one progresses. This is not achieved in one step. A yogi must zero-in on sectors of his interest, isolate those, observe their ways and means, wrestle with the need for them, and then as inspired and by trial and error subdue and eliminate them.

Verse 17

वितर्कविचारानन्दास्मितारूपानुगमात्सम्प्रज्ञातः ॥ १७ ॥

vitarka vicāra ānanda asmitārūpa anugamāt saṁprajñātaḥ

vitarka – analysis; vicāra – deliberation, reflection; ānanda – introspective happiness; asmitārūpa – I-ness self-consciousness; anugamāt – by accompaniment, occurring with; saṁprajñātaḥ – the observational linkage of the attention to a higher concentration force.

The observational linkage of the attention to a higher concentration force occurs with analysis, reflection and introspective happiness or with focus on self-consciousness.

Analysis:

Suddenly and without warning, *Śrī Patañjali* jumped from the cultivation of non-interest in the mundane world to the observational linkage of the attention to higher concentration force. If a yogin is successful at stopping the ordinary functions of his mento-emotional energies, he will enter a neutral stage from which his attention can linked to or become fused to higher concentration forces in the sky of consciousness, the *cit ākāśa*.

In the beginning, the yogi will be affected by four other forces from this side of existence. These are the analytical power of the intellect, the reflective mood of it, the introspective happiness felt during *pratyāhār* sensual withdrawal practice and the I-ness or self-consciousness which directed the attention to be linked to the higher concentration force.

Some other commentators categorized *saṁprajñātaḥ* as a type of *samādhi*. In other words it has come down in the yogic disciplic succession that *saṁprajñātaḥ* is a type of *samādhi* or a lower stage of the eighth and final level of yoga practice. However, this writer informs readers that *saṁprajñāta* is part of *dhāraṇā* practice which is the sixth stage of yoga. In that stage, the linkage is deliberate and is done by the yogi through the mystic force applied. In the next stage, that of *dhyāna*, the yogi is able to realize his sense of identity and its forceful application. He finds that his will power is drawn into the higher concentration force of its own accord. In the eighth stage, that of *samādhi*, his will is not only effortlessly drawn but it is continually pulled for periods of time exceeding twenty minutes.

In the *saṁprajñāta* observational linkage, the yogin sometimes finds that he must analyze his state of linkage. This is preliminary. All yogis experience this as they progress. One does not move permanently from a lower to a higher stage until one has integrated the transition. At first when the deliberate linkage occurs, there is an analysis of what one is linked to, as to what level and its value, what it will evolve into and the extent of transcendence.

After this one reflects on it, for the purpose of integrating it fully for the sake of being able to explain it to others at a later date. Writings such as this were made on the basis of due reflection in this stage. It is for the integration of the writer himself and for use later in teaching and explaining. After one advances beyond this, one reaches a stage of introspective happiness. This is due to full *pratyāhār* when one loses interest in others and totally retracts all sensual energies and is able to direct oneself purely without looking back for support.

When this stage is completed, one reaches a stage of self-awareness in feeling the limits of one's spiritual radiation. At that stage one links with the cosmic intellect and the cosmic sense of identity, which are bright lights on the supernatural planes. This causes an enrichment of one's personality and a surcharging of one's spirituality. If one is not careful at this stage, one may attract many disciples, thus bringing one's spiritual practice to an end.

Student yogins must remember that *saṁprajñāta* absorption is observational. That is its flaw. However it is part of the course of development. One must perform it and do so carefully so that one can reach a higher stage. On any stairway, some steps might be slippery, some might be rough, some might have partial treads, but regardless one has to use all of them if one is to go higher. Thus one should not feel that one can bypass the *saṁprajñāta* stage of absorption. If one completes it properly one will progress upward without having to come down again.

Application:

Initially, you will notice that your attention becomes linked to higher psychological states, but there will still be some analysis, reflection, inner joy and focus on self-consciousness. Each of these will have their detached analysis and resulting conclusions, regarding if they cause a return to lower planes or act as staging points to higher levels.

Analysis has an ultimate value as a way of describing transcendental experiences to other human beings. Thus when one graduates from the need for human association, one drops this.

Reflection has as its benefit, self-assessments for finding worth in identity. Once the yogi gets placement in higher dimensions the worth of the lower planes loses relevance. Their comparison and consideration become a whimsical aspect.

Introspective happiness is the contrasting feature which helps the yogi to break away from sensual dependence. Once he is relocated to the spiritual plane and his focus is permanently applied there, the introspective happiness reaches saturation and no effort is required to reach or maintain it.

The random focus on self-consciousness, which is the boomerang effect of sensual energy outpouring, is abandoned by the yogi when the sensual energies and displays from lower levels no longer dazzle his psyche.

Verse 18

विरामप्रत्ययाभ्यासपूर्वः संस्कारशेषोऽन्यः ॥ १८ ॥

virāmapratyayaḥ abhyāsapūrvaḥ
saṁskāraśeṣaḥ anyaḥ

virāma – losing track of, dropping; pratyayaḥ – objective awareness, opinions and motives of mind content; abhyāsa – practice; pūrvaḥ – previous, before; saṁskāraśeṣaḥ = saṁskāra – impression in the mento-emotional energy + śeṣaḥ – what is remaining; anyaḥ – other.

The other state is the complete departure from the level where the remaining impressions lie in the mento-emotional energy.

Analysis:

The previous practice of losing track of opinions and motives, results in the other state which is awareness of remaining impressions left in the mento-emotional energy.

Most commentators agree that this is the stage of *asaṁprajñāta samādhi* or a state of fusion to a higher plane without maintaining any opinions or motivations.

Provided that one has a previous habit of repeatedly losing track of one's opinions and motivations, one can automatically attain this other state in which there is awareness of the remaining impressions as they exist in the mind compartment and in the emotions. The yogi must repeatedly practice to attain this state, just as *Śrī Patañjali* told us of the long practice *(dīrgha kāla)* required. In this state there is no foothold on any form or forms, and therefore the yogi must be very determined, patient and persistent.

Application:

Periodically and with good luck, one may experience the transcendence in which the memory of all things mundane seems not to exist at all. Though possible, this state is rarely achieved. However, one should endeavor and not overburden the self with lofty aspirations which keeps it in a state of negative excitation. It is sufficient to know that as one progresses, one will, sooner or later, break away from the mass energy on lower planes. In one consideration it is hardly likely that one will ever do so and in another, it is the only reason to persist with transcendental practice.

The brace is the association with more advanced yogis and with divine beings like Krishna and Shiva. Their support supplements any deficiency.

Verse 19

भवप्रत्ययो विदेहप्रकृतिलयानाम्॥ १९॥

bhavapratyayaḥ videha prakṛtilayānām

bhava – inherent nature, psychology; pratyayaḥ – mental content, objective awareness; videha – bodiless persons; prakṛtilayānām – of those who are diffused into subtle material nature.

Of those who are diffused into subtle material nature and those who exist in a bodiless state, their psychology has that content.

Analysis:

This is another jolt put to us by *Śrī Patañjali,* as he explained why one yogi gets a certain advancement, which is different from another and why without any current practice, some attain the benefits of yoga. In this case, those who are diffused into the subtle material nature without any effort on their part, without endeavor, are able to do so because of their inherent nature. A question remains as to whether this is the inherent nature of the spirit or of the psyche which is fused to it.

Śrī Patañjali answered that question by using the word *pratyayaḥ*, which means mental content, the psychological make-up. However, even though it is not their spirits, still they have to adhere to that nature.

Certain other individuals attain the bodiless state and remain in material nature. They sometimes take birth but are unable to remain tied down to a material body due to the inherent tendency to be bodiless.

Bengali Baba, in his commentary on these sūtras, stated that the *videhas*, the bodiless ones, are the persons who, after performing virtuous actions such as *Agnihotra* ceremonies of the Vedas, attain the state of freedom, which is similar to absoluteness. He referred to *Māṇḍūkopaniṣad*, Chapter 2, Part 1. He wrote that they are not to return to human life but they will become presiding officers in future creations. He cited King *Suratha* who will be the eighth *Manu* after the reign of the current *Manu* who is *Vaivasvata*.

Such persons attain a permanent status as small-time gods of these worlds. They have no need to take a gross body. They either use a subtle form or spatial existence, but their energy affects this creation.

Application:

Even a split second transit out of the mento-emotional energy, gives one a glimpse of the status of the released souls, who are diffused into the subtle material nature requiring no gross existence and those divine beings who exist without a subtle or super-subtle material body. Their mind and emotions do not comprise of subtle energies of material nature.

There will be occasions during meditation, when even a neophyte will experience the self when it is out of contact with the normal mento-emotional energy. Those rare contacts with supernatural reality will allow insight into the mental and emotional content of the yogis whose existences are without lower transmigrations. A great appreciation for the divine beings arises in the yogi.

Verse 20

श्रद्धावीर्यस्मृतिसमाधिप्रज्ञापूर्वक इतरेषाम्॥ २०॥

śraddhā vīrya smṛti samādhiprajñā pūrvakaḥ itareṣām

śraddhā – confidence; vīrya – vigor, stamina; smṛti – introspective memory; samādhi – continuous effortless linkage of the attention to a higher concentration force; prajñā – profound insight; pūrvakaḥ – previously practiced; itareṣām – for others.

For others, confidence, stamina, introspective memory, the continuous effortless linkage of the attention to a higher concentration force, and profound insight, all being previously mastered, serve as the cause.

Analysis:

These are the requirements for those who want full success in attaining what *Patañjali* described in the second *sūtra*.

yogaḥ cittavṛtti nirodhaḥ

The skill of yoga is demonstrated by the conscious non-operation of the vibrational modes of the mento-emotional energy. *(Yoga Sūtra 1:2)*

One must have confidence in the practice of yoga and be satisfied with it to such an extent that one becomes attached to it above everything else and will do it to completion. If one does not have such confidence one will either be stalled at the lower stages, give up the practice and take a position in the material world, or become detached from gross existence but remain attached to subtle mundane life.

One must have stamina which arises with sufficient vigor to spur one to practice. There are many energies which contravene or undermine spiritual efforts. If one does not have the stamina, one will be influenced by a negative force. This results in termination of practice.

One must practice *samādhi* repeatedly. *Samādhi* is the continuous effortless linkage of the attention to any of the higher concentration forces, which a yogi experiences. He or she should practice repeatedly.

The yogin must have profound insight gained through development of the *buddhi* intellect organ which sees beyond the material world into the super-physical planes and beyond.

Śrī Patañjali, though acknowledging those persons who are natural mystics, wrote these sūtras expressively for those yogis who endeavor with such stamina that they will adhere to yoga, life after life, until they reach the culmination. There are many people who without any record of yoga practice in their current or perhaps even in their past lives, are able to switch themselves to psychic or supernatural levels. These fortunate persons rely on an inherent nature either to be accustomed to being bodiless or to being diffused into particular subtle phases of material nature *(prakṛtilāya).*

Application:

Since we have neither the diffused status nor the divine one, and since we still have a fixation with the memory of things mundane, our success in cultivating the required lack of interest hinges on confidence in what Patañjali *recommends. We require stamina. We should train ourselves to retain transcendental experiences, even the slightest ones. We should study this text so as to recognize the state of* samādhi *which is continuous and spontaneous contact between the attention and someone or some energy which is beyond the normal range of perception. By this, a profound insight will manifest.*

By confidence in a great yogi, a divine being or a transcendental experience, one may suddenly experience a transit from this frail reality to a spiritual one which supports full existential security. Even though it is not likely and the probability of it is very low, still it is possible.

By stamina and persistence in spiritual disciplines, one may get a transcendental transfer to a realm of spiritual objects.

Introspective memory which is deep and which is in the causal body, can cause a transit to a transcendental environment. In the memory of the causal form there are instances of previous existence in supernatural and spiritual places. If perchance either through endeavor or by grace one makes contact with the causal level, one may be transited to a transcendental world.

The definite and perhaps most difficult method is samādhi practice, which is the continuous effortless linkage of one's attention to a spiritual person or spiritual environment. The two are synonymous since a spiritual environment has spiritual persons and spiritual persons are present in a spiritual environment. Continuous effortless linkage to a transcendental domain is a rare accomplishment for a yogi. He can achieve that by persistent meditation following guidelines from teachers like Patañjali and books like Bhagavad Gītā.

Profound insight which occurs causelessly or which is realized as being caused by a teacher or deity, can transit a fortunate person to a transcendental locale. Such an experience may change the lifestyle of a person permanently.

Verse 21

तीव्रसंवेगानामासन्नः ॥२१॥

tīvrasaṁvegānām āsannaḥ

tīvra – very intense; saṁvegānām – regarding those who practice forcibly; āsannaḥ – whatever is very near, what will occur soon.

For those who practice forcefully in a very intense way, the skill of yoga will be achieved very soon.

Analysis:

Even though *Śrī Patañjali* stated that yoga is attained after a long time, he qualified that statement by saying that it is achieved much sooner by those who have an intense practice. In fact, one cannot conclude yoga practice in any life without intensity and persistence.

Application:

Know with certainty that anyone who practices forcefully in a very intense way, will be a masterful yogi in the near future. However, only a few persons carry such a motivational energy as he or she transmigrates. The vast majority of seekers do not have the energy of persistence required, but one may be inspired by a teacher or divinity, or one may force oneself to practice after experiencing a deep disgust for being in the material world.

Verse 22

मृदुमध्याधिमात्रत्वात्ततोऽपि विशेषः ॥ २२ ॥

mṛdu madhya adhimātratvāt tataḥ api viśeṣaḥ

mṛdu – slight; madhya – mediocre; adhimātratvāt – from intense; tataḥ – then; api – even; viśeṣaḥ – rating.

Then there are even more ratings, according to intense, mediocre, or slight practice.

Analysis:

Yoga practice yields results according to the intensity of correct practice. One person might practice intensely but with wrong methods. His result will be the realization of the incorrect practice. Another person might practice very little with the correct method but he too might not get the results because his practice does not have forcefulness.

Patañjali gave four ratings: Very intense *(tīvra saṁvega),* intense *(adhimātratvā),* mediocre *(madhya),* and slight *(mṛdu).*

Application:

Not everyone can apply themselves with intensity. One person might be mediocre. Another might practice infrequently. To be fair to oneself, one should honestly assess the time and effort applied and mold the expectations accordingly.

A sure way to become discouraged about yoga is to imagine grand results while investing little time and effort to practice. One may also reach a dead end if one exerts strenuously in the wrong way while expecting rapid advancement. A theoretical understanding of the states of yoga and the techniques mastered in each could help someone to scale down their presumptions of the process.

Verse 23

ईश्वरप्रणिधानाद्वा ॥ २३ ॥

īśvara praṇidhānāt vā

īśvara – The Supreme Lord; praṇidhānāt – derived from profound religious meditation; vā – or.

Or by the method of profound religious meditation upon the Supreme Lord.

Analysis:

Śrī Patañjali, in another abrupt statement, gave an alternative method, profound religious meditation upon the Supreme Lord. Readers who want to inquire further into the meaning and application of this verse should examine the word *praṇidhāna*. The root word, *dha*, means to put, to lie upon, to fix upon, to hold, to contain, to seize. *Nidhāna*, means putting down, depositing, or a place where anything is placed.

Praṇidhāna, joint together, indicates a profound and deep reflection of the mind upon the Supreme Lord. This is very deep meditation. If one can achieve that without practicing yoga, one is demonstrating the culmination of yoga even without practice.

Application:

The profound religious meditation upon the Supreme Lord is a very special method. Few can use this successfully since it hinges on an intimate and deep relationship with the Personality of Godhead. This involves linkage of emotional and devotional life from the spiritual body of the devotee to that of the divinity. The difficulty on this path is that the mento-emotional energy in the psyche is condemned since it mimics but is not the required spiritual energy.

It is all well and good for the time being to enact a pretence of love and devotion to the personal God but if the impure mento-emotional energy is used for that action, it will never cause the devotee to be transited to the spiritual plane.

Verse 24

क्लेशकर्मविपाकाशयैरपरामृष्टः पुरुषविशेष ईश्वरः ॥ २४ ॥

kleśa karma vipāka āśayaiḥ aparāmṛṣṭaḥ puruṣaviśeṣaḥ Īśvaraḥ

kleśa – affliction, troubles; karma – action; vipāka – developments; āśayaiḥ – by subconscious motivations; aparāmṛṣṭaḥ – unaffected; puruṣa – person; viśeṣaḥ – special; īśvaraḥ – Supreme Lord.

The Supreme Lord is that special person who is not affected by troubles, actions, developments or by subconscious motivations.

Analysis:

Lest there be confusion, *Śrī Patañjali* defined the Supreme Lord, the *Īśvara*, as the person who is ever-free from all afflictions, actions and developments in the material world and from subconscious motivations. Such a person wherever he may be found, would cause the devotee to enter into the higher consciousness for being free from the normal operations of the mento-emotional energy, as stated in the previous verse:

īśvara praṇidhānāt vā

"Or by the method of profound religious meditation upon the Supreme Lord." (Yoga Sūtra 1:23)

Application:

This person is that special individual who is not affected by troubles, actions, developments or by subconscious motivations, which are based on the urgings of subtle material nature. Contact with this person must be made from the spiritual body of the devotee, not from the material form or subtle body. There is authorized worship of God using a material body and using a subtle form, but that is not under discussion by Patañjali.

For practice in Patañjali's *method, one has to use the spiritual body directly and not relate through a material form.*

Verse 25

तत्र निरतिशयं सर्वज्ञबीजम्॥ २५॥

tatra niratiśayaṁ sarvajñabījam

tatra – there, in Him; niratiśayaṁ – unsurpassed; sarvajña – all knowing; bījam – origin.

There, in Him, is found the unsurpassed origin of all knowledge.

Analysis:

This is a further description of the Supreme Lord. *Śrī Patañjali* did not name this Lord as Krishna or Shiva or Brahma, Jesus Christ or anyone else. He gave only the Lord's special characteristics through which this person may be identified.

Application:

The Supreme Person is for all practical purposes the ultimate knower. He is the most experienced person. One does not have to accept this deity to benefit from this manual of Patañjali. *He does not say that one should be a theist to use the information.*

The profound religious meditation upon the Supreme Lord is one of the methods for attaining deep samādhi. *One can use any other.*

Verse 26

स पूर्वेषामपि गुरुः कालेनानवच्छेदात्॥ २६ ॥

sa eṣaḥ pūrveṣām api guruḥ kālena anavacchedāt

sa = sah – He; eṣaḥ – this particular person; pūrveṣām – of those before, previous authorities, the ancient teachers; api – even; guruḥ – the spiritual teacher; kālena – by time; anavacchedāt – unconditioned.

He, this particular person being unconditioned by time, is the guru even of the ancient teachers, the previous authorities.

Analysis:

To further clarify this Supreme Person, *Patañjali* reveals that God as the teacher even of ancient authorities. That person is ever-existing as the supreme master and teacher of everyone.

Application:

This God, being unconditioned by time, is the teacher even of the ancient theistic masters of yoga, the pioneers of the process of release. There are atheistic masters of yoga who became proficient in samādhi. *Regardless of a belief or disbelief in God and with right endeavor, one is privileged in transiting to higher levels of consciousness.*

Verse 27

तस्य वाचकः प्रणवः॥ २७॥

tasya vācakaḥ praṇavaḥ

tasya – of him; vācakaḥ – what is denoted or named; praṇavaḥ – the sacred syllable āuṁ (Oṁ).

Of Him, the sacred syllable* āuṁ (Oṁ) *is the designation.

Analysis:

Oṁ is the standard designation given to the Supreme Being by the Vedic sages, who transcended this world before. In the *Bhagavad Gītā*, *Śrī* Krishna identified Himself with this *āuṁ (Oṁ)*.

Application:

In India, teachers before *Patañjali* designated the sacred syllable *ĀUM (Oṁ)* as being related to the Supreme Person. An *oṁ* sound may be created with the vocal cords and repeated with or without prayer beads. *Oṁ* may be intonated in the mind. Either method has validity. Therefore one should use a method which suits one's psychology.

Verse 28

तज्जपस्तदर्थभावनम्॥ २८॥

tajjapaḥ tadarthabhāvanam

taj = tat – that sound; japaḥ – murmuring; tadarthabhāvanam = tat = that + artha – value + bhāvanam – with deep feelings.

That sound is repeated, murmured constantly for realizing its meaning.

Analysis:

The *japa* murmuring must be done with deep feeling and intense concentration. This leads into a deeper state of mind and to a quietude in which reverberates the sounds from the supernatural world. These sounds are the actual *āuṁ (Oṁ).* The yogi recognizes them after purifying his mento-emotional energy through *prāṇāyāma* and a lack of interest in the material world.

A key factor is to disengage the gears of memory from the engine of the intellect. So long as the memory wanders autonomously, the yogi cannot be free from the chatter and image flashing in the mind. Thus he will not experience what comes from the supernatural and spiritual worlds.

Application:

Many ancient teachers constantly repeated and murmured ĀUM (Oṁ) for realizing its effects and meaning. One may practice in that tradition.

Verse 29

ततः प्रत्यक्चेतनाधिगमोऽप्यन्तरायाभावश्च॥ २९॥

tataḥ pratyakcetana adhigamaḥ api antarāya abhāvaḥ ca

tataḥ – thence, what is resulting; pratyak – backwards, inwards, in the opposite direction; cetana – sense consciousness; adhigamaḥ – accomplishment; api – also; antarāya – obstacle; abhāvaḥ – not existing; ca – and.

As a result there is an inwardness of the sense consciousness and the disappearance of obstacles to progress.

Analysis:

The act of chanting *oṁkāra* culminates in the attainment of the stage of *pratyak (pratyāhāra)*, or the internalization of the sense consciousness. Usually this consciousness flows outward into the subtle and gross material world. If *āuṁ (Oṁ)* is repeated properly, one develops introspection so that the same outward-going sense energy reverses and begins to flow inwards.

This causes conservation of psychological energy in the realms of thinking and feeling. The mento-emotional energy becomes restrained and conserved. The yogi then gets a boost of pranic energy charge and experiences supernatural and spiritual realities. This leads into *dhāraṇā* practice which is the sixth stage of yoga.

Once one masters the internalization of the sense consciousness, many obstacles vanish and one is lifted out of the dimension where such hindrances exist. The obstacles remain for others who have not advanced to that stage.

Application:

When oṁ *is uttered correctly, one's sense energy develops the urge to turn away from objects outside of one's material body. The sense energy then seeks psychological objects. The extrovert tendency which is an obstacle to progress is greatly decreased. Chanting of* oṁ *may be done as the vibration of the Sanskrit letters* ā-u-ṁ *or as two letters* o-ṁ. *In either case the sound begins in the front of the mouth and recedes gradually to the back into the head. The resonation of* oṁ *causes effects which silence all other sounds in the brain. In the head of the subtle body, the resonation of* oṁ *causes the organs in the subtle head to become stabilized and to jump frequencies to higher dimensions. Chanting of* oṁ *with meditation, while sitting and focusing on the central forehead, causes rapid acceleration of spiritual progress. There is an instruction from Krishna about this:*

omityekākṣaraṁ brahma vyāharanmāmanusmaran
yaḥ prayāti tyajandehaṁ sa yāti paramāṁ gatim (8.13)
ananyacetāḥ satataṁ yo māṁ smarati nityaśaḥ
tasyāhaṁ sulabhaḥ pārtha nityayuktasya yoginaḥ (8.14

Controlling all openings of the body, and restricting the mind in the core of consciousness, situating the energizing energy of the soul in the brain, remaining fixed in yoga concentration,

...uttering Om, the one-syllable sound which represents the spiritual reality, meditating on Me, the yogi who passes on, renouncing the body, attains the highest objective. (*Bhagavad Gītā 8.12-13*)

Verse 30

व्याधिस्त्यानसंशयप्रमादालस्याविरतिभ्रान्तिदर्शनालब्धभूमिकत्वानवस्थितत्वानि

चित्तविक्षेपास्तेऽन्तरायाः ॥ ३० ॥

vyādhi styāna saṁśaya pramāda ālasya avirati bhrāntidarśana alabdhabhūmikatva anavasthitatvāni cittavikṣepaḥ te antarāyāḥ

vyādhi – disease; styāna – idleness; saṁśaya – doubt; pramāda – inattentiveness; ālasya – lack of energy; avirati – proneness to sensuality; bhrāntidarśana – mistaken views; alabdhabhūmikatva – inability to maintain the progress made, not holding the ground (bhumi); anavasthitatvāni – unsteadiness in the progression; cittavikṣepaḥ – scattered mental and emotional energy; te – these; antarāyāḥ – obstacles.

These obstacles are disease, idleness, doubt, inattentiveness, lack of energy and proneness to sensuality, mistaken views, inability to maintain the progress attained, unsteadiness in progression, scattered mental and emotional energy.

Analysis:

Pratyāhār practice, which was described in the previous verse as being the main benefit from murmuring the *āuṁ (Oṁ)* sound, is the turning point in the practice of a yogi. If he masters that, there is really no turning back for him. He will thereafter consolidate the progress. Those who do not master *pratyāhār* are subjected to numerous types of discouragement in yoga practice. It is mainly because they did not master *prāṇāyāma*.

Under a false notion *(bhrāntidarśana)*, a neophyte gets an idea that he does not have to do any painstaking strenuous *prāṇāyāma*. Thus he neglects a very important stage and is unable to displace the lower pranic energies in his subtle body.

Let us consider the obstacles.

Disease *(vyādhi)*

Disease is an obstacle to any yogi who acquires a gross body for the practice of yoga. That body is our means of deliverance but if unhealthy, our minds and emotions will cause us to desist from practice for some time. A yogi should be realistic. He is a limited being and cannot expect that his human form will always be free from disease.

Some advanced yogis maintain the practice even with disease. This is to maintain the spirit of the practice. If one passes on from a diseased body and does not attain liberation, one will carry to the next human body the tendency to do yoga, which will be an asset in the new form. Thus even if there is disease, a yogin should maintain whatever portion of the practice he can do with the diseased form.

One who mastered the seventh stage of yoga, that of *dhyāna*; effortless linkage of the attention to the higher concentration forces, is not put down by disease, but others definitely are. Since one's liberation is reliant on the status of the human body, one should do as much as possible to protect it from malfunction.

Laziness / Idleness *(styāna)*

By constitution some people possess a fickle mind and lack determination. Such persons attend yoga class for quick liberation. Without understanding the requirement, they adopt the view that everyone can attain instant liberation or that a great yogin should be able to liberate everybody. The truth is that everyone cannot become liberated because by constitution some spirits do not have the gomsha or inner drive to strive for liberation.

Nonetheless, a person who is by nature idle-minded, might become liberated if his *ātma* or spirit is connected existentially to a great yogin. If a boat has too small of an engine, then a tug, a small boat with an over-size engine can pull it along. Similarly if another boat has a large engine that is defective, it too can be pulled by a powerful tug. It is more a question of how long such a tug can pull the powerless craft. How long can a great yogi drag an idle-minded disciple?

Idle-mindedness can be overcome after long, long practice, especially in *prāṇāyāma* and *pratyāhār*, the breath infusion and sensual restraints. It is the outpouring of the sensual energies which cause a person to have a scattered mind. This is why, in the last sutra, *Patañjali* indicated that if one chants the *Oṁkāra* one can develop internalization.

Doubt *(saṁśaya)*

Doubt is removed by personal experience of spiritual truths. Such experience comes after persistent practice. Some student yogis are doubtful by instinct. Even after having a few experiences, they remain troubled about the aim of yoga. This stresses their minds and causes them to go slower in the progressions.

A doubtful student will leave the path unless he or she is sustained in the practice by the association of a great yogin.

Inattentiveness *(pramāda)*

This is related to idleness and is based on innate tendencies of the scattering energies of the mind. It is by mastery of *pratyāhār*, the fifth stage of yoga, that this is achieved. Inattentiveness is a state of mind which is driven by certain types of pranic forces which latch on to a particular living entity. If he or she can change that pranic energy, taking in a more concentrated type, the inattentiveness goes away.

Lack of energy *(ālasya)*

In yoga one must endeavor. If there is a lack of energy, there will be no progress.

Proneness to sensuality *(avirati)*

This is also driven by the type of pranic energy in the mind. Hence one needs *prāṇāyāma* and *pratyāhār* practice to change the nature of the mind by purifying the energy content. The mental and emotional energy which we use has certain inherent dysfunctions.

Mistaken views *(bhrāntidarśana)*

Mistaken views come about according to the status of the intellect which is used for analyzing. That subtle organ, regardless of its accurate or inaccurate deductions, is prone to receiving information from the senses. The senses in turn accept information in a prejudiced way, depending on the type of sensual energy used and on the basis of what comes up in the memory circuits. Purification of the *buddhi* brings about a dismissal of the mistaken views and that process is called *buddhi* yoga which is described in detail in chapter two and three of the *Bhagavad Gītā*.

One must purify the life force, the *kuṇḍalinī* chakra, as well as all parts of the subtle body. One must be celibate by practicing the yoga austerities. Then the intellect assumes a brighter glow and becomes capable of avoiding mistaken views.

Inability to sustain progress *(alabdhabhūmikatva)*

A person who adopts yoga and who, by association with a great yogi, makes progress, may not be able to maintain the advancement. He or she might digress into a lower stage after sometime. This is due to the assertion of the lower nature. It is due also to the distractions which come by virtue of the power of the memory. Instead of shedding off previous negative tendencies, the person is motivated by these, because of the probing and prompting of the memory circuits. Thus the person becomes distracted from yoga and is driven to live a life which is similar to the one used by non-yogis. Thus whatever progress made is lost for the time being, when the lower tendencies take over the psyche and force their way of operation.

Unsteadiness in progress *(anavasthitatvāni)*

Unsteadiness in progression occurs because of the force of cultural activities. These acts force their way into the life of an aspiring yogi and cause him to abandon yoga altogether or to see it as being a side feature. When the cultural activities assert themselves as the priority, the yogi is unable to maintain a consistent practice. His progression becomes sporadic and he loses faith, thinking that yoga will give him no results.

A yogi in such a position needs to consult with a person who understands karma yoga as it is taught in the *Bhagavad Gītā* to Arjuna. If one works under the direction of the Universal Form in helping with duties in karma yoga, then one can ultimately be free from cultural acts.

Scattered mental and emotional energy *(cittavikṣepaḥ)*

The only way to abandon the scattered mental and emotional energy is through *prāṇāyāma* and *pratyāhār* practice. *Pratyāhār* practice causes one not to need much association from others because one conserves the sensual powers and enriches oneself while becoming being less and less dependent on social associations. *Prāṇāyāma* practice makes the yogin see that it is possible to displace the lower pranic energies in the psyche with higher ones which accelerate yoga.

Application:

*The **obstacles** to the practice of yoga are: physical and mental diseases, idleness, doubts about the power of the practice, inattentiveness while practicing, lack of energy to invest in an intense practice, proneness to sensuality in terms of always being drawn to forms in this world, mistaken views due to the inability to side-step cultural activities and scattered mental and emotional energy which is due to the influence of subtle matter.*

A student should tackle those features one by one. Their removal requires detailed observation, analysis and elimination. Any of these facets can forestall progress and blight a yogi.

***Disease** is more than a physical danger and a distracting preoccupation. Disease could be physical and psychological simultaneously. Getting rid of a physical disease does not put an end to its psychic counterpart. The condition of the subtle body is a separate study in yoga which takes place during the practice of* prāṇāyāma. *Ultimately escape from disease can happen by jumping into higher dimensions, where a lower subtle form is abandoned in a previous realm and one scuttles and assumes a new subtle configuration that is spontaneously generated in a higher world.*

Idleness *is a vast danger in meditation and it is due to absorption in voids. Since one is conditioned to physical variety and activity, one may be discouraged for meditation if there are no psychological objects during a session. This can cause one to turn away from a blank mind and return to physical reality.*

Void states need be tolerated if one is to reach beyond the subtle mundane realities. If one is afraid of the voids, one is condemned to physical activities and to the lower subtle planes. There is one meditation that rids one of voidal boredom. It is listening to the naad oṁ *sound which resonates in the subtle head. This is a high frequency sound which occurs on the right or left side near either subtle ear. By constantly listening to naad one escapes from the danger of idleness. In his instruction to Uddhava, Krishna said this:*

piṇḍe vāyv-agni-saṁśuddhe
hṛt-padma-sthāṁ parāṁ mama
aṇvīṁ jīva-kalāṁ dhyāyen
nādānte siddha-bhāvitām

In performing full purification within his body, by air and by fire, he should meditate on the effortless linking of his attention to the concentration force which connects with My subtle but supreme partial manifestation, which is situated on a lotus in the bosom area, and which the perfected yogis experience at the end of their progression through naad subtle sound resonation. (*Uddhava Gītā* 22.23)

Doubt *occurs in advanced practice because of the fluidity of the dimensions and the unsettling nature of reality. Like an albatross which cannot find a place to rest its feet as it flies above a vast ocean, the yogi eventually succumbs to doubts about higher existence, and makes a fatal decision that life on this material planet is the only substantial thing there is.*

To escape from being such a loser, a yogi has to aspire under the shelter of a divine being, who can and does reveal spiritual territories where stability reigns and suitable spiritual forms can be assumed. The situation which causes doubts at an advanced stage is described in this way by Krishna:

kleśo'dhikatarasteṣām
avyaktāsaktacetasām
avyaktā hi gatirduḥkhaṁ
dehavadbhiravāpyate (12.5)

The mental exertion of those whose minds are attached to the invisible existence is greater. The goal of reaching that invisible reality is attained with difficulty by the human beings. *(Bhagavad Gītā 12.5)*

Inattentiveness *comes on in meditation when a yogi hits a void and meditates for weeks or months and finds no dimension with an environment and other beings. He loses interest in subtle existence. Since gross life is filled with unfavorable circumstances, he becomes inattentive to it with no recourse to anything else. To escape such a fate, a yogi needs to hitch himself to a great teacher or a divine being.*

Lack of energy *assails those mystics and psychics who are ignorant of the energizing benefits of* prāṇāyāma *breath infusion techniques. Sooner or later, the subtle body is de-energized and drained by an aging physical form. As nature would have it, a material body causes energization of the subtle form soon after birth, and subsequent de-energization when the new form deteriorates. This is a* kuṇḍalinī *procedure. It is older than the duration of even primitive life on this planet. It is older than the birth of the universe. No one is going to nudge it out of existence, not even God.*

The ultimate escape from exhaustion is relocation to a world where everything is spiritual, where all materials are spiritual energy. In the meantime, exhaustion can be modified and minimized by breath infusion, the processes of prāṇāyāma *practice.*

Proneness to sensuality *is eradicated by shifting one's sensual quest to higher dimensions. Some mystics propose that the sensual quest be scrapped entirely. That was the idea left for us by Gautama Buddha. However such an idea though logical is useless in the face of reality, since one cannot abolish sensuality. The secret to its control is relocation to a place where sensual expression reinforces spirituality. In this existence it wreaks havoc on one's sense of security.*

Mistaken views *stall a yogi or mystic when that person remains stubbornly attached to concepts which arose as a result of many births of frustration in the material world.*

Persons who are distressed by their individuality may develop a need to be wiped out, to commit spiritual suicide. Since that is not their existential right, they eventually become totally frustrated as they find that they must keep on existing through states of unconsciousness. Since they are allergic to a Supreme Being, they resort to mistaken views about the deity.

The inability to sustain progress *occurs because of an overestimation of one's prowess and a lack of appreciation of the assistance rendered by advanced yogis and divine beings. These persons give help to all entities everywhere. If one fails to recognize* *their silent and non–assertive assistance, one will fail to maintain the progress attained.*

Denial of a Supreme Person is a serious miscalculation in the life of a mystic or yogi. Thus Patañjali's *alert should be heeded:*

kleśa karma vipāka āśayaiḥ aparāmṛṣṭaḥ
puruṣaviśeṣaḥ Īśvaraḥ
sa eṣaḥ pūrveṣām api guruḥ kālena anavacchedāt
tatra niratiśayaṁ sarvajñabījam

The Supreme Lord is that special person who is not affected by troubles, actions, developments or by subconscious motivations.

There, in Him, is found the unsurpassed origin of all knowledge.

He, this particular person being unconditioned by time, is the guru even of the ancient teachers, the authorities from before. *(Yoga Sutras 1.24-26)*

***Unsteadiness in progression** is due to karmic complexities which are thrown on the life path of a yogi. Such destined mess-ups forcibly distract the yogi and engage him in social affairs. The way out is a serious study of the power of providence and an agreement to settle differences with fate on fate's terms.*

***Scattered mental and emotional energy** is the main problem for the meditator. It has to do with the core-self's lack of psyche control. As ordered by material nature, the core-self is just like a cog in a complicated ticking machine. To break the control of nature the self should shut down the scattered mental and emotional energies. This literary gift of* Patañjali *discusses how to meet that goal.*

Verse 31

दुःखदौर्मनस्याङ्गमेजयत्वश्वासप्रश्वासा विक्षेपसहभुवः ॥ ३१ ॥

duḥkha daurmanasya aṅgamejayatva
śvāsapraśvāsāḥ vikṣepa sahabhuvaḥ

duḥkha – distress; daurmanasya – of mental depression; aṅgamejayatva – nervousness of the body; śvāsapraśvāsāḥ – labored breathing; vikṣepa – distraction; sahabhuvaḥ – occurring with the symptoms.

Distress, depression, nervousness and labored breathing are the symptoms of a distracted state of mind.

Analysis:

Physical distress, mental distress, emotional distress (causing nervousness of the body) and labored breathing occur as symptoms of a distracted mind. These manifest in old age as a matter of course. To decrease these occurrences, consistent *āsana* and *prāṇāyāma* practice is required.

These distractions and the obstacles to progress mentioned in the previous verse must be avoided by a yogin. He must recognize how these come about. He must stay away from their causes. He must side-step the associations which bring on or aggravate these conditions.

Application:

It would be necessary to remove the tendency for distracted states of mind. These come about by distress, depression, nervousness and labored breathing. All of which are triggered by impulsive emotional states. While in psychology these are treated in a direct way which relates to their effects on social living, in meditation these are regarded as superficial symptoms of a deeper trauma in the subtle body.

The behavior of the subtle form is directly controlled by its subtle energy (pranic) intake. Thus a yogi treats distracted mental states by displacing low-vibration mental energy with high-frequency breath infusion.

Verse 32

तत्प्रतिषेधार्थमेकतत्त्वाभ्यासः ॥ ३२ ॥

tatpratiṣedhārtham ekatattva abhyāsaḥ

tat – that; pratiṣedha – removal; ārtham – for the sake of; eka – one; tattva – standard method in pursuit of reality (tattva); abhyāsaḥ – practice.

For the removal of the obstacles, there should be the practice of a standard method used in the pursuit of the reality.

Analysis:

One has no alternative but to practice, using methods which yogis in the past were successful in applying. Each yogin should use a method that applies to his state of development. In the *Bhagavad Gītā*, we find a similar statement about the practice:

śrī-bhagavān uvāca
asaṁśayaṁ mahā-bāho mano durnigrahaṁ calam
abhyāsena tu kaunteya vairāgyeṇa ca gṛhyate

The Blessed Lord said: Undoubtedly, O powerful man, the mind is difficult to control. It is unsteady. By practice, however, O son of Kunti, by indifference to its responses, also, it is restrained. (*Gītā 6.35*).

Application:

To remove any of these obstacles, one should practice a standard method, which was effective for a more advanced yogi and which he recommends. One should be careful to find remedies which apply in the pursuit of reality, which is to say, solutions which accelerate spiritual advancement. Superficial cures may fulfill the social mission but they will not help in the spiritual quest and if anything they discourage deeper insight.

Verse 33

मैत्रीकरुणामुदितोपेक्षाणां सुखदुःखपुण्यापुण्यविषयाणां भावनातश्चित्तप्रसादनम्॥ ३३ ॥

maitrī karuṇā muditā upekṣānāṁ
sukha duḥkha puṇya apuṇya
viṣayāṇāṁ bhāvanātaḥ cittaprasādanam

maitrī – friendliness; karuṇā – compassion; muditā – joyfulness, cheerfulness; upekṣaṇam – indifference, neutrality, non-responsiveness; sukha – happiness; duḥkha – distress; puṇya – virtue; apuṇya – vice; viṣayāṇāṁ – relating to attractive objects; bhāvanātaḥ – abstract meditation; citta – mento-emotional energy; prasādanam – serenity.

The abstract meditation resulting from the serenity of the mento-emotional energy comes about by friendliness, compassion, cheerfulness and non-responsiveness to happiness, distress, virtue and vice;

Analysis:

This reverts back to the second verse where the skill of yoga is defined:

yogaḥ cittavṛtti nirodhaḥ

"The skill of yoga is demonstrated by the conscious non-operation of the vibrational modes of the mento-emotional energy." (Yoga Sūtra 1:2)

The turbulence in the mental and emotional energies causes the living entity to be unsettled in the material creation and to strive after that which is temporary. This causes stress and ends in frustration because the temporary state of manifested energy always changes either in a favorable or unfavorable way.

For stability of that energy, one must practice yoga for a long time. Most persons are disinclined to austerities and do not regard yoga as a priority. They are beholden to the sensual energies and the promises transmitted to them by such powers, promises that for the most part, are fulfilled partially.

By cultivating friendliness, by administering compassion, by maintaining a cheerful demeanor and by an attitude of neutrality in response to the lower energies, the yogin develops serenity of nature, which allows him to practice the abstract meditation through which he is allowed to break free and enter into the supernatural and spiritual dimensions.

Application:

When the obstacles temporarily subside or when they are removed altogether, an abstract meditation ensues. In that state, the creative urges disappear. This is directly related to the successful cultivation of friendliness, compassion, cheerfulness and non-responsiveness to happiness, distress, virtue and vices. Failure to cultivate and express friendliness, compassion, overall cheerfulness and resistance to the need for happiness, distress, virtue and vice, results in a failed yoga practice. Without these attributes, a yogi finds that providence becomes hostile and dampens the enthusiasm for practice.

Non-responsiveness to moods and social incentives is the single method for conserving psychological energy. This conservation provides inner stability which is needed for a steady practice. Hours upon hours of silent meditation, while retracting the sensual energies are required.

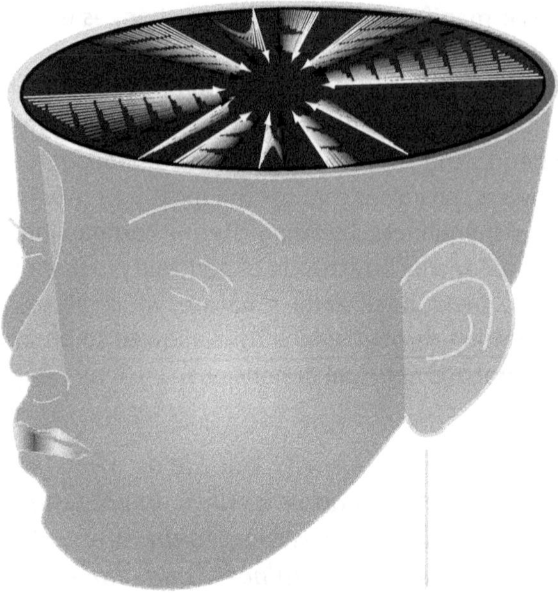

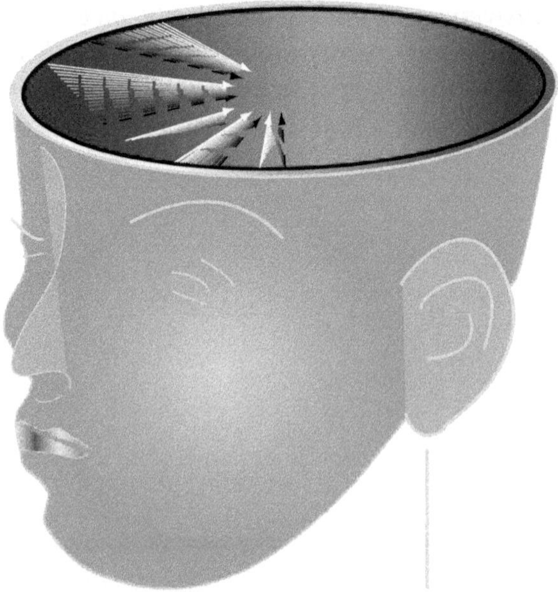

Verse 34

प्रच्छर्दनविधारणाभ्यां वा प्राणस्य ॥ ३४ ॥

pracchardana vidhāraṇābhyāṁ vā prāṇasya

pracchardana – exhalation; vidhāraṇābhyāṁ – by inhalation; vā – or; prāṇasya – of the vital energy.or by regulating the exhalation and inhalation of the vital energy.

or by regulating the inhalation and exhalation of the vital energy;

Analysis:

This is the practice of *prāṇāyāma*, the fourth stage of yoga. This must be learned from a knowledgeable yogin who practices and knows the benefits of the methods taught. It may be discovered by the most diligent students of yoga.

Application:

That abstract meditation may be caused by practicing a method of breath infusion wherein the vital energy of the gross and subtle bodies is enhanced, causing the creative lower urges to be displaced by a higher grade of subtle energy. Prāṇāyāma *is worth the while but one may have to practice for some time to derive its benefits.*

Verse 35

विषयवती वा प्रवृत्तिरुत्पन्ना मनसः स्थितिनिबन्धिनी ॥ ३५ ॥

viṣayavatī vā pravṛttiḥ utpannā
manasaḥ sthiti nibandhanī

viṣayavatī – like normal sensuality, something different but similar to a normal object; vā – or; pravṛttiḥ – the operation; utpannā – produced, brought about; manasaḥ – of the mind; sthiti – steadiness; nibandhanī – bond, fusion.

Or fusion and steadiness of the mind is produced by the operation of the mento-emotional energy towards an object which is different to but similar to a normal thing;

Analysis:

This refers to the supernatural and or spiritual perception, which is developed in the psyche of a yogi, especially in his intellect through the curbing of the imagination faculty. Then the yogi sees beyond the gross and subtle material energy into the super-physical and spiritual realities. Such perception brings steadiness of mind and fusion of the attention into the higher level of reality, the *cit ākāśa*.

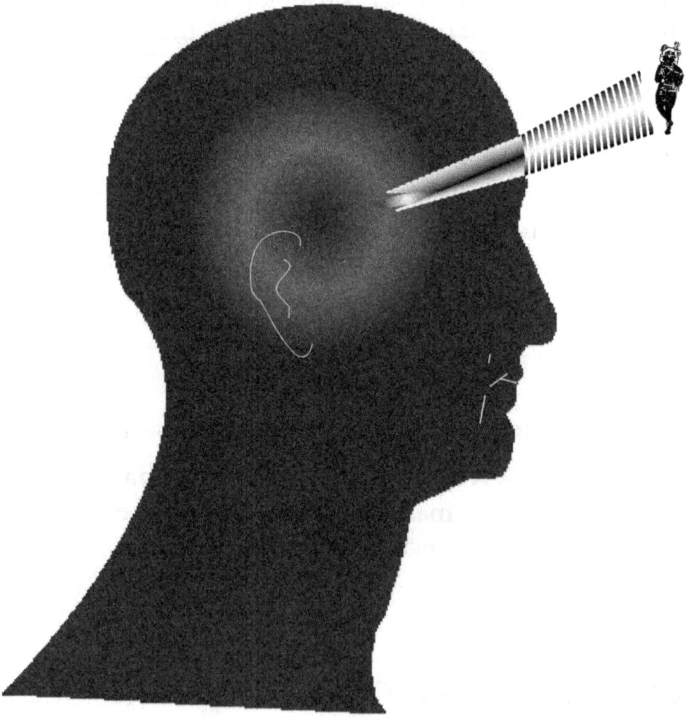

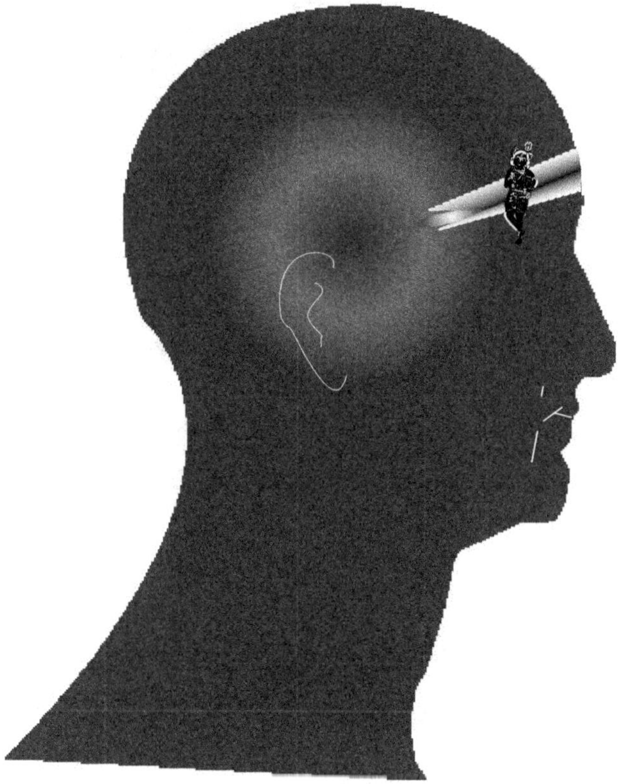

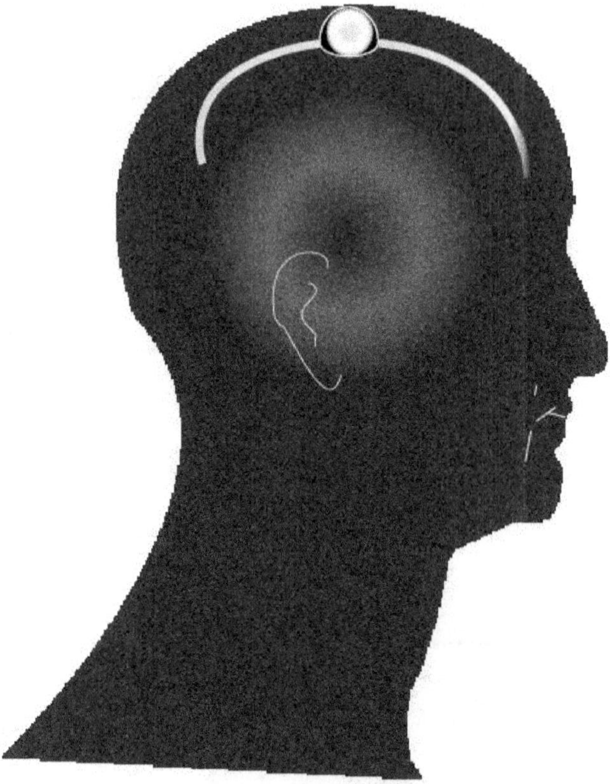

Viṣaya is a normal sense object of this world, something to which our normal senses are usually attracted, either for attaching itself or for repulsing itself. *Vatī* means something similar, something that bears resemblance. Objects in the sky of consciousness are also objects but they do not cause the self to be degraded as objects in this world do.

The term *pravṛtti* means operation, for active function. Even though the aim of yoga is to stop the conventional operation of the mental and emotional energies, still this means that they must be stopped on this side of existence. Hence the functioning of that energy for perception of spiritual objects causes the fusion of the energized mental-emotional force with a higher reality.

Application:

One may attain fusion to higher states or steadiness of mind by directing the mind towards a supernatural or spiritual object. Such an object would be just as real and objective as a physical one. In some meditations, one may become linked to higher states even without endeavoring or desiring. Those experiences cause increase of faith and removal of procrastination and doubts. Reaching the spiritual environments by transiting there in meditation, the yogi discovers spiritual objects and spiritual social relationships. Thus his speculations about a voidal state in liberation are banished. The need for association is asserted in reference to spiritual reality which is similar and yet different to social life on the physical plane.

Verse 36

विशोका वा ज्योतिष्मती॥ ३६ ॥

viśokāh vā jyotiṣmatī

viśokāh – sorrowless; vā – or; jyotiṣmatī – spiritually-luminous.

or by sorrowless and spiritually-luminous states;

Analysis:

The various experiences of student yogis differ, but these experiences cause them to have faith in the practice of yoga. It increases their drive for progress. It is not stereotyped. One person might see beyond this physical world into the sky of consciousness. Another might feel a sorrow-less energy or experience sheer spiritual light.

Any of these experiences which are valid alternatives to this subtle and gross material existence, will result in the stability of mind required to curtail the operations of the mental and emotional energy, thus leading to personal experiences of the transcendence and mastership over one's interaction with the material world.

Application:

Sorrow-less and spiritually-luminous states may occur in environments with no visibility of forms. Thus many who get these experiences spread the word that the Absolute is formless.

What does this really mean?

It amounts to being limited to one's experiences. Other yogis and mystics testify reliably about spiritual domains in which there is social life with divine beings.

The conclusion is that both realms exists; spiritual locales with and without persons.

Verse 37

वीतरागविषयं वा चित्तम्॥ ३७॥

vītarāga viṣayaṁ vā cittam

vīta – without; rāga – craving; viṣayaṁ – an object or person; vā – or; cittam – mento-emotional energy.

or by fixing the mento-emotional energy on someone who is without craving;

Analysis:

One may, by association with a great yogi who is free from craving, develop stability to stop the haphazard operations of the mental and emotional energies. Such associations can definitely cause this.

Application:

One may attain super-consciousness by linking one's attention to a person who is without craving. Since that person's psychology is quiescent, linking with that person may cause one's psyche to become energized sufficiently to transit into transcendental domains.

Verse 38

स्वप्ननिद्राज्ञानालम्बनं वा॥ ३८॥

svapna nidrā jñāna ālambanaṁ vā

svapna – dream; nidrā – dreamless sleep; jñāna – information; ālambanaṁ – taking recourse; vā – or.

or by taking recourse to dream or dreamless sleep.

Analysis:

Some yogis gain steadiness of mental and emotional energy by keeping track of dreams and by remaining objectively conscious in dreamless sleep. Through these mystic observations, they study the movements of consciousness and are able to discern reality and non-reality and to situate themselves in state which is detached from normal operations of the mental and emotional force. For success in this course, a yogi must distance himself from the memory, because its impressions encourage mental instability and motivate the emotional energies to create picture sensations for further cultural activity in the material world.

Application:

In some cases, super-consciousness may occur after one takes recourse to dreams or dreamless sleep. Dimensional switching occurs in dreams, dreamless sleep and day dreaming. This may take place spontaneously, even if one does not desire it.

Verse 39

यथाभिमतध्यानाद्वा ॥ ३९ ॥

yathābhimata dhyānāt vā

yatha – as, according; ābhimata – what is dearly desired; dhyānāt – from effortless linkage of the mind to a higher concentration force; vā – or.

Or it can be achieved from the effortless linkage of the mind to a higher concentration force which was dearly desired.

Analysis:

This verse hints that through love and endearment, one may attain the cessation of the undesirable operations of the mental and emotional energy. The process of *bhakti* or devotion is mentioned in this verse under the term *ābhimata* which means agreeable, beloved or endearing.

Application:

Spontaneous linkage of the attention to a higher concentration force or person, who was dearly desired, may occur when the yogi is graced by a divine being or when higher energy is infused into the psyche by higher authority.

Verse 40

परमाणुपरममहत्त्वान्तोऽस्य वशीकारः ॥ ४० ॥

paramāṇu paramamahattvāntaḥ asya vaśīkāraḥ

paramāṇu = parama – smallest + aṇu – atom; parama – greatest; mahattva – largeness, cosmic proportions; āntaḥ – ending, extending to; asya – of his, him; vaśīkāraḥ – mastery of the psyche.

The mastery of the psyche results in control of the relationship to the smallest atom or to cosmic scale.

Analysis:

Some commentators explain this as the yogi gaining control over what is atomic *(aṇu)* and what is cosmic *(mahatva)*. However, on a close study of the Sanskrit term *vaśīkāraḥ*, it is clear that *Patañjali* meant otherwise. He means the yogi can control not the atomic and cosmic but rather his relationship to the same. By controlling his psychological energies, he acquires a greater degree of control over his response to what is cosmic and atomic. Those aspects remain the same in the universe he inhabits, but his response to them reflects a position of relative immunity to their spiritually-detrimental influences. This occurs because of the yogin's detachment, his lack of interest, as described in verses 12 and 15.

While a human being is compelled to react in a preset way to a set of circumstances or to a type of energy, the yogin, because he switched his energy intake to a higher concentration force, sidesteps most influences and remains unbiased through proficiency of yoga.

Application:

The mastery over the function and movement of the urges, results in the control of one's relationship to the smallest portions of energy or to the largest conglomerations. The power of the individual limited spirit is used most efficiently when it can regulate its sensual intake. All social connections function though sensuality. Hence control has to do with maintaining a disciplined relationship with the senses.

Verse 41

क्षीणवृत्तेरभिजातस्येव मणेर्ग्रहीतृग्रहणग्राह्येषु तत्स्थतदञ्जनता समापत्तिः ॥४१॥

kṣīṇavṛtteḥ abhijātasya iva maṇeḥ grahītṛ
grahaṇa grāhyeṣu tatstha tadañjanatā samāpattiḥ

kṣīṇa – great reduction; vṛtteḥ – concerning the mento-emotional operations; abhijātasya – of what is produced all around or transparent; iva – like; maṇeḥ – of a gem; grahītṛ – perceiver; grahaṇa – flow perception; grāhyeṣu – in what is perceived; tatstha – basis foundation; tad = tat – that; añjanatā – assuming the nature of or characterization of (añj – to smear with, to mix with); samāpattiḥ – linkage fusion.

In regards to the great reduction of the mento-emotional operations, there is fusion of the perceiver, the flow of perceptions and what is perceived, just like the absorption of a transparent jewel.

Analysis:

This fusion also happens in ordinary experiences when a person becomes totally preoccupied with gross objects or experiences an endearing feeling. So what is special about a yogin who achieves this fusion after greatly reducing the impulsive operations of his mento-emotional energy?

Indeed, there is a difference in the accomplishment of the yogi. For one thing, the ordinary person is driven impulsively. He has not practiced to stop the automatic operations in the mind. He has no control over the fusion of consciousness with the various forces that attract the mind and pull the emotions. He does not have purity in the psyche which the yogi earned by higher yoga practice. Therefore, the yogin's linkage with higher concentration forces is quite different to the ordinary man's absorption of subtle and gross energy, through an impure psyche.

Application:

For great reduction of the urges in your mind and emotions, one has to sort between the perceiver in the mind, the related flow of the ideas or images and the objects perceived. This is similar to knowing the state of a transparent jewel, the light which it absorbs from a colorful source, and that source itself. In this comparison the perceiver is like the jewel. The ideas and images are like the colored light reflected.

Meditation in silence with keen observation brings clarity in sorting the observant core-self, an object and the flow of energy between. Practice to stop the flow of energy from the mind to an external object. Then practice full retraction of the energy flow from the core-self to the edge of the mind.

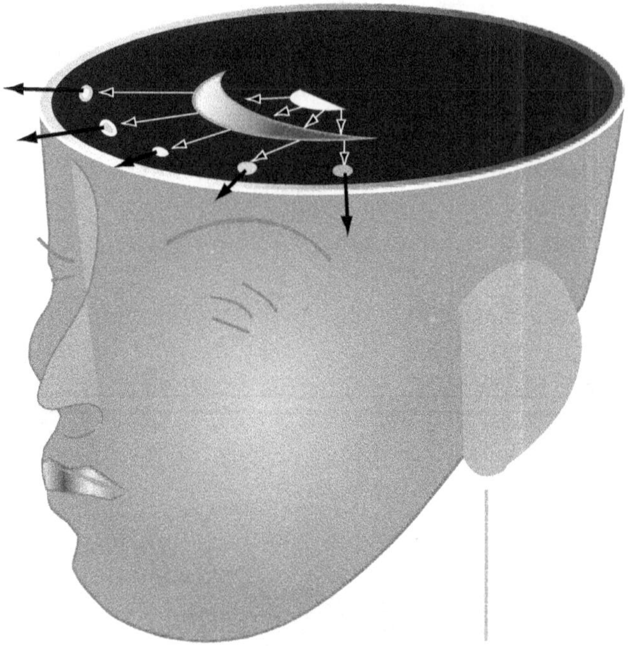

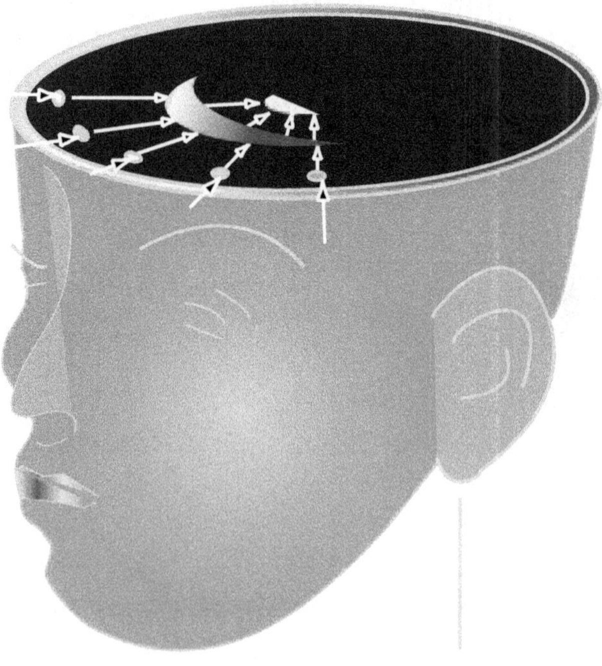

Verse 42

तत्र शब्दार्थज्ञानविकल्पैः सङ्कीर्णा सवितर्का समापत्तिः ॥४२॥

tatra śabda artha jñāna vikalpaiḥ
saṅkīrṇā savitarkā samāpattiḥ

tatra – there, in that case; śabda – word; artha – meaning; jñāna – knowledge concerning something; vikalpaiḥ – with option, alternative, doubt, uncertainty; saṅkīrṇā – blending together, mixed; savitarkā – thoughtfulness, reasoning, deliberation; samāpattiḥ – fusion, linkage.

In that case, the deliberate linkage of the mento-emotional energy to a higher concentrating force occurs when a word, its meaning and the knowledge of the object alternate within the mind, blending as they was.

Analysis:

There are various types of linkage between the yogin's partially or fully purified attention and some other person or force. It might be a person or force residing in his psyche or one that is exterior to it. When that linkage occurs with the analytical organ being operative, then it is called deliberative linkage or *vitarkā samāpattiḥ*. *Śrī Patañjali* defined each type of higher linkage to clarify the levels of accomplishment of a yogi and to remove any vagueness regarding lower accomplishment and higher yoga.

Application:

Even in ordinary usage of consciousness, one may deliberately link one's attention to a higher concentration force by a careful observation of how the mind-attention mechanism operates when a word, its meaning and the knowledge of the object alternate within the mind, blending as they were, with one of those facets permeating the other. This occurs through the anxiety of the core-self and its craving for conclusions. This craving increases the speed of the operations up to the step of displaying the conclusion. When the core-self develops an interest in understanding the details of mental moves and constructions, the system slows down and every change of ideas during a mental construction is revealed

A word, as well as its meaning and knowledge about the object, are stored in the mind in different compartments. This information is procured by the intellect. Once it cycles through this appropriation process, the intellect displays a conclusion to the core self, along with a suggestion about a possible response. When perceived in slow motion, every step in the process is seen.

In locating a word in the mind, one will find the vibration or energy for the word in one place, the meaning of the word in another, and knowledge about the object named in yet another. One can observe how each of these subtle stuffs are moved from one mental place to another, like files in a government building which are transported to different rooms upon request.

Verse 43

स्मृतिपरिशुद्धौ स्वरूपशून्येवार्थमात्रनिर्भासा निर्वितर्का ॥ ४३ ॥

smṛtipariśuddhau svarūpaśūnya iva arthamātranirbhāsā nirvitarka

smṛti – memory; pariśuddhau – on complete purification; svarūpa – essential nature of something; śunya – devoid of; iva – as if; artha – meaning; mātra – only; nirbhāsā – shining; nirvitarka – fusion or linkage without deliberation or analysis.

Non-analytical linkage of the attention to a higher concentration force occurs when the memory is completely purified and the essential inquiring nature disappears as it were, so the value of that higher force shines through.

Analysis:

When a yogi engages in non-analytical linkage of his attention to a higher concentration force with a purified memory and when he finds that the analytical urges of the intellect cease functioning, then he discovers the value of the higher concentration force or person to which he is linked.

Readers should keep in mind that these are advanced explanations. *Patañjali* described subtle super-physical and spiritual phenomena that are not easily understood. It gives us an appreciation of the accomplishments of the great yogins.

Śudda means purity but *pari śudda* means complete purity. When the memory is cleansed by consistent and thorough practice, which stops impulsive activations and silences influences and biases, then the yogi can disarm the intellect.

Because the intellect *(buddhi)* carries the weapon of analysis, it is able to blackmail and intimidate the self into cooperating with the plan of the impulsive and blind life force and the shortsighted senses. Thus when the yogin silences the weapon of analysis, he becomes freed from its harassments.

At that time the senses become powerless to bother him, because they lose the protective support of their powerful ally, the analytical intellect organ (*buddhi)*. The yogin no longer has to fight the memory to stop it from whimsically and impulsively showing so many impressions in their visual and auditory forms. With such distractions reduced to nil, he progresses quickly and is able to move his attention into the realm of the *cit ākāśa*, the sky of consciousness.

Application:

Even though analysis is useful in material existence, it does not serve the purpose in higher yoga practice. In fact such analysis is discarded completely in the highest stages. When the memory is completely purified where it no longer reminds the self to pursue vices and when the inquisitive nature disappears, then the higher concentration forces and the divine personalities are experienced objectively.

Analysis is necessary in the beginning. During the advanced stages it is discarded because then, one does not work with lower references and with survival anxieties. One must start with analysis; let me be clear on that issue. Do not discard analysis until one breaks away from the need to survive. Be very honest about this.

The memory is a hindrance in higher yoga, because it impulsively tries to impose itself on the analytical orb. Once the orb is influenced, it conveys the acquired prejudices to the self, which usually accepts what is presented to it.

The memory is purified when the core-self disengages from schemes of survival. This allows for the gradual erasure of memory impressions. Over time these faded ideas disappear.

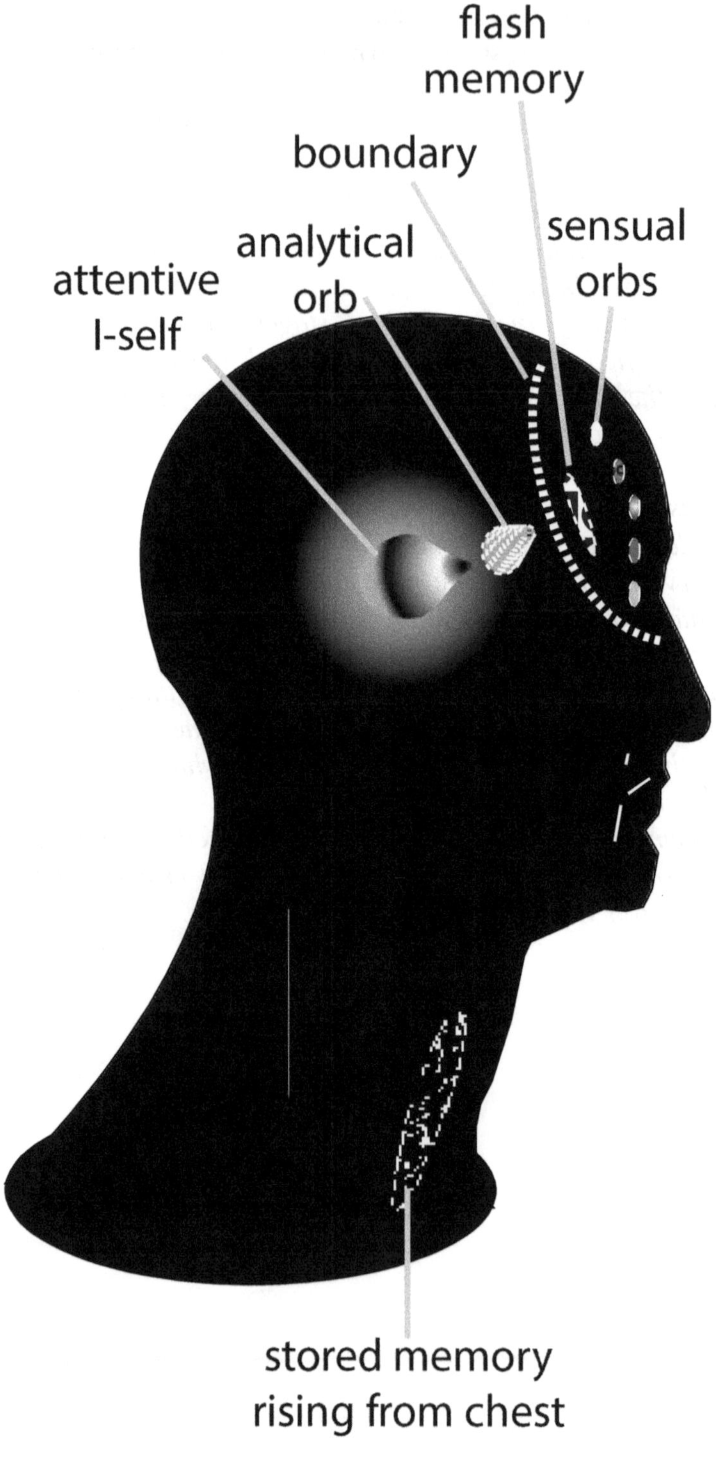
flash
memory
boundary
sensual
orbs
analytical
orb
attentive
I-self
stored memory
rising from chest

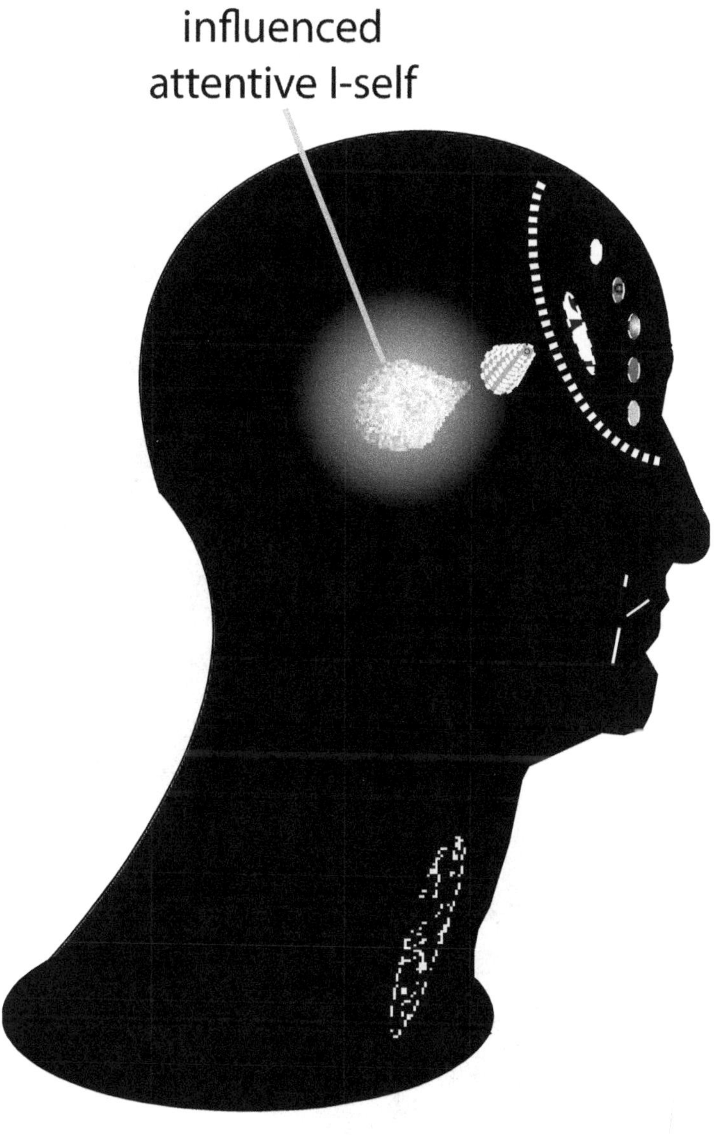
influenced
attentive I-self

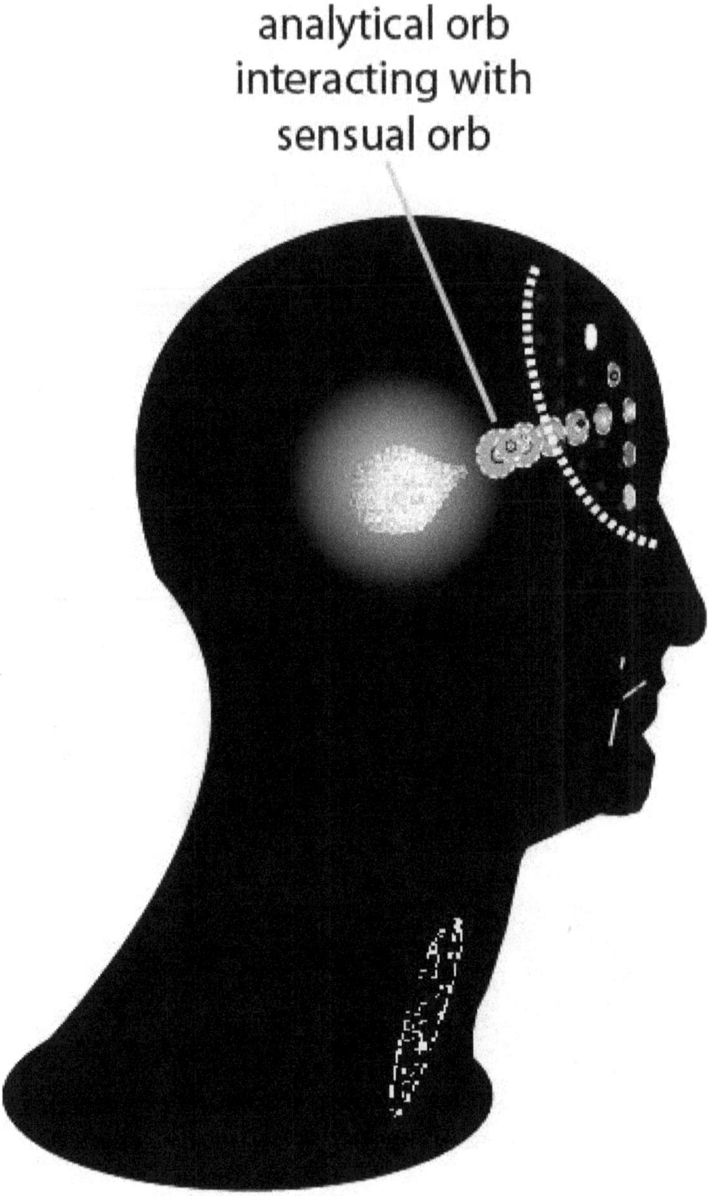
analytical orb
interacting with
sensual orb

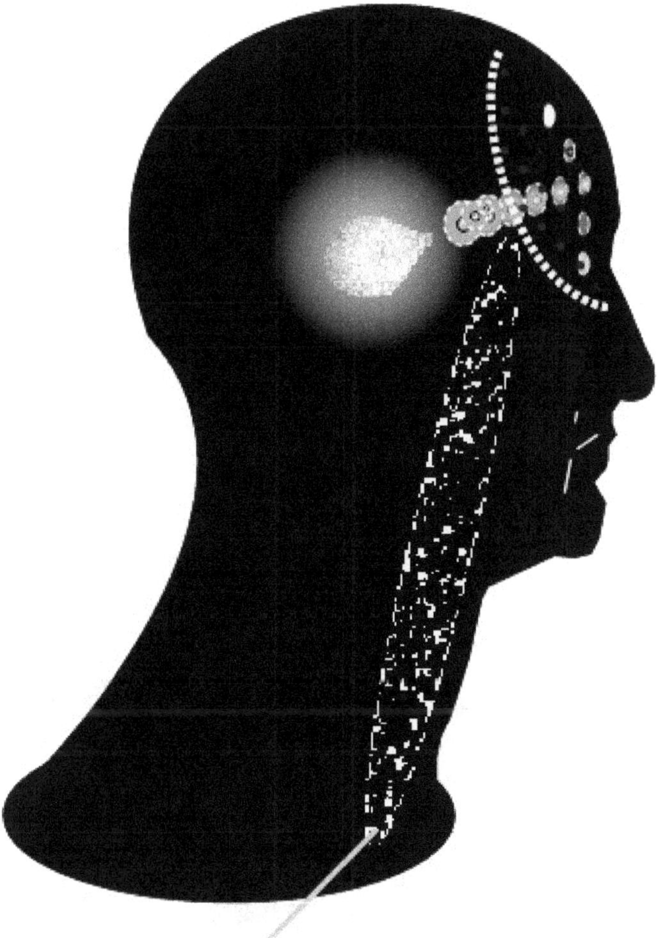

Stored memory rises from chest
to interact with current ideas and images

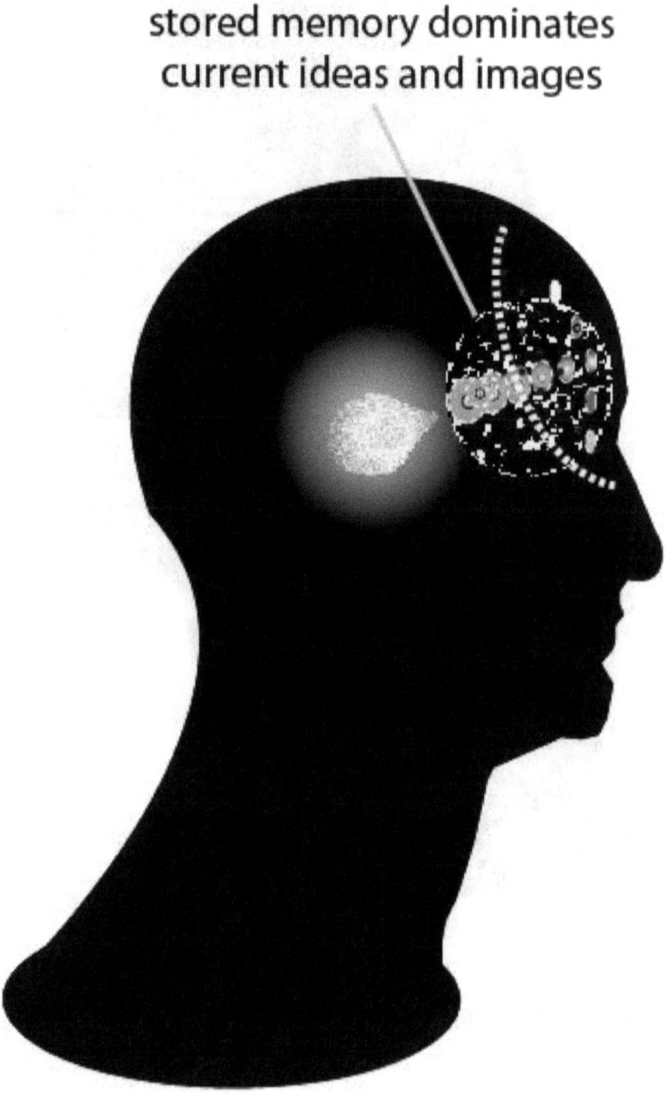
stored memory dominates
current ideas and images

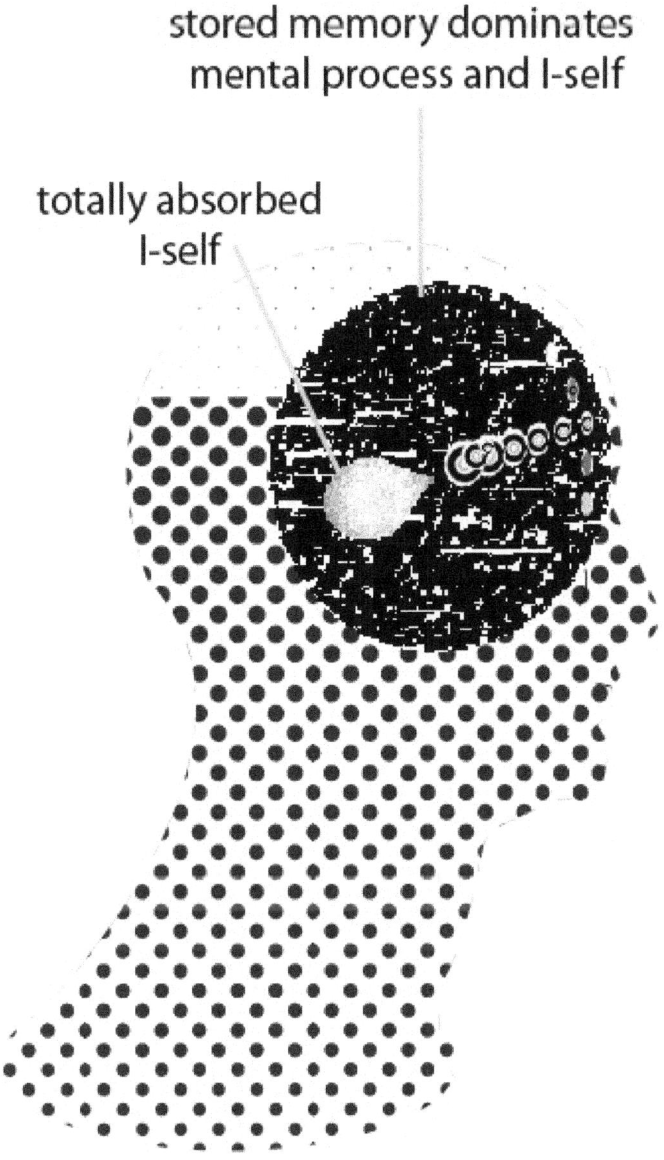

Verse 44

एतयैव सविचारा निर्विचारा च सूक्ष्मविषया व्याख्याता ॥ ४४ ॥

etayaiva savicārā nirvicāra ca
sūkṣmaviṣayā vyākhyātā

etaya – by this; eva – only; savicārā – investigative linkage of one's attention to a higher concetration force; nirvicāra – non-investigative linkage; ca – and; sūkṣma – subtle; viṣayā – object; vyākhyātā – explained.

By this, the investigative linkage and non-investigative linkage of one's attention to a higher concentration force consisting of subtler objects, was explained.

Analysis:

There is a slight difference between an analytical linkage and an investigative one. It depends on the yogi's interest in particular subtle phenomena and on the influence of the higher concentration force to which he is linked. At a higher stage, he regards the subject of interest without the bias of an analytical or investigative approach. This is called surrender to the higher concentration force, person or object.

Application:

One may investigate very subtle objects after dropping the usual analysis and after mastering the linkage of the attention as stated above. For beginners, the investigative linkage is the method, since a neophyte does not have the sensitivity to objectify subjective states. Hence, even though investigative mystic research is not the higher level, it is necessary and it brings one a step closer to the advanced levels.

Functioning in the subjective states without the required sensitivity to be conscious at those levels has to be achieved through mastership of subjective research. Meditation, therefore, takes time, patience and honesty for advanced practice.

Verse 45

सूक्ष्मविषयत्वं चालिङ्गपर्यवसानम्॥४५॥

sūkṣmaviṣayatvaṁ ca aliṅga paryavasānam

sūkṣma – subtle; viṣayatvaṁ – what is concerning the nature of gross objects; ca – and; aliṅga – without characteristics; paryavasānam – termination.

The insight into the subtle nature of gross objects terminates when one becomes linked to the higher concentration force which has no characteristics.

Analysis:

Regarding matter, a yogin should research it by linking his attention to its subtle states. Ultimately, he will reach a stage where he connects with the undifferentiated state of matter, the ultimate state. At that point, his research into it terminates. Yet he still has to discover the role played by the Supreme Lord *(īśvara)* in activating and manifesting matter.

Śrī Patañjali graciously informed all student-yogins that when they reach the featureless state of the subtle material energy, they have reached the end of their research into it. Even so, this must be discovered individually by each yogin during the linkage of his attention to higher concentration forces.

Application:

The insight gained by that mystic research terminates, when one becomes linked to the higher concentration force which has no gross characteristics and which is not directly linked to a gross object. This marks the end of research into the origin and behavior of all aspects of material existence. At this stage the curiosity of the yogi or yogini terminates. This is that person's terminal fulfillment in the subtle and gross material worlds. Limited entities who gain this achievement either align themselves to a Personality of Godhead or create their own supernatural territory from which sub-dimensions evolve. They are the gods of such systems where their imaginative powers are supreme.

Verse 46

ता एव सबीजः समाधिः ॥४६॥

tā eva sabījaḥ samādhiḥ

tā – they; eva – only; sabījaḥ – with motivation from the mento-emotional energy; samādhiḥ – effortless continous linkage of the attention to a higher concentration force.

The previous descriptions concern the effortless and continuous linkage of the attention to a higher concentration force, as motivated by the mento-emotional energy.

Analysis:

After progressing in higher yoga, a yogin realizes that his practice was being motivated by the same mental and emotional energy which he endeavored to transcend. A psychic and motivational force in his psyche derived fulfillments from the endeavors. He traces and discovers that these forces derived pleasure from the practice.

At that stage advancement begins in earnest and the purpose of the material energy in the life of the yogi is revealed. Accrediting the mental and emotional mundane energy in his psyche, he moves on in appreciation. The purpose for which the Supreme Being caused the limited self, His eternal partner, to come in contact with a mundane life force and an investigative subtle organ called the analytical orb (*buddhi),* now becomes evident to the yogin.

Application:

Initially, all of this is motivated by the creative urges, in the sense that they caused the inquiring tendency in the first place. Thus the previous descriptions were of higher experiences which were motivated because the spirit made contact with energies on this side of existence. All spiritual efforts are made on the basis of the same troublesome mento-emotional energy. Before being manifested in this creation, a limited spirit had no idea about a desire for liberation. The impulse for that arises because of the challenges the individual is confronted with after it discovers itself on this side of existence. Thus the initial motivation to inquire and achieve is based on the subtle material nature.

Prior to finding itself existing in the material world, a limited spatial spirit has only subjective consciousness. With that it can do nothing besides being conscious in the moment without information, without a past, without a future and without a sense of individual identity.

Thus the material existence causes a sense of identity to be invoked but it does so with the disadvantage of tagged responsibilities. Sooner or later any spirit which finds itself in this predicament aspires for freedom from ignorance. The approach to this varies from individual to individual, with some desiring to cancel the sense of identity and others wanting to expand it.

Verse 47

निर्विचारवैशारद्येऽध्यात्मप्रसादः ॥४७॥

nirvicāra vaiśāradye adhyātmaprasādaḥ

nirvicāra – non-investigative linkage of one's attention to a higher concentration force; vaiśāradye – on gaining competence; adhyātma – relationship between the Supreme Soul and the limited one; prasādaḥ – clarity and serenity.

On gaining competence in the non-investigative linkage of one's attention to the higher concentration force, one experiences the clarity and serenity which results from the linkage of the Supreme Soul and the limited one.

Analysis:

When the yogin passes beyond the realm of material nature, his attention links with spiritual energy in total. Then he may, if he continues to progress, gain competence. That causes his limited spirit to link with the Supreme Personality. From that connection, a serenity of spirit and clarity of relation between him and that Supreme Person develops.

Application:

In the advanced states the lower urges lose their hold on the self. The self is no longer motivated by them and no longer reacts to them, either for fulfilling the urges or for becoming indifferent to them. Thus new motivations come from the Supreme Soul to whom the limited soul becomes linked. That association brings clarity and serenity. After becoming proficient in continuous effortless linkage, the yogi is directly attuned to the Supreme Spirit and abandons the supports in the subtle material nature.

A limited being does not become absolute and independent at any stage, but a direct reliance on the Supreme Person is preferred.

Verse 48

ऋतम्भरा तत्र प्रज्ञा ॥ ४८ ॥

ṛtaṁbharā tatra prajñā

ṛtaṁbharā – reality-perceptive, truth discerning; tatra – there, at that time; prajñā – insight.

There with that competence, the yogin develops the reality-perceptive insight.

Analysis:

The *ṛtaṁbharā buddhi* is referred to differently in the Vedic literatures like the *Bhagavad Gītā*. It is termed as *jñāna-dīpena* and *jñāna chakṣusa*, meaning the lighted *(dīpena)* insight *(jñāna)* or the vision *(chakṣusa)* of insight *(jñāna)*. In yoga parlance it is often called the cleansed brow chakra or third eye. This insight comes after much practice, when the mental and emotional energy *(citta)* is silenced, when it stops vibrating in reference to the subtle and gross material energy and when it stabilizes and converts the imagination orb into exacting visual insight.

Śrīla Yogeshwara of Gangotri, a great yogin, rated this *ṛtaṁbharā buddhi* highly and recommended its development. *Śrī Patañjali* explained that until one reaches the stage of *nirvicāra samādhi*, that of non-investigative linkage of one's attention to a higher concentration force in the *cit ākāśa*, one cannot develop this *ṛtaṁbharā buddhi.*

Application:

With competence after much practice, the yogi develops the reality-perceptive insight, which is inherent to the Supreme Soul and which the limited soul develops in the supreme association. This insight is direct spiritual perception. It includes clear visual sensing which allows spiritual forms to be perceived. In the material world, anyone using a healthy material body has certain automatic perceptive rights just by virtue of being fused into that form. Similarly a spirit in a spiritual psyche perceives spiritual objects without extraneous means.

Verse 49

श्रुतानुमानप्रज्ञाभ्यामन्यविषया विशेषार्थत्वात्॥ ४९ ॥

śruta anumāna prajñābhyām
anyaviṣayā viśeṣārthatvāt

śruta – what is heard; anumāna – what is surmised or reasoned out; prajñābhyām – from the two methods of insight; anya – other; viṣayā – object; viśeṣa – particular aspect; arthavāt – because of an object.

It is different from the two methods of insight which are based on what is heard and what is reasoned out, because those are limited to a particular aspect of an object.

Analysis:

Direct perception with the reality-perceptive insight is different to conventional perception which is based on what is heard or read and what is surmised or reasoned out on the basis of lower sense information. In lower perception, the mind can only deal with one aspect at a time. It presents this one aspect to the intellect for analysis and comparison. Then through prejudiced notions, it forms haphazard opinions.

Application:

Spiritual perception differs from the normal perception, which is based on what is heard of or reasoned in the material world. When the analytical orb gets information in the material world, it is restricted to a partial aspect of an object and never reveals comprehensively. It can gather information in bits and pieces and then put that together for a comprehensive conclusion but it cannot make a spherical analysis all at once.

In contrast the spiritual perception does assessments from the inside of an object and thoroughly.

Verse 50

तज्जः संस्कारोऽन्यसंस्कारप्रतिबन्धी ॥५०॥

tajjaḥ saṁskāraḥ anyasaṁskāra pratibandhī

taj = tat – that; jaḥ – which is produced from; saṁskāraḥ – the impressions; anya – other; saṁskāra – impression; pratibandhī – the preventer, that which effectively suppresses something else.

That impression which is produced from the reality-perceptive insight, acts as the preventer of the other impressions.

Analysis:

Patañjali did a great favor by explaining the stages of higher yoga, a process which is vague even to many yogins who reached the higher practice. This is due to the subtlety of the experiences and the failure of yogins to observe minute details. By a careful study of the information, one will get an idea of where one is located on the path.

In this verse, *Śrī Patañjali* informed that the impression derived from the reality-perceptive insight acts to prevent other impressions in the psyche which were formed by the lower faculty and which hinder advanced practice.

This information is significant, because in higher yoga one wonders when and where one will get rid of the impressions which repeatedly arise in the mind and jar loose the focus. The answer is that until one develops the reality-perceptive insight, one will be unable to completely suppress the distracting impressions. One will instead tolerate them to a degree and use other ineffective methods. This clears misconceptions and gives the student yogi hope that a time will come when the bothersome memories are suppressed.

Application:

Once the association of Supreme Soul is repeatedly attained, the impressions of that contact act as the preventer of the other impressions which previously contravened yoga practices. In this advanced stage, meditation to shift the attention away from the mento-emotional energy and its allied forces becomes irrelevant. With the psyche ordered as preferred and with the mento-emotional force relegated for subordination to the core-self, the yogin no longer has to go through the routines of prāṇāyāma *breath infusion,* pratyāhār *sensual energy withdrawal and* dhāranā *deliberate focus out of normal consciousness. This is a very blessed state. All students should long for it.*

Verse 51

तस्यापि निरोधे सर्वनिरोधान्निर्बीजः समाधिः ॥५१॥

tasyāpi nirodhe sarvanirodhāt nirbījaḥ samādhiḥ

tasya – of that (preventative impression); āpi – also; nirodhe – on the non-operation; sarva – all; nirodhāt – resulting from that non-operation; nirbījaḥ – not motivated by the mento-emotional energy; samādhiḥ – continuous effortless linkage of the attention to the higher concentration force

The continuous effortless linkage of the attention to the higher concentration force which is not motivated by this mento-emotional energy, occurs when there is a non-operation, even of that preventative impression which caused the suppression of all other lower memories.

Analysis:

When all the impressions cease to be activated, the highest contemplation occurs, a contemplation which is not motivated by this end of existence. It is controlled by and operated by the spiritual level of existence, the *cit ākāśa*.

Traditionally this first chapter is called *samādhi* pāda, which means the chapter defining *samādhi*. The Second chapter is *sādhana pāda*, which deals with the practice of yoga. That is of special interest to the students.

Application:

When there is linkage of the attention to the higher concentration force, it must be effortless and continuous (not with effort and not momentarily). This is considered to be samādhi, *the highest stage of yoga. In that state there is a complete departure from the memory. Its power of reminding the self of its contents is completely nullified. The self then becomes freed. With the reference of material existence gone, the yogi or yogini is free to roam through pure spiritual energy, either in touch with divine personality or with spiritual bliss energy, or with both aspects simultaneously.*

Chapter 2
Sādhana Pāda:
Practice Accomplishment

Verse 1

तपःस्वाध्यायेश्वरप्रणिधानानि क्रियायोगः ॥ १ ॥

tapas svādhyāya Īśvarapraṇidhānāni kriyāyogaḥ

tapaḥ – austerity; svādhyāya – study of the psyche; īśvarapraṇihānāni = īśvara – Supreme Lord + praṇidhānāni – profound religious meditation; kriyāyogaḥ – dynamic yoga practice.

Austerity, study of the psyche and profound religious meditation on the Supreme Lord is the dynamic kriyā yoga practice.

Analysis:

Many *Vaiṣṇava* teachers deride *Śrī Patañjali* as an impersonalist, because they misunderstand these *sūtras* and have a negative bias towards yoga. Even though *Śrīla* Vyāsadeva, his son *Śuka* and others like *Nārada*, themselves being leading *Vaiṣṇavas*, did perfect the dynamic *kriyā* yoga practice, still today many Vaiṣṇava leaders who hail in their name, denounce the very process as being devoid of *bhakti* or devotion to *Īśvara*.

However, it is clear that this dynamic *kriyā* practice was taught to Uddhava by *Śrī* Krishna in their final conversation. The three aspects mentioned, namely austerity *(tapaḥ)*, study of the psyche *(svādhyāya)* and profound religious meditation upon the Supreme Lord *(īśvarapraṇidhānāni)* are absolutely essential for the liberation of a living being. Whether one cultivates this by long practice, as *Patañjali* described or one does so effortlessly as *Śrī Caitanya Mahāprabhu* did, it will still be necessary in one way or the other.

Those who practice dynamic *kriyā* and avoid profound religious meditation upon the Supreme Lord, must substitute a profound type of religious meditation toward the yogi guru who gives them techniques. Ultimately, the offering of devotion to that person reaches the Supreme Lord, either directly or through the chain of *siddhas*, who are connected to that ultimate teacher, the spiritual master of the ancient yogis. The profound religious meditation cannot be avoided in the course of dynamic *kriyā* yoga. This explains why someone may become a *siddha* even though he is not an avowed devotee of that Supreme Lord. That person has an indirect but very effective connection through a yogi-guru to God.

Application:

Kriyā *yoga is strongly recommended because it is definite. It is a hands-on personal process. It is not reliant on mere good luck or on accidental process.* Kriyā *yoga has scientific austerity, careful introspective study of the psyche and religious meditation on the Supreme Lord, as its practice. Some* kriyā *masters however either minimize or deny the religious meditation on the Supreme Lord. The success of such masters in reaching the Absolute may be taken as evidence that the Supreme Lord does not mind neglect or denial.*

Patañjali *however gave definite information about the layout of kriya yoga:*

1. austerity
2. study of the psyche
3. profound religious meditation on the Supreme Lord

This is compliant with the requirements mentioned by Krishna in Bhagavad Gītā, *where the 3rd aspect is stressed:*

abhyāsayogayuktena cetasā nānyagāminā
paramaṁ puruṣaṁ divyaṁ yāti pārthānucintayan (8.8)
kaviṁ purāṇamanuśāsitāram aṇoraṇīyāṁsamanusmaredyaḥ
sarvasya dhātāram acintyarūpam ādityavarṇaṁ tamasaḥ parastāt (8.9)
prayāṇakāle manasācalena bhaktyā yukto yogabalena caiva
bhruvormadhye prāṇam āveśya samyak sa taṁ paraṁ puruṣamupaiti divyam (8.10

With a mind that does not venture outwards, which is disciplined by yoga practice, a person goes to the divine Supreme Person, while deeply meditating, O son of Pṛthā.

He who meditates on the Person Who knows everything, the most ancient of people, the Supreme Supervisor, the most minute factor, the one with unimaginable form, with a radiant body, free of grossness,

...and that meditator who even at the time of death, with an unwavering mind, being connected devotedly, with psychological power developed through yoga practice, and having caused the energizing breath to enter between the eyebrows with precision, goes to the Divine Supreme Person. *(Bhagavad Gita 8.8-10)*

Verse 2

समाधिभावनार्थः क्लेशतनूकरणार्थश्च ॥ २ ॥

samādhi bhāvanārthaḥ kleśa tanūkaraṇārthaś ca

samādhi – continuous effortless linkage of the attention to a higher concentration force or person; bhāvana – producing; arthaḥ – for the value or purposes of; kleśa = mento-emotional afflictions; tanū – thought-reducing; karaṇa – cause, causing; arthaś = arthaḥ – for the value of purpose; ca – and.

It is for the purpose of producing continuous effortless linkage of the attention to a higher concentration force and for causing the reduction of the mental and emotional afflictions.

Analysis:

Without the reduction of the mental and emotional afflictions, there can be no *samādhi* or continuous effortless linkage of the attention to a higher concentration force or person. The afflictions serve as distractions to keep the intellect engaged in lower pursuits, effectively barring it from synchronizing with higher levels of consciousness. The dynamic *kriyā* yoga is necessary. It is the only process that systematically reduces the mental and emotional botherations and gradually puts the psyche at a distance from them. It does not postpone or put them into dormancy or drown them out with sounds and images. It brings them to an end.

Application:

Kriyā *yoga causes a reduction of the mental and emotional conflicts and their short-termed or long-termed negative effects. It is the definite way for attaining* samādhi, *which is the continuous effortless linkage of the attention to higher dimensions and their contents. The mental and emotional afflictions doggedly follow a living entity, no matter where it goes in the material creations. It is an achievement to escape from their impositions.*

Verse 3

अविद्यास्मितारागद्वेषाभिनिवेशाः क्लेशाः ॥ ३ ॥

avidyā asmitā rāga dveṣa abhiniveśaḥ kleśāḥ

avidyā – spiritual ignorance; asmitā – misplaced identity; rāga – a tendency of emotional attachment; dveṣa – impulsive emotional disaffection; abhiniveśaḥ – strong focus on mundane existence which is due to an instinctive fear of death; kleśāḥ – the mento-emotional afflictions.

The mental and emotional afflictions are spiritual ignorance, misplaced identity, emotional attachment, impulsive emotional disaffection and a strong focus on mundane existence, which is due to an instinctive fear of death.

Analysis:

The prime cause of the mental and emotional afflictions is spiritual ignorance *(avidyā)*. Unfortunately this ignorance is primeval for many of the living entities who end up in the material creation. They have no idea of their spiritual whereabouts. They assume that their existence is mundane. By not understanding their essential selves *(sva-bhāva)*, they are subjected to endless misidentities. It is by the grace of a spiritually advanced person that one gets some idea about the essential self. It is by the example of such a person that one makes the endeavor to release the self.

The misplaced self identity *(asmitā)* causes numerous afflictions in daily affairs. Through it, one attaches one's psychological energy to persons and things in a harmful way. By yoga discipline, one develops the power to control the sense of identity, so that it may focus only on higher realities and ultimately cause one to be situated in a permanent non-painful condition.

The tendency for emotional attachment *(rāga)* is an impulse which is curbed after one masters the *pratyāhār* fifth stage of yoga practice, by withdrawing the sensual energies from their external pursuits and conserving that energy within the psyche for application to higher realities.

The impulsive emotional disaffection occurs on the basis of justified or unjustified biases acquired in present and past lives. It is impulsive in nature and hard to control. By higher yoga, one can end this.

The strong focus on mundane existence due to an instinctive fear of death *(abhiniveśaḥ)* is removed by realization of the self. One must gain mystic experiences whereby one finds oneself in one's subtle body when it is separated from the gross one. Gradually, by repeated experiences of this sort, one loses the instinctive fear of death and finds that it is no longer necessary to maintain a strong focus on material existence, since one will definitely survive the perishable body. These five causes of the mental and emotional afflictions must be removed before one can enter *samādhi* on a regular basis.

Application:

There are five generalizations of the mental and emotional conflicts which are stored in the psyche. These are the inability to know the difference between one's spirit and its subtle sensing tools, the compelling tendency to react to other influences, the tendency to link with other factors emotionally, the strong urge to dislike certain other factors, and the instinctive fear of death which fosters a strong focus on mundane existence. Little by little, a yogi overcomes these expressions of his confrontation with spiritual ignorance. Though an eternal spirit with an imperishable core identity, the living entity is nonetheless lacking in some technical information. It is not familiar with all aspects of reality. That is ignorance. Its sojourn in the material world makes that lack of knowledge become self-evident.

Verse 4

अविद्या क्षेत्रमुत्तरेषां प्रसुप्ततनुविच्छिन्नोदाराणाम्॥ ४॥

avidyā kṣetram uttareṣāṁ prasupta
tanu vicchina udārāṇām

avidyā – spiritual ignorance; kṣetram – field, existential environment; uttareṣāṁ – of the other afflictions; prasupta – dormant; tanu – reducted; vicchina – alternating, periodic; udārāṇām – expanded.

Spiritual ignorance is the existential environment for the other afflictions, in their dormant, reduced, periodic or expanded stages.

Analysis:

Spiritual ignorance *(avidyā)* is the root cause of the mental and emotional distresses which come upon a living entity, and which are perceived as an impediment by aspiring yogins. Afflictions form on the basis of spiritual ignorance. They arise in the psychological environment of a person who is spiritually ignorant of self-identity, due to a lack of objective experience and too strong of a focus on gross existence.

Application:

The inability to know the difference between one's spirit and its subtle sensing tools is not just that lack of knowledge. It serves as a mental and emotional environment, which produces and supports other conflicts of identity and energy. These conflicting energies may be dormant, reduced, periodical in nature, or fully expanded. If there is a purpose for being in touch with material nature it is the recognition and subsequent remorse of this ignorance. The ease with which a spirit identifies itself with material nature, and the attraction between it and nature, acts like a booby trap to confine the spirit in a very uncomfortable way. That inconvenience is the first motivation for the spirit to segregate itself from material nature. Thus nature itself sponsors the spirit's self realization.

Verse 5

अनित्याशुचिदुःखानात्मसु नित्यशुचिसुखात्मख्यातिरविद्या ॥ ५ ॥

anitya aśuci duḥka anātmasu nitya
śuci sukha ātma khyātiḥ avidyā

anitya – not eternal, temporary; aśuci – not clean, not pure; duḥkha – distress; anātmasu – in what is not the spirit; nitya – eternal; śuci – pure; sukha – happiness; ātma – spirit; khyātiḥ – what is known or identified; avidyā – spiritual ignorance.

Spiritual ignorance is exhibited when what is temporary, impure, distressful and mundane, is identified respectively as being eternal, pure, joyful and spiritual.

Analysis:

This exhibition of spiritual ignorance is rooted in the strong focus on gross existence which is due to an instinctive fear of death (*abhiniveśaḥ*, verse 3). By that focus, one mistakes what is temporary, feeling that it is or can be permanent, if it is maintained by one's interest in it. One feels that what is impure can be purified by external means and by decorations. One does not recognize what is distressful but instead feels that it is joy-yielding. One mistakes what is not the spirit for the spirit. For example, one feels that one's body is oneself, and that it might be possible for one to live as the body indefinitely.

Application:

That spiritual ignorance is revealed to someone when he realizes that what he considered to be eternal was temporary, what was pure was actually impure, what was joyful was in fact distressful, and what was spiritual was mundane. The spirit who initially was just a subjective existence in pure awareness, finds itself with objective awareness in material existence. It is circumstantially forced to dig its way out of this perplexity. Searching and searching, using speculation, trial and error, it eventually reecognizes the distinctions in the various realities.

Verse 6

दृग्दर्शनशक्त्योरेकात्मतेवास्मिता ॥ ६ ॥

dṛg darśanaśaktyoḥ ekātmatā iva asmitā

dṛg = dṛk – supernatural vision; darśana – what is seen; śaktyoḥ – of the two potencies; ekātmatā – having one nature, identical; iva – as if, seems to be; asmitā – mistaken identity.

Mistaken identity occurs when the supernatural vision and what is seen through it, seem to be identical.

Analysis:

The *dṛg śakti* or *dṛk śakti* is the supernatural visionary power which emits from the spirit itself. It is not what is seen, even though it is the medium which is used directly or in conjunction with other perceiving instruments. Hence it is mistaken identity when one feels that what is seen is identical to his own vision.

First of all, the supernatural vision is experienced as one's attention on this level of existence. On this level one uses a subtle and gross instrument for focusing attention. The subtle instrument is the *intellect*, the main organ in the head of the subtle body. The gross instrument is the physical brain with its auxiliary nerves. When the attention is focused through the subtle reality, it is altered by the energy. Thus its prejudices should be realized and taken into account.

Application:

The compelling tendency to react to other influences occurs when one cannot distinguish between the viewing-sensing power and what is seen through it. Identification is commonly considered to be subjective to the viewing self. As endowed by nature with a psychology which is fused to the self, the core-person rarely distinguishes between itself and its subtle viewing apparatus. Higher yoga concerns distinguishing between the perceiving energy in the psyche and the core-self. Thus one has to meditate until one becomes proficient at sorting this self from its fusion into a psychological viewing mechanism.

Verse 7

सुखानुशयी रागः ॥ ७ ॥

sukha anuśayī rāgaḥ

sukha – happiness; anuśayī – connected to, devotedly attached to; rāgaḥ – craving.

Craving results from a devoted attachment to happiness.

Analysis:

A yogin must study his psychology to see how it operates and then take steps to curb it for success in yoga. Each yogi needs to pay attention to his nature, find its defects and alter it in the interest of progress.

Human nature increases craving by being devotedly attached to happiness. Happiness is derived from sensual contact in terms of smelling, tasting, seeing, touching and hearing. In the *pratyāhār* sensual withdrawal stage, a yogi understands how he becomes attached to various types of happiness and how those attachments develop into craving, which forms compulsive habits. Each yogi should systematically review his conduct to understand and then correct the compulsive habits.

Application:

The impulsive urge to link with other factors emotionally creates as a result, a craving for repeated contact with those factors and a devoted attachment to any pleasure experienced in the process. This however is a natural function in creature existence. By the grace of nature, all species are endowed with it. Species need to grow, mature and reproduce. This is sponsored by craving which drives consumption of nutrients which in turn promotes growth, maturation and reproduction. It is nature's way. A yogin has to break away from this and still allow the life force in his body to pursue its natural course.

Verse 8

दुःखानुशयी द्वेषः ॥८॥

duḥkha anuśayi dveṣaḥ

duḥkha – distress; anuśayi – connected to, devotedly attached to; dveṣaḥ – impulsive emotional disaffection.

Impulsive emotional disaffection results from a devoted attachment to distress.

Analysis:

Impulsive emotional disaffection manifests as an instinctive dislike for something or someone. One can become habituated to such disaffection. This results in a cynical attitude and abhorrence towards one object or the other.

Distress, though painful on the emotional level, may be liked by someone. Thus the person is repeatedly drawn into distressful situations in an effort to derive emotional satisfaction by linking emotions to painful situations. When this is discovered by a yogin, he can wean himself from distress and its causes.

Application:

The strong urge to dislike certain factors arises as a need for conflict and disharmony. It is an attachment to distress. Even though distress is not preferred, one can become addicted to it. A human being finds itself liking and disliking the same thing simultaneously. Within the liking energy there might be a disliking force. Within a disliking energy there might be a liking force. Thus a yogi should endeavor for equipoise or neutrality.

Verse 9

स्वरसवाही विदुषोऽपि तथारूढोऽभिनिवेशः ॥९॥

svarasavāhī viduṣaḥ 'pi tatha rūḍho 'bhiniveśaḥ

svarasavāhī = sva – own + rasa – essence + vāhī – flow, current, instinct for self-preservation (svarasavāhī – its own flow of energy of self preservation); viduṣaḥ – the wise man; 'pi = api – also; tatha – just as, so it is; rūḍho = rūḍhah – developed produced; 'bhiniveśaḥ = abhiniveśaḥ – strong focus on mundane existence due to instinctive fear of death.

As it is, the strong focus on mundane existence, which is due to the instinctive fear of death, which is sustained by its own potencies, and which operates for self-preservation, is developed even in the wise man.

Analysis:

Even if wise, a person must curb the instinctive life force. Mastership of *kuṇḍalinī* yoga is necessary before one can attain salvation. The fear of death is due to the natural sense of self-preservation present in the subtle body, which instinctively fears not having a gross form and having to leave such a form permanently.

Unless one effectively resists the life force in the subtle body, one's wisdom or knowledge cannot remove the fear of death. The resistance to this fear is acquired by intake of higher pranic energies, through *prāṇāyāma* and other methods which form part of the elementary *kriyā* yoga practice.

Mastery of the life force, the *kuṇḍalinī* chakra, gives a yogin the ability to infuse the subtle body with a lack of fear. When the subtle body is experienced objectively in subtle existence, it releases itself from dependence on this gross manifestation, and the fear of death *(abhiniveśaḥ)* departs it.

In his translation, the *rāja* yogi, I.K. Taimni, gave riding and dominating as the meaning of *rūḍhah*. His translation reads that *abhiniveśa* is the strong desire for life which dominates even the learned (or the wise). In his purport, he stated that the universality of *abhiniveśaḥ* shows a constant and universal force inherent in life which automatically finds expression in this "desire to live".

In higher yoga one traces that urge to the life force in the subtle body and then to the cosmic life force which dominates the psyche, using urges and motivations to dictate how it should procure gross existences, maintain these and fight to remain rooted in these.

It is only when a yogin has developed a yoga *siddha* body that he becomes totally free of that life force impulse which forces him to procure a foothold in gross existence and struggle for survival in lower worlds.

Application:

The instinctive fear of death is the subtle body's way of showing its dislike for having to repeatedly give up gross forms in an unpleasant way. To counteract the effects of this, the subtle form exhibits a strong focus on mundane existence. These energies operate even in the psyche of a wise man. The reason being that one's liberation does not change the nature of matter.

Verse 10

ते प्रतिप्रसवहेयाः सूक्ष्माः ॥ १० ॥

te pratiprasavaheyāḥ sūkṣmāḥ

te – these, they; prati – opposing, reverting back; prasava – expressing, going outwards; heyāḥ – what is fit to be left or abandoned; sūkṣmāḥ – subtle energies.

These subtle motivations are to be abandoned by reverting their expression backwards.

Analysis:

This verse refers to the practice of *rāja* yoga or mystic actions which effectively curb and totally curtail what is unwanted in the psyche and what thwarts completion of the objectives of yoga.

Pratiprasava is otherwise known as the fifth stage of yoga which is *pratyāhāra (prati-āhāra),* reverting the sensual expressions back into the psyche, so they do not manifest outwards. This allows conservation of valuable psychic energy through which one develops supernatural perception.

Many subtle motivations can be abandoned or made powerless so that they do not degrade the yogi's psyche. One must develop the power to shut down or squelch such energies.

Application:

The mental and emotional conflicts are to be nullified by squelching their eruptions so that when they arise within the mind or emotions, their urges are inhibited or forced back into dormancy or potentiality. A yogi will realize that no matter what, material nature will continue in its own way for eternity. No one, not even God, will affect any permanent changes in it. The conclusion is that to stop its motivation, one has to extract the self from its territories.

If I cannot stop an eruption, my way out is to leave the environment where it takes place. So long as he must be in the material world, a yogi may revert psychic motivation into dormancy. If he is successful he will gain proficiency in advanced practice.

Verse 11

ध्यानहेयास्तद्वृत्तयः ॥ ११ ॥

dhyānaheyāḥ tadvṛttayaḥ

dhyāna – effortless linking of the attention to the higher concentration force or person; heyāḥ – what is fit to be abandoned or left aside; tad = tat – that; vṛttayaḥ – vibrational modes of the mento-emotional energies.

Their vibrational modes are to be abandoned or ceased by the effortless linkage of the attention to a higher concentration force or person.

Analysis:

This advice is direct. It does not state that there are alternate methods for dealing with the vibrational motivations which spring from the *abhiniveśaḥ* urges which cause a yogi and others to pursue mundane life with wanton passion. The attempt at effortless linkage of the attention to higher concentration forces or persons is the only method that reveals to the yogin the various parts of the psyche and the complications he faces in trying to displace the impure nature. The vibrational modes which apply to the lower psychic level and to the physical planes, are not to be silenced except by causing the mind to abandon those lower planes. The techniques are realized by practicing introspective yoga.

Application:

The mental or emotional eruptions are to be squelched by developing a meditation habit whereby the attention effortlessly links to a higher concentration force or person. The potential for eruption will remain. That will continue to rule others from within. The yogi must accept that his power has only one fully-effective application, which is to transit his psyche into a fail-safe dimension.

Verse 12

क्लेशमूलः कर्माशयो दृष्टादृष्टजन्मवेदनीयः ॥ १२ ॥

kleśamūlaḥ karmāśayaḥ dṛṣṭa
adṛṣṭa janma vedanīyaḥ

kleśa – mento-emotional distress; mūlaḥ – root, cause; karma – cultural activities; āśayaḥ – storage, reservoir; dṛṣṭa – perceived, realized; adṛṣṭa – not perceived, not realized; janma – birth; vedanīyaḥ – what is experienced or realized.

The psychological storage of the impressions left by performance of cultural activities which is itself the cause of the mental and emotional distress, is experienced in realized and non-realized births.

Analysis:

This *karma āśayaḥ* or psychological storage-compartment, which holds the compacted impressions which are left by the performance of cultural activities, is manifested to us in meditation as memory. It is very troublesome and stalls the yogi in his attempts to master *pratyāhār*, *dhāraṇā*, and *dhyāna*. A yogi may be stalled for years by motivations which spring from the memory compartment. When the memory emits impressions, they are translated by the mento-emotional energy, the *citta*. Then the intellect takes possession of the pictures and sounds and creates further impressions, causing the psyche to create desires and motivations to act. This is the bane of higher yoga. Until a yogin can control this, he does not progress in the *dhāraṇā* and *dhyāna* practice.

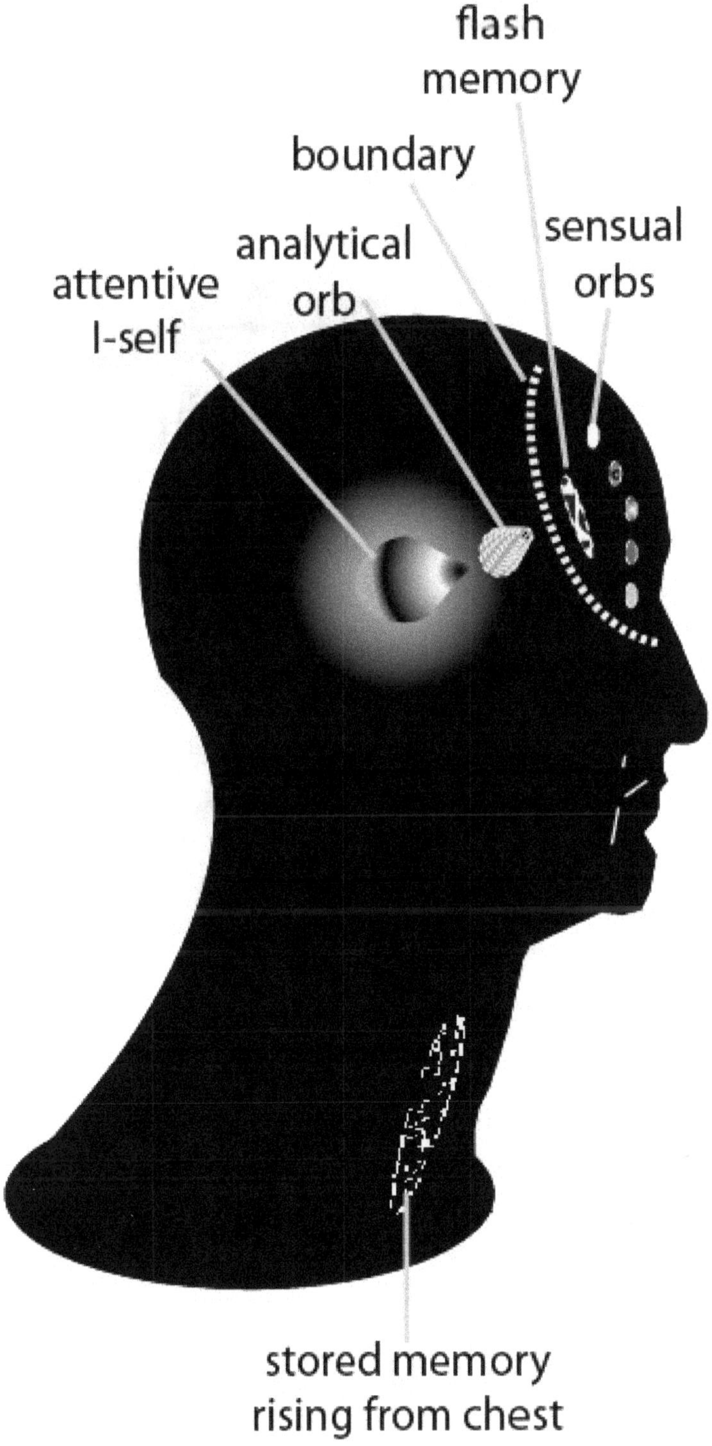
flash
memory
boundary
sensual
orbs
analytical
orb
attentive
I-self
stored memory
rising from chest

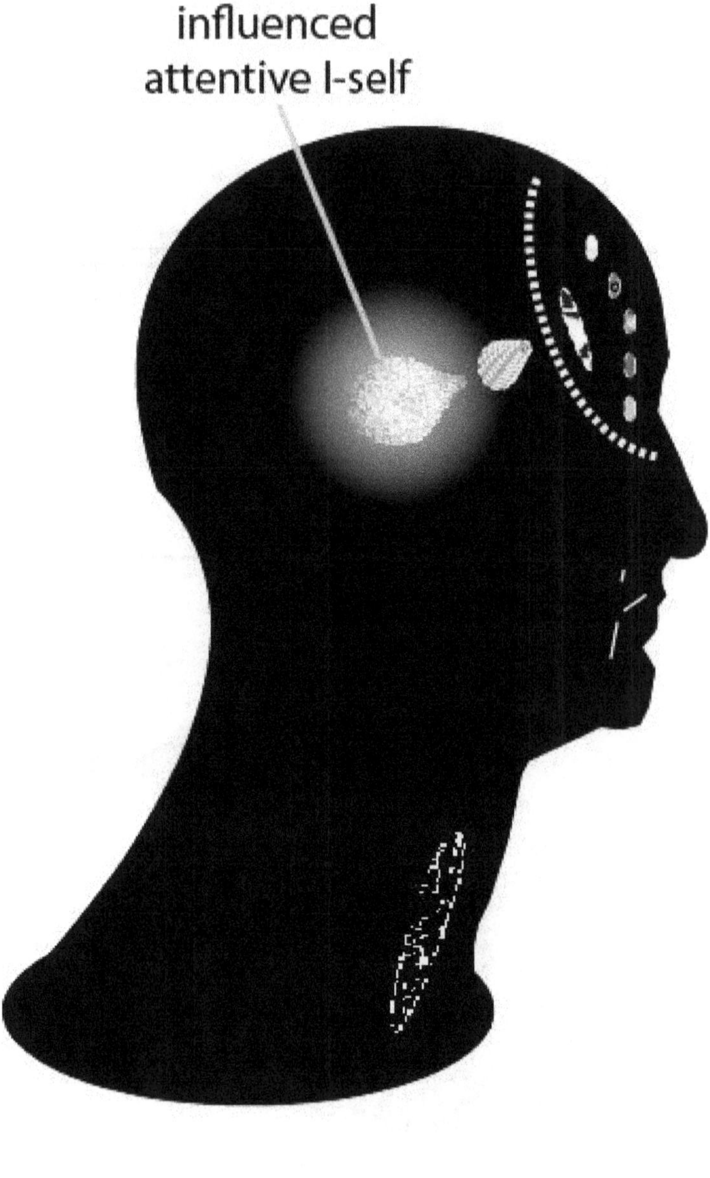
influenced
attentive I-self

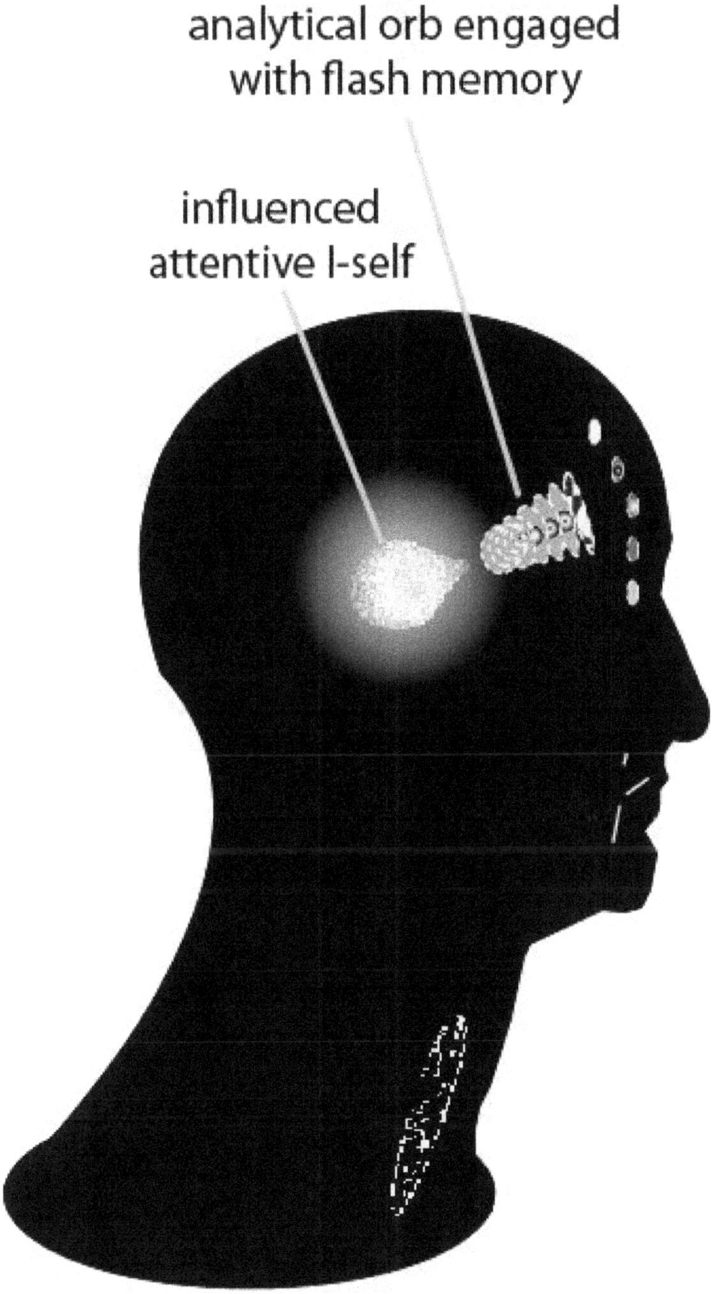
analytical orb engaged
with flash memory
influenced
attentive I-self

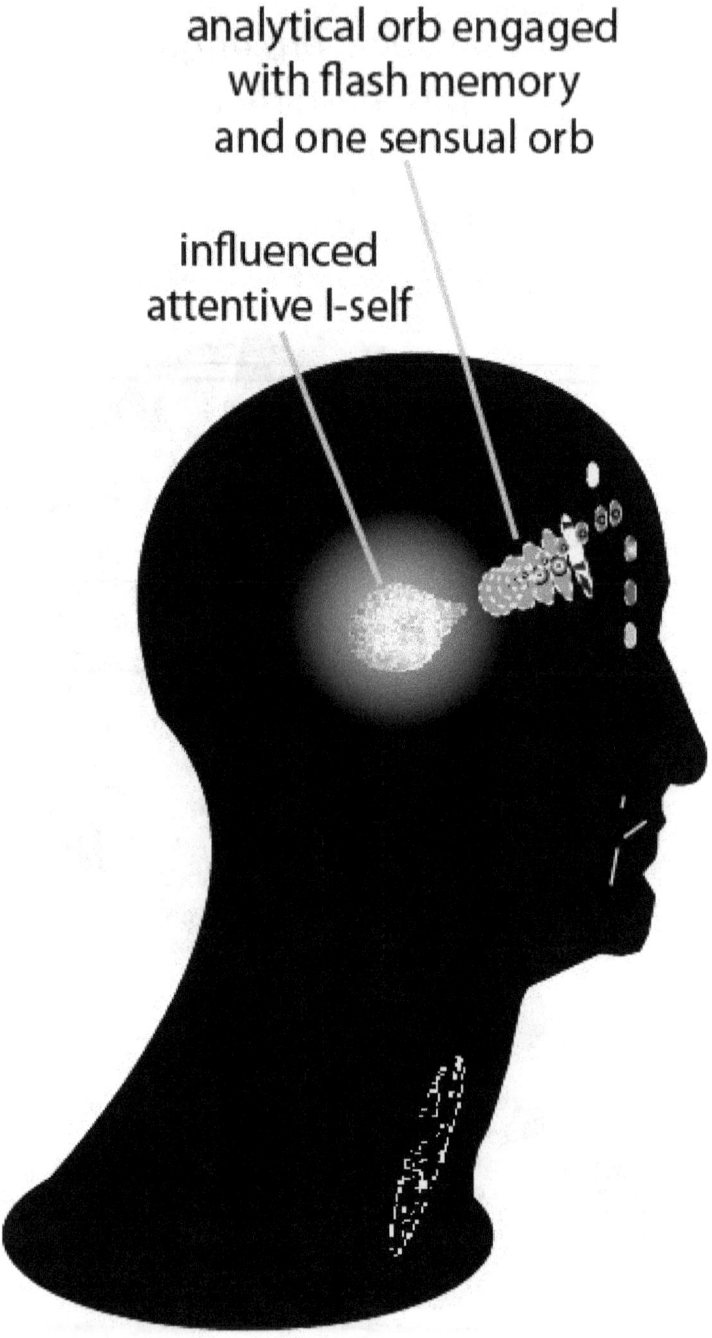
analytical orb engaged
with flash memory
and one sensual orb
influenced
attentive I-self

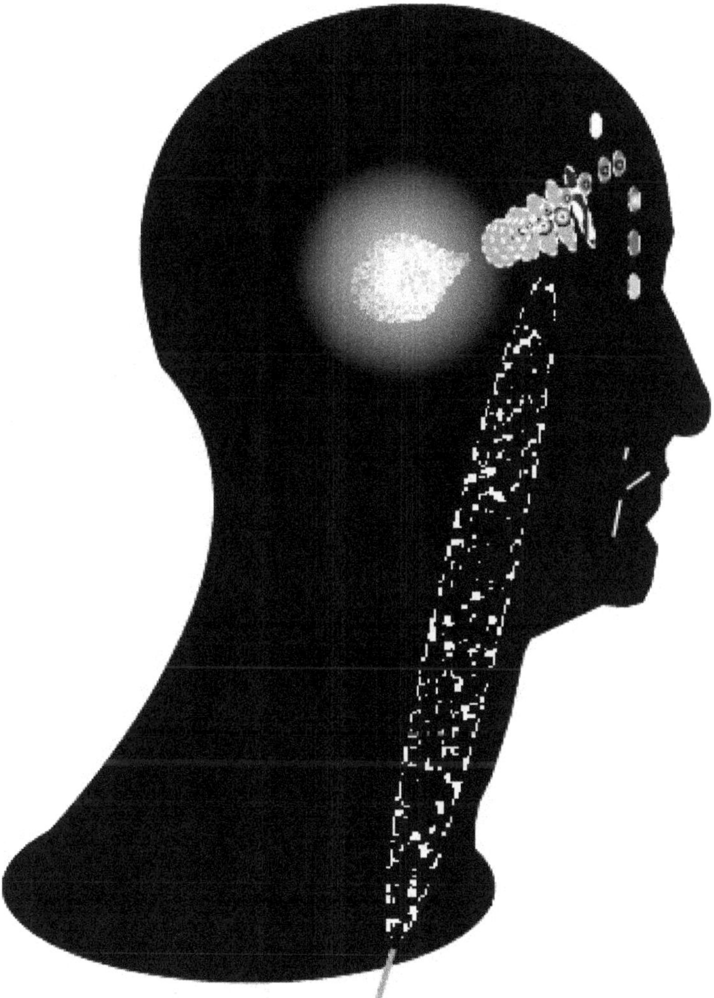

stored memory elongates
to penetrate interaction

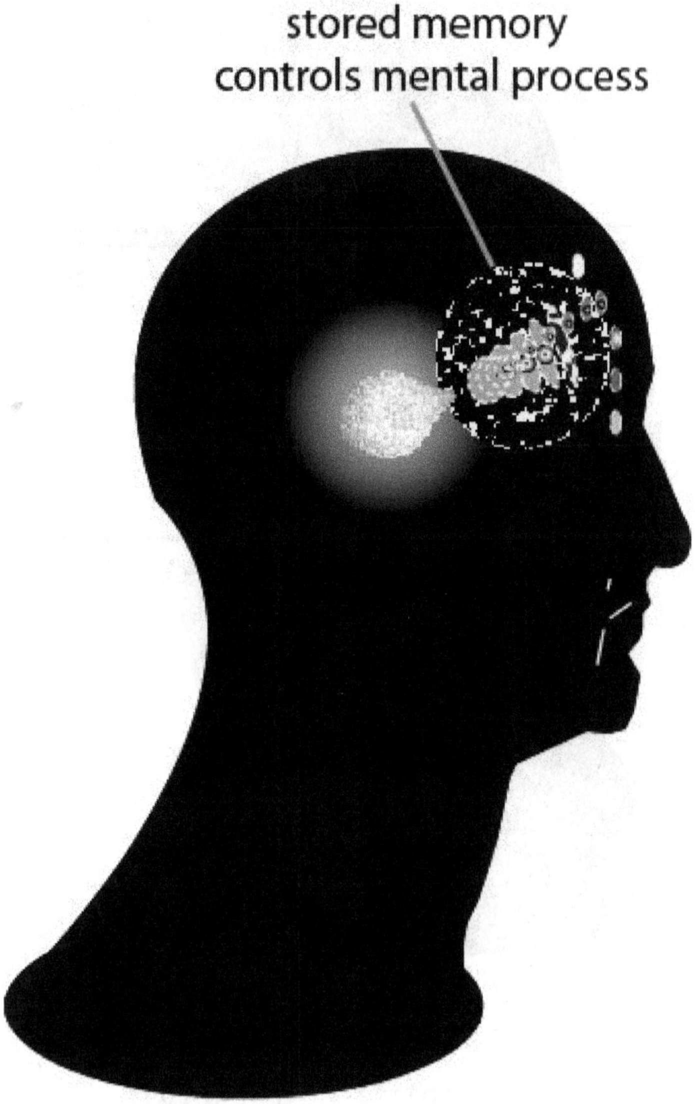
stored memory
controls mental process

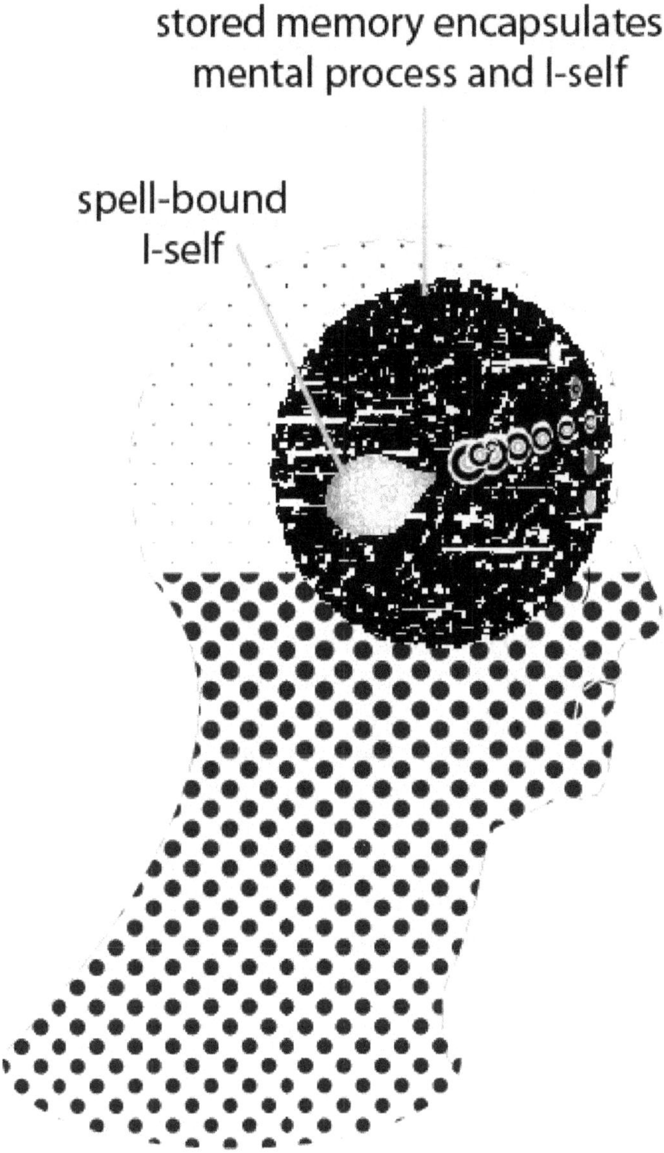
stored memory encapsulates
mental process and I-self
spell-bound
I-self

Some translators have innocently translated *dṛṣṭa adṛṣṭa janma* as present and future births, but that is a mistake. *Dṛṣṭa* does not mean what is present in terms of time and adṛṣṭa does not mean what is absent today. *Dṛṣṭa* means observing, seeing, or perceiving. *Adṛṣṭa* is the opposite, meaning births that a yogi does not objectively realize. In other words, in some births one can realize that it is a temporary circumstance one has entered into and in other births due to limited perception one does not realize this. For instance, in the case of souls who take animal or vegetative forms, they have no idea that they are in a birth for a limited amount of time. Still, as *Śrī Patañjali* stated, the person will experience the impressions which were in its psyche and which were left behind by its past acts in the cultural world. It cannot avoid those experiences even though it may not understand why the impressions go through its mind.

The impressions are experienced even by animals and trees but they do not understand what they perceive. Spiritually-ignorant human beings do not understand the impressions either. They try to rationalize all of it in terms of what they remember in the present life. A yogi, by higher practice, has a big advantage, because according to his level of advancement, he may understand the impressions to a lesser or greater degree. He may also get help from teachers who are conversant with the forces in the psyche.

Application:

Impressions of everything encountered do lodge in the mind. These stored energies are itchy and troublesome. An advanced yogi may perceive those impressions which erupt as mental and emotional distress. In deep meditation, a yogi sees the storage compartments of memory. These are located in the chest area of the subtle body, in the head and in the gullet of that form. The interaction of these impressions with the analytical orb drives a living being into haphazard transmigrations. By quarantining the memory compartment, a yogi gains control over his transfers to new bodies.

3 segregated memory components

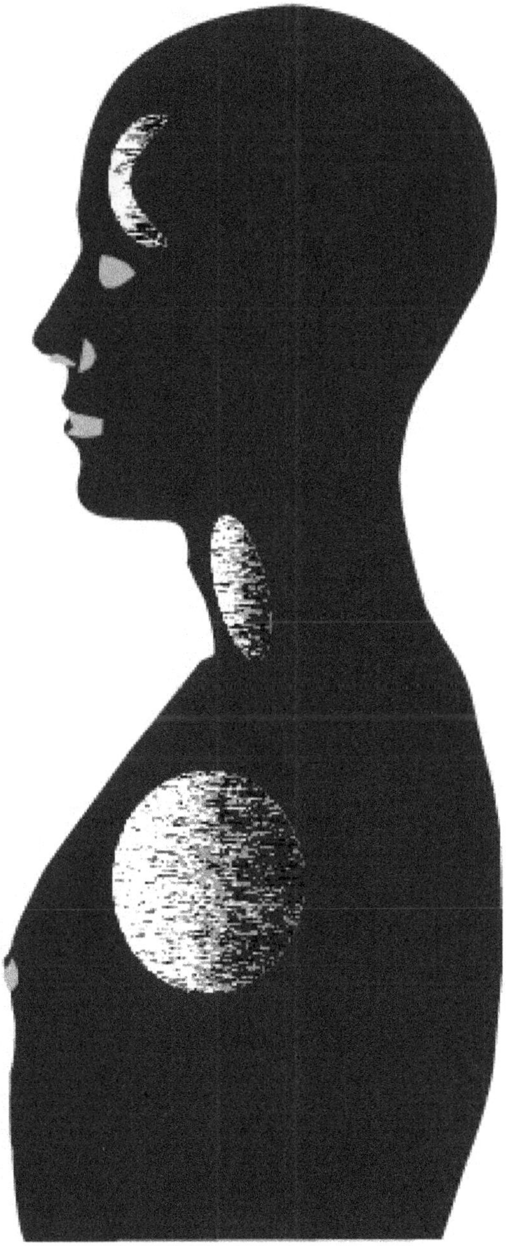

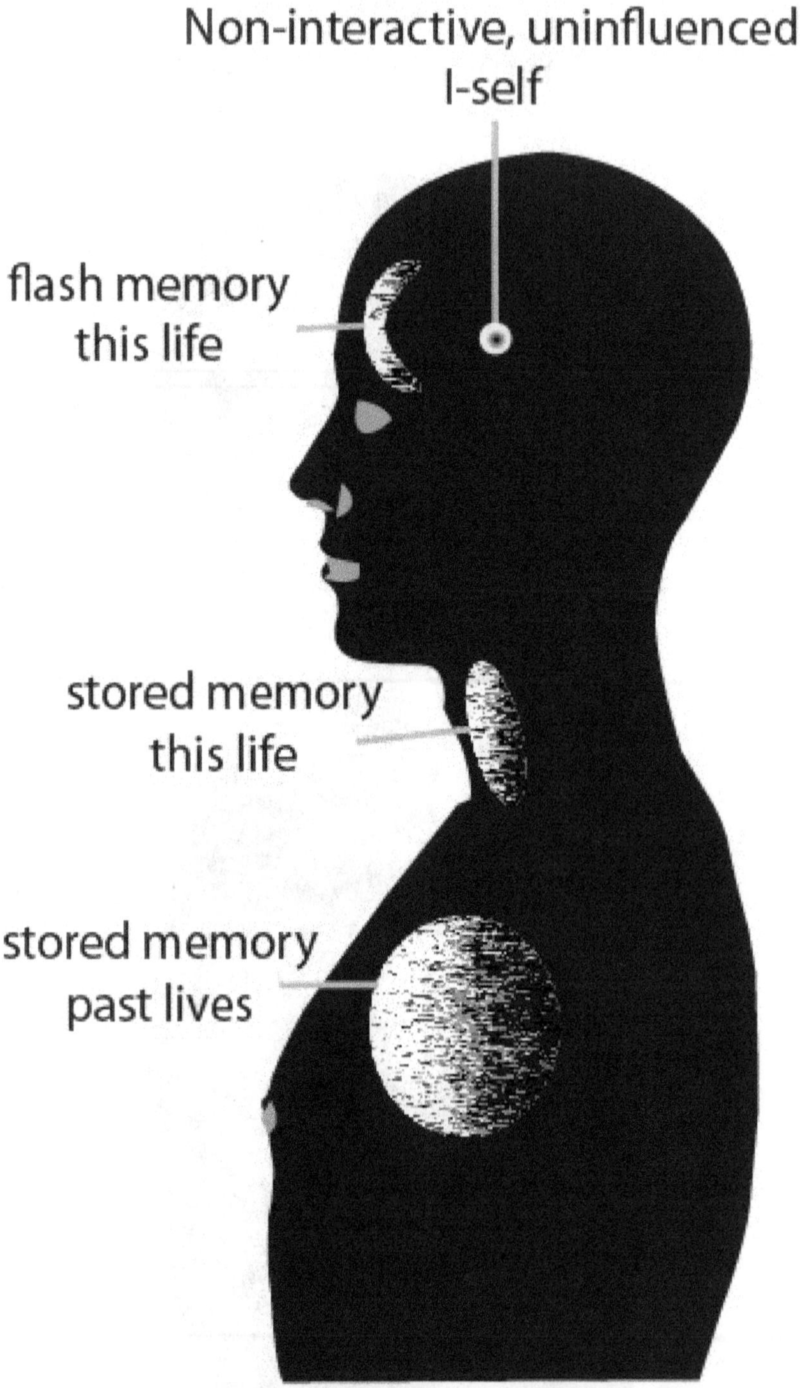
Non-interactive, uninfluenced
I-self
flash memory
this life
stored memory
this life
stored memory
past lives

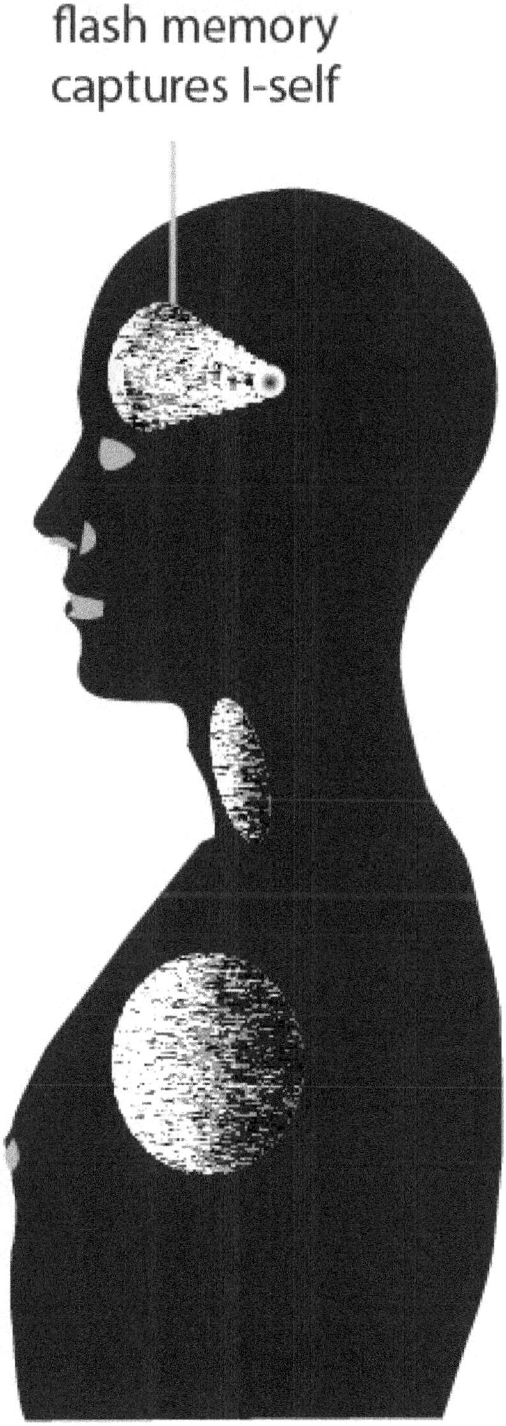
flash memory
captures I-self

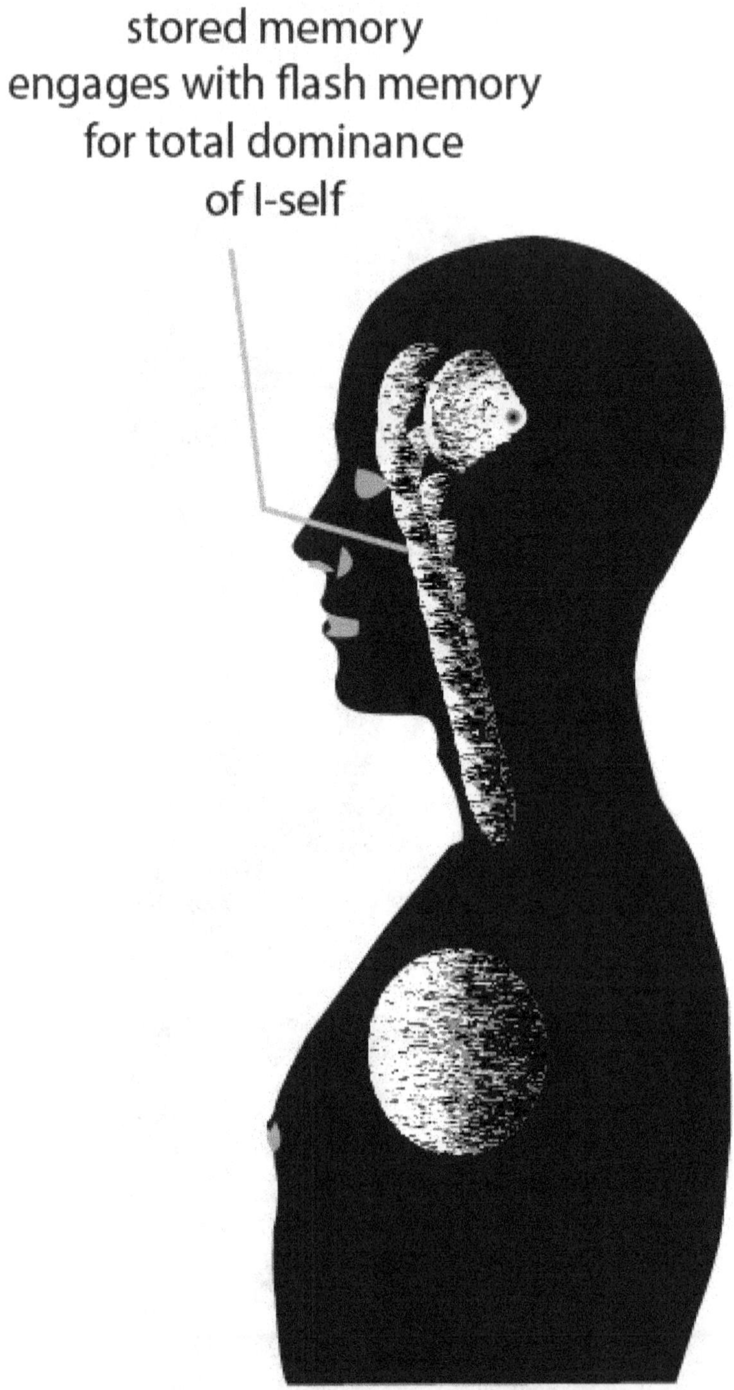
stored memory
engages with flash memory
for total dominance
of I-self

Previous lives stored memory
engages with present life stored memory
and present life flash memory
for complete dominance
of I-self

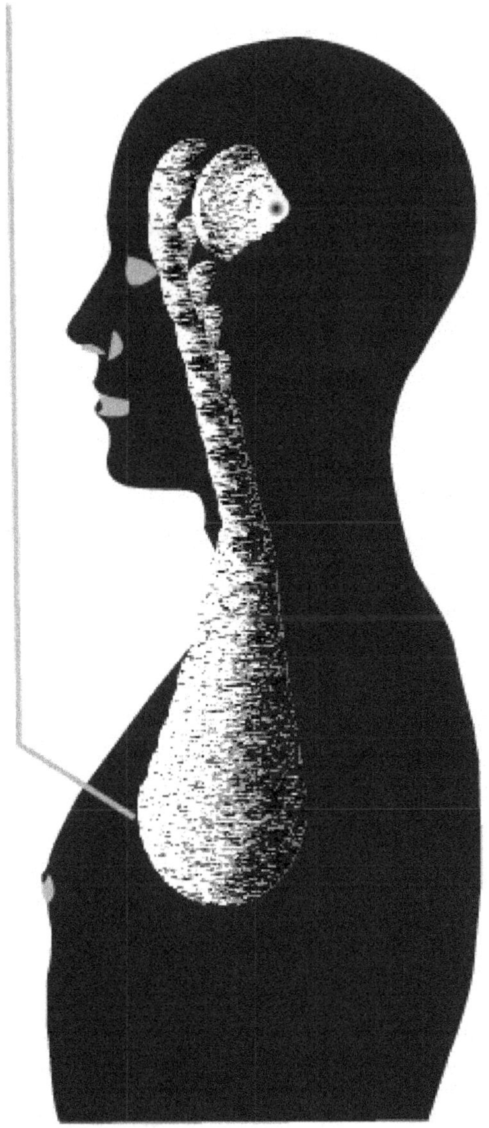

Verse 13

सति मूले तद्विपाको जात्यायुर्भोगाः ॥ १३ ॥

sati mūle tadvipākaḥ jāti āyuḥ bhogāḥ

sati – there is existing; mūle – in the cause; tat – that, it; vipākaḥ – what is resulting; jāti – species, status of life; āyuḥ – duration of life; bhogāḥ – type of experience.

In the case aforementioned, there exist the resulting effects which manifest as a particular species of life with certain duration of body and type of experiences gained in that form.

Analysis:

One develops a certain type of body with a duration for its existence along with the experience gained through that form, on the basis of the impressions which were formed before by the performance of cultural activities. All species of life are engaged in cultural acts. The human is more deliberate. This is its only advantage. Even though one forgets the cultural acts from past lives, still one's life is, to a greater degree, determined by the type of cultural acts one previously performed. The psychological storage compartment holds the impressions of the past cultural acts, as motivations to take advantage of certain situations. This is done impulsively.

Application:

Those bodies which are assumed as well as the various climatic and geographic environments, come about on the basis of those stored impressions. They are the origin. Thus the control of that stored energy is vital for the liberation of any limited being. Material nature carries out its algebraic computations regarding when and where to afford birth opportunities. It has the advantage because a living entity can only act after the fact, or after the creation and subsequent evolution of an environment, and only for as long as the environment supports a particular life form.

Verse 14

ते ह्लादपरितापफलाः पुण्यापुण्यहेतुत्वात् ॥ १४ ॥

te hlāda paritāpa phalāḥ puṇya apuṇya hetutvāt

te – they; hlāda – happiness; paritāpa – distress; phalāḥ – results; puṇya – merits; apuṇya – demerits; hetutvāt – that which causes.

They produce happiness and distress as results, on the basis of merits and demerits.

Analysis:

The impressions from previous cultural activities form happy or unhappy times according to the laws of nature, not according to what human beings believe. The rationalization of human beings, particularly the fundamental religious ones, does not necessarily tally with the laws of nature.

The merits are those which are approved by nature. The demerits form from her disapproval. However, a living being must sometimes wait for many years, or even many thousands of years before it can enjoy or suffer for complying with or disrupting a law of nature.

The past cultural acts which left impressions in the subconscious memory *(karmāśayaḥ)* remains there until it senses a favorable circumstance for conformity to the matching meritorious or demeritorious reaction.

Application:

With those bodies functioning in the outcome-environments like this earth, we perform austerities which produce a culture or way of life. And this in turn causes happiness and distress as results, all occurring on the basis of merits and demerits which are defined by the relationship of the energies. Our control is applied after we acquire creature forms, and thus we cannot adjust the pre-set situations. We are left to act or react to whatever providence hurls before us, like a clumsy batsman missing a ball thrown towards him.

Verse 15

परिणामतापसंस्कारदुःखैर्गुणवृत्तिविरोधाच्च दुःखमेव सर्वं विवेकिनः ॥ १५ ॥

pariṇāma tāpa saṁskāra duḥkaiḥ guṇavṛtti virodhāt ca duḥkham eva sarvaṁ vivekinaḥ

pariṇāma – circumstantial change; tāpa – strenuous endeavor; saṁskāra – impulsive motivations; duḥkhaiḥ – with distress; guṇa – quality, features of material nature; vṛtti – vibrational mode of the mento-emotional energy; virodhāt – resulting from confrontation or clashing aspects; ca – and; duḥkham – distress; eva – indeed; sarvaṁ – all; vivekinaḥ – the discriminating person.

The discriminating person knows that all conditions are distressful because of circumstantial changes, strenuous endeavor, impulsive motivations, clashing aspects and the vibrational modes of the mento-emotional energy.

Analysis:

This discrimination is gained by virtue of yoga practice. It is an insight into the nature of the material world rather than only a theoretical understanding. By this, a yogi sees the complications in cultural activities. He becomes reluctant to participate. One cannot control the features of material nature. If one does not advance into higher yoga, one cannot control the vibrational modes of one's mental and emotional energies.

Therefore a yogi has no alternative but to back away from the cultural world and neutralize himself by performing higher yoga, mastering it and then applying it while performing any remaining cultural obligations efficiently, in a way that causes disengagement from the cultural circuit.

The conditions in these lower existences are always distressful whether in the short or long range. That is the nature of it. Too many circumstantial changes occur outside the control of a limited being. He cannot at all times regulate his mind's entry into or admittance of emotional distresses. And he cannot always side-step the involuntary motivations which lead to further distress. Therefore, the only alternative is to perfect the higher yoga practice of *dhyāna* effortless linkage of his attention to higher concentration forces and persons. That is the method for getting rid of the psychological disturbances which cause instability, anxiety and emotional distress.

Application:

An advanced yogi has a special discriminating ability, whereby he can sort between his spirit and his psychological viewing aids. Thus he recognizes the potential for distress posed by cultural activity and the resulting impressions. There will be circumstantial changes beyond the performer's control that may aid or frustrate his enterprise. He must exert himself frequently. He must submit to impulsive motivations from time to time, and he must react to some clashing aspects whether he wants to or not. Finally, he cannot always suppress the urges which grow out of his mind and emotions.

In the end, one realizes that the odds are not in one's favor. They never were and never will be. Thus one abandons the quest to be a somebody.

Verse 16

हेयं दुःखमनागतम्॥ १६ ॥

heyaṁ duḥkham anāgatam

heyaṁ – that which is to be avoided; duḥkham – distress; anāgatam – what has not manifested.

Distress which is not manifested is to be avoided.

Analysis:

For liberation, a yogin will have to reach a stage where he can willfully side-step all the merits and demerits which are due to him from providence. Both happiness and distress on the basis of cultural activities from the past, are to be avoided at all costs. However a yogin has to first advance sufficiently. It requires insight into the psychological receptacles that are submissive towards the manifestation of the merits and demerits. A yogin must then close such receptacles by practicing *kriyā* yoga.

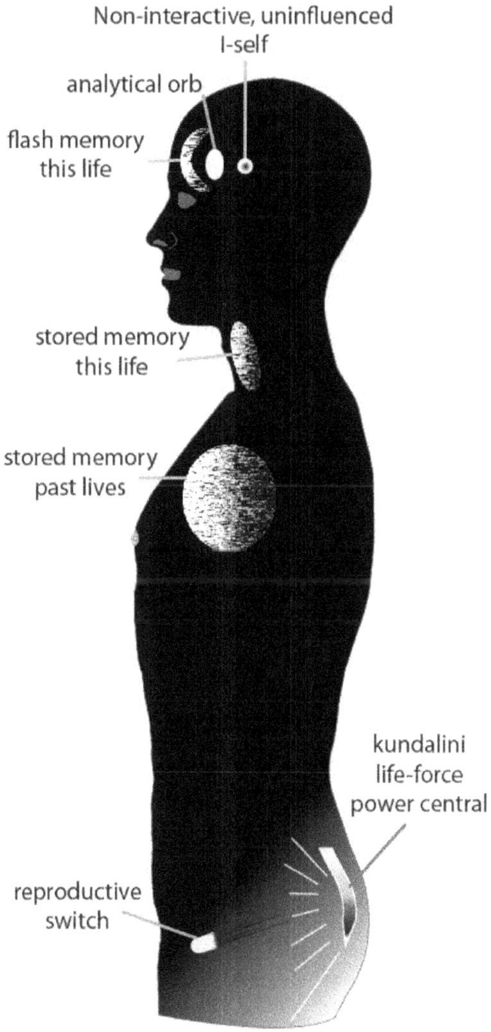

Application:

Distress which is not manifested should be avoided. Thus one should develop the ability to thwart the impressions which could produce that. The desired attitude towards happiness which is the flipside to distress, is to be neutral to it. Anything besides neutrality causes craving which hurls the person to a lower level.

Verse 17

द्रष्टृदृश्ययोः संयोगो हेयहेतुः ॥ १७॥

draṣṭṛdṛśyayoḥ saṁyogo heyahetuḥ

draṣṭṛ – the observer; dṛśyayoḥ – of what is perceived; saṁyogo – the indiscriminate association; heya – that which is to be avoided; hetuḥ – the cause.

The cause which is to be avoided is the indiscriminate association of the observer and what is perceived.

Analysis:

When we identify wholly and solely with what we perceive, we lose objectivity and become attached, rather than detached. This causes a misplaced identity with things not in our interest and makes us lose objectivity. Then we experience an impulsive interaction between the new impressions received through the senses and the old impressions stored in the memory *(karmāśayaḥ)*. The analytical part of the intellect then hashes over the matter and comes to a conclusion which is shown to us internally in the mind through the magical imagery of the imagination orb. Thus we again come under the spell of the function of that psychic organ.

If a yogi reaches a stage of control, whereby he stops the impulsive sensual intakes or puts a damper on them as soon as they enter the psyche, he realizes himself as being the perceiver or observer. Then he sees the operations of the senses and the machinations of memory as being counterproductive. These interact to produce new images which he usually identifies with, to his detriment.

In higher yoga, one is trained in how to distinguish the various parts of the intellect subtle mechanism and the *citta* mento-emotional energy gyrations. Then one puts an end to the impressions and their varied motivations which destroy one's ability to see beyond the material world.

Application:

Remember that the cause which can definitely be adjusted is the indiscriminate association of the observer and what is perceived. But since that linkage is impulsive and very natural, efforts will be required to change it. Nature granted each life form a very convenient but dangerous allowance for automatic connection between objects and means of perception. This is advantageous in certain situations and degrading in others. A yogi has to forego this free bestowal of nature if he would be freed from the influence of the mento-emotional energies.

Verse 18

प्रकाशक्रियास्थितिशीलं भूतेन्द्रियात्मकं भोगापवर्गार्थं दृश्यम्॥ १८॥

prakāśa kriyā sthiti śīlaṁ bhūtendriyātmakaṁ bhogāpavargārthaṁ dṛśyam

prakāśa – clear perception; kriyā – action; sthiti – stability; śīlaṁ – form, disposition; bhūta – mundane elements; indriya – sense organs; ātmakaṁ – self, nature; bhoga – experience; apavarga – liberation; arthaṁ – value or purpose; dṛśyam – what is perceived.

What is perceived is of the nature of the mundane elements and the sense organs and is formed in clear perception, action or stability. Its purpose is to give experience or to allow liberation.

Analysis:

Whatever we perceive in the subtle or gross mundane energy depends on the condition of the seeing instrument, the intellect in the subtle body. According to how it is influenced and powered by the modes of material nature, it either allows clear perception, impulsive action, or inertia. The purpose behind the interaction of the seer and what is seen, is experience for involvement or experience which results in either consumption or liberation.

Material nature serves to give either increasingly varied pleasurable or harmful experiences or to allow liberation from both. While others chase after what is pleasurable and try to avoid what might render pain, the yogin strives for liberation by curbing the intellect so that he possesses clear perception *(prakāśa)*.

Application:

What is perceived in this world with this psychology is of the nature of the mundane elements and the sense organs, and is formed in clear perception, action or stability. Its purpose is to give experience or to allow liberation. Yet to gain liberation, one has to abandon the need for the experiences in this world. Our situation is described in this verse in brief. Nature awards a place in its panoramic display but it does so using our energy while affording perceptions of its activity and stability. We are attracted to its organic and inorganic properties.

Eventually a living entity gives up on material nature and no longer exhibits enthusiasm about or abhorrence of any of her fancy or drab displays. One turns to introspection for reviewing the possibility of life without material nature.

Verse 19

विशेषाविशेषलिङ्गमात्रालिङ्गानि गुणपर्वाणि ॥ १९ ॥

viśeṣa aviśeṣa liṅgamātra aliṅgāni guṇaparvāṇi

viśeṣa – that which is specific; aviśeṣa – what is regular; liṅgamātra – a mark, that which is indicated; aliṅgāni – that which has no indication; guṇa – influences of material nature; parvāṇi – phases, stages, parts.

The phases of the influences of material nature are those which are specific, regular, indicated or not indicated.

Analysis:

By higher yoga, a yogin clearly sees how material nature has certain over-riding phases which it shifts into by its own accord, and which the yogi can enter once he masters *dhāraṇā* linkage of attention to higher concentration force, either in or beyond material nature.

The specific objects are those perceivable on the gross plane of existence and highlighted to our senses because of strong attraction. The non-specific are those gross objects that exhibit mild attraction.

These are regular items like dirt. Even though a gem is a form of dirt, still it is specific. Contrarily, a speck of mud or a grain of sand is regular, being non-specific. These all have subtle counterparts which are categorized in the same way and which can be seen through the subtle body when it is highly energized.

That which is indicated is the subtle matter which we can detect with electronic instruments or discover by mystic techniques in higher yoga. That which has no indication is the material energy in its quiescent stage where it has no differentiation. It is as it was, simply nothing at that stage. In higher meditation, one perceives each of these.

Application:

Some of the experiences afforded by material nature occur in clear perception, some in the fervor of action, some in any of the states of stability which make one form regrettable decisions. These experiences may be specific, regular, indicated beforehand, or not anticipated. Does material nature really target a living entity? Is the displacement of material energy a random expression with no focal point?

Regardless of how one answers either question with or without scientific evidence, the fact remains that the fused condition of a living entity makes it a focus of electrostatic charges in the environment. As such one should realize the flow of energy which is in and which affects sensual perception.

Verse 20

द्रष्टा दृशिमात्रः शुद्धोऽपि प्रत्ययानुपश्यः ॥२०॥

draṣṭā dṛśimātraḥ śuddhaḥ api pratyayānupaśyaḥ

draṣṭā – the perceiver; dṛśi – perception, consciousness; mātraḥ – measure or extent; śuddhaḥ – purity; api – but; pratyayaḥ – conviction or belief as mental content; anu – following along, patterning after; paśyaḥ – what is perceived.

The perceiver is the pure extent of its consciousness but its conviction is patterned by what it perceives.

Analysis:

In actuality the *dṛśi* or consciousness which spiritually emanates from the individual self, is itself that self and that self alone. However, due to its absorbent nature, the self loses track of itself and adopts patterns which form in its consciousness as conviction. On the assumption of these convictions one is motivated into cultural activities.

Patañjali used the technical term *mātra* which means a measure of or to an extent. The individual soul is limited. His consciousness radiates only to a certain extent, before it becomes attenuated or is linked to lower or higher concentration forces which help to offset its limited range.

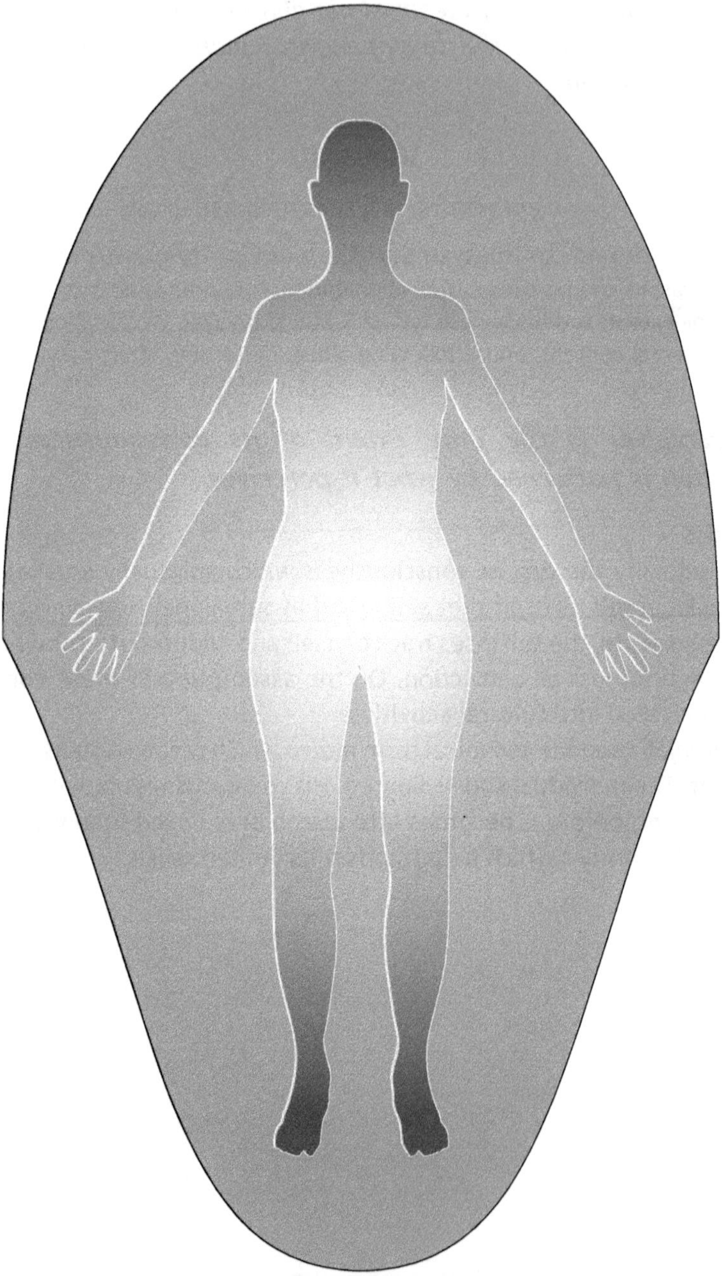

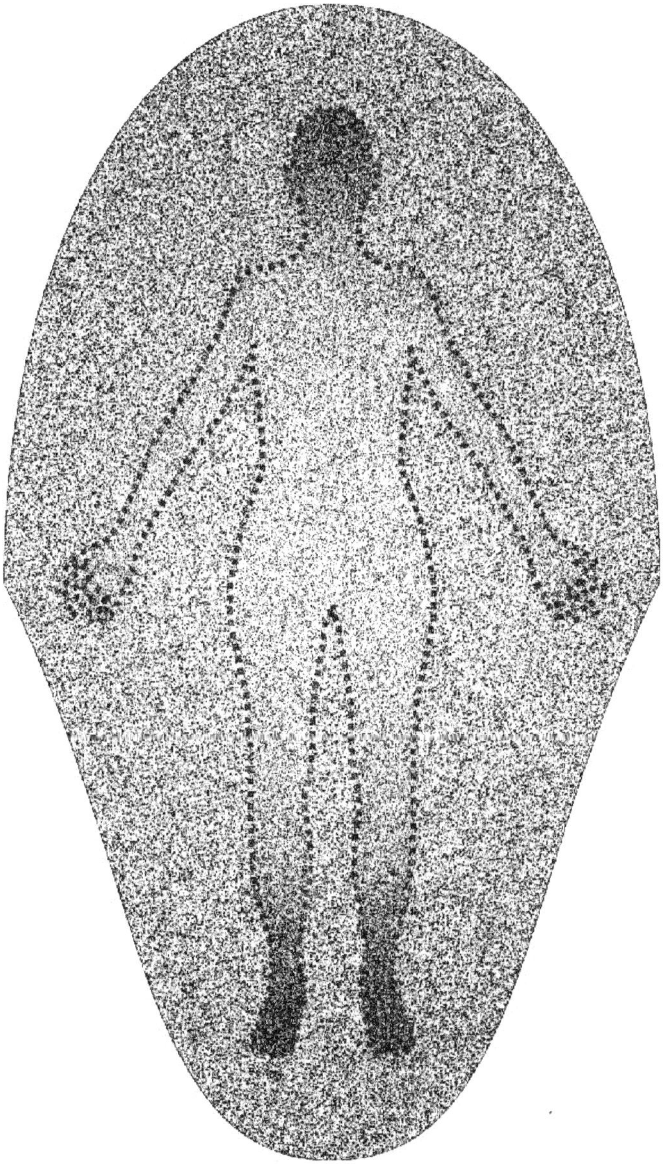

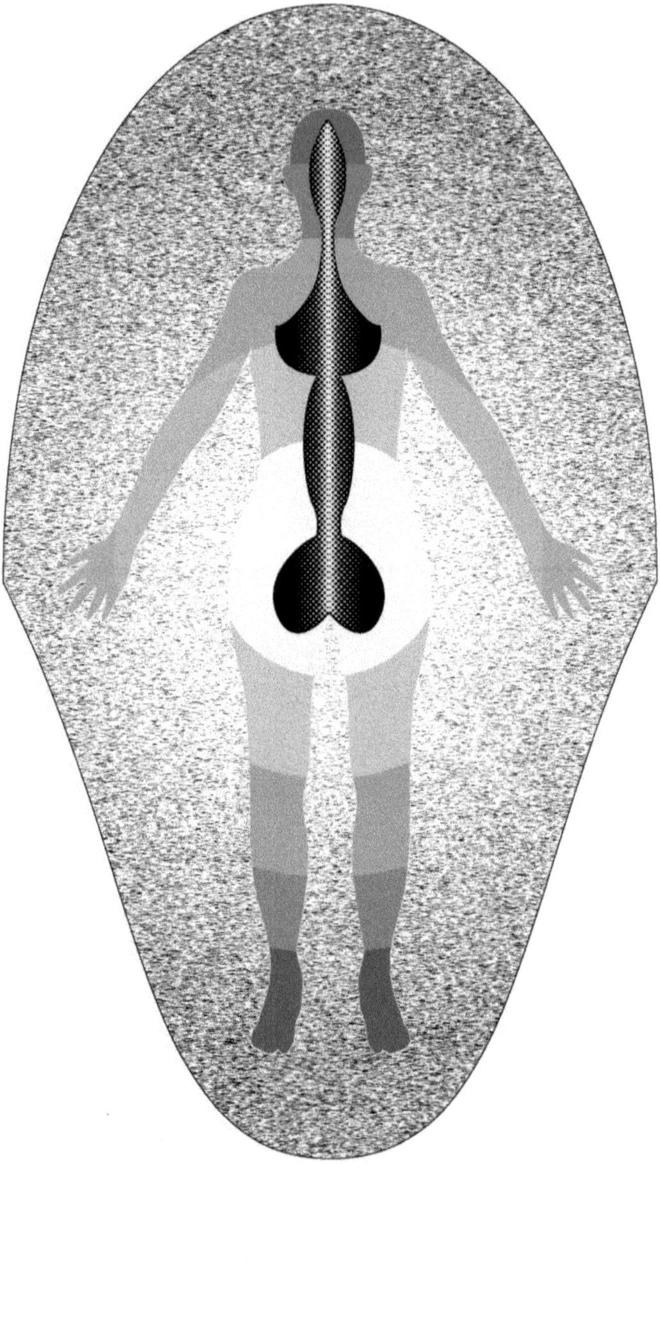

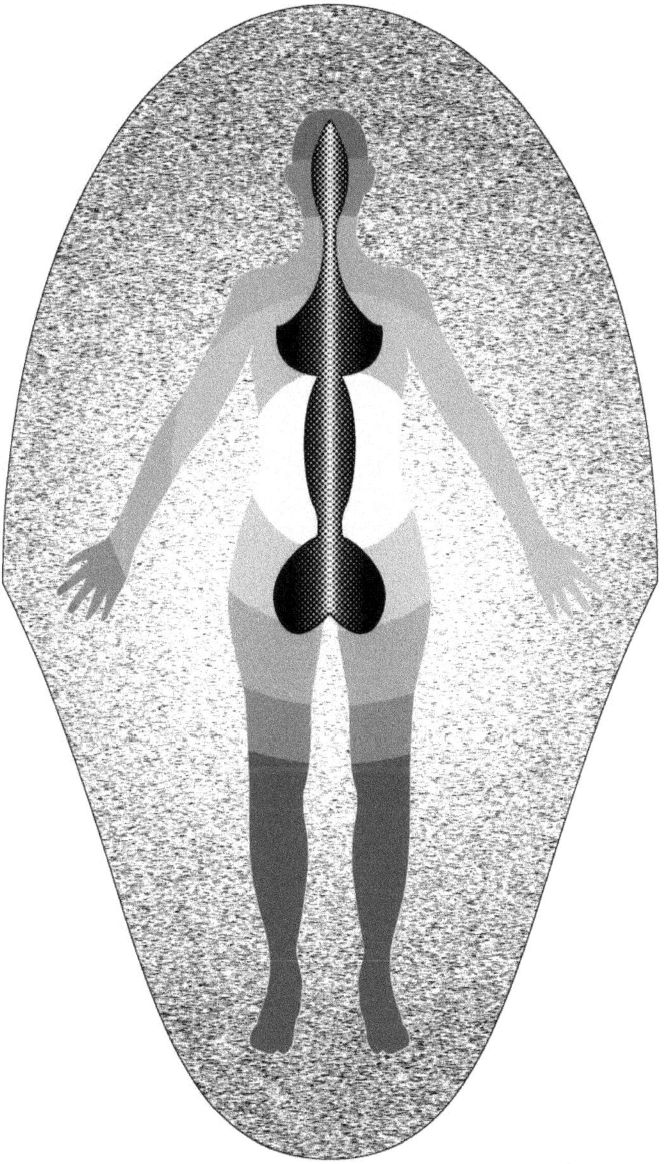

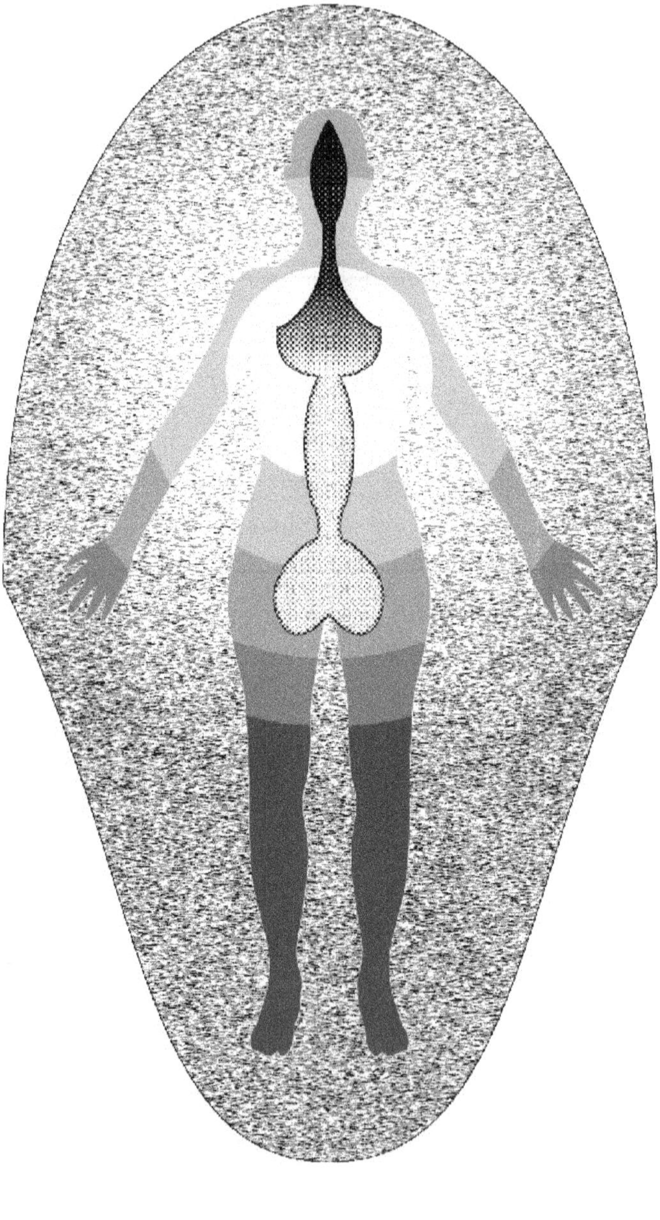

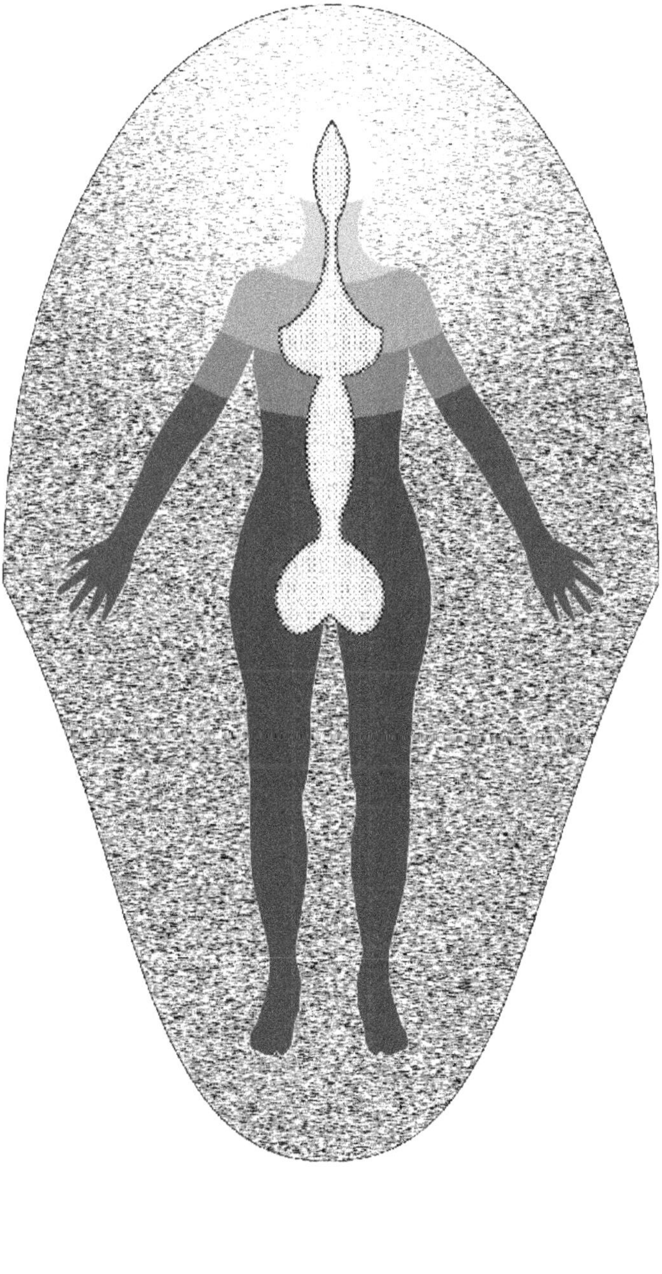

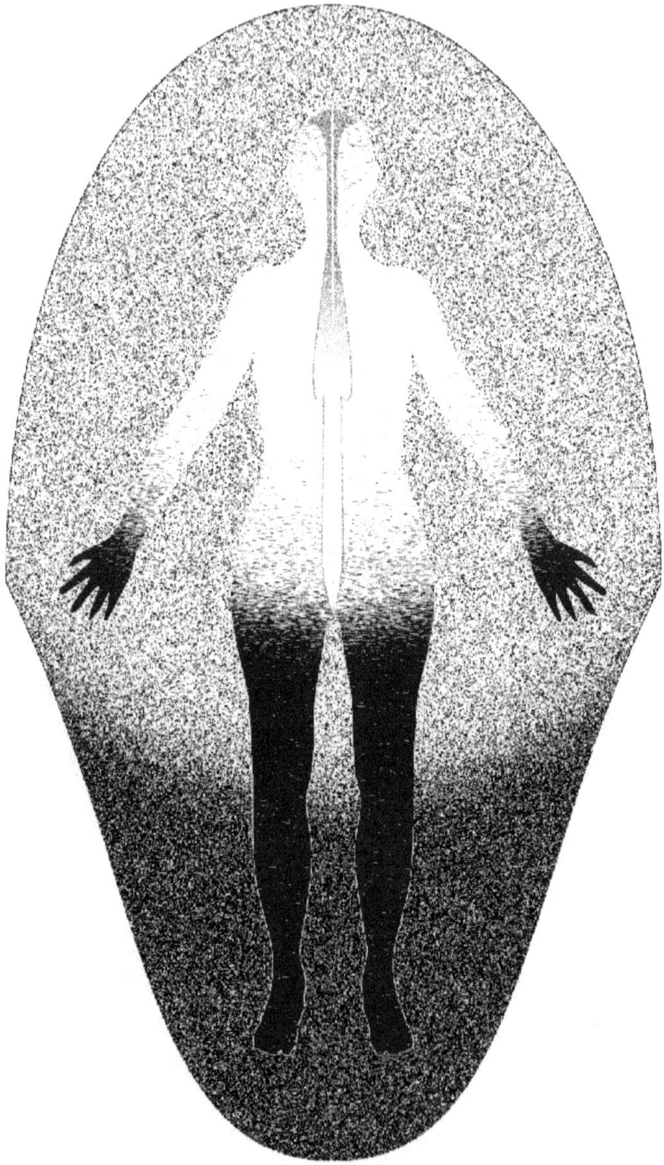

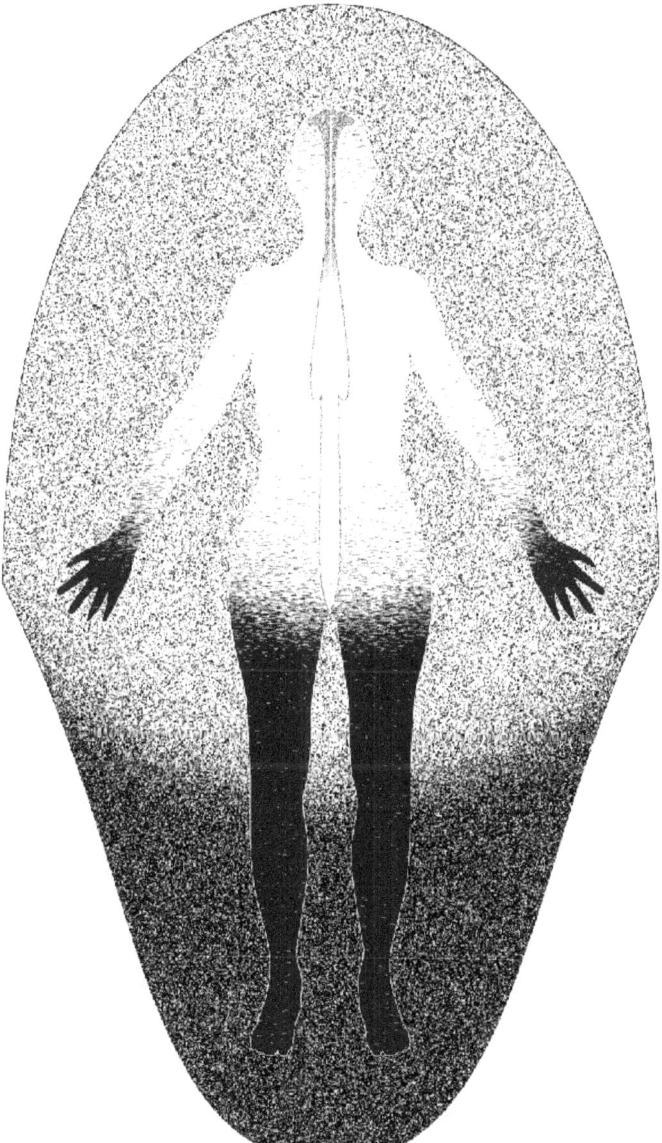

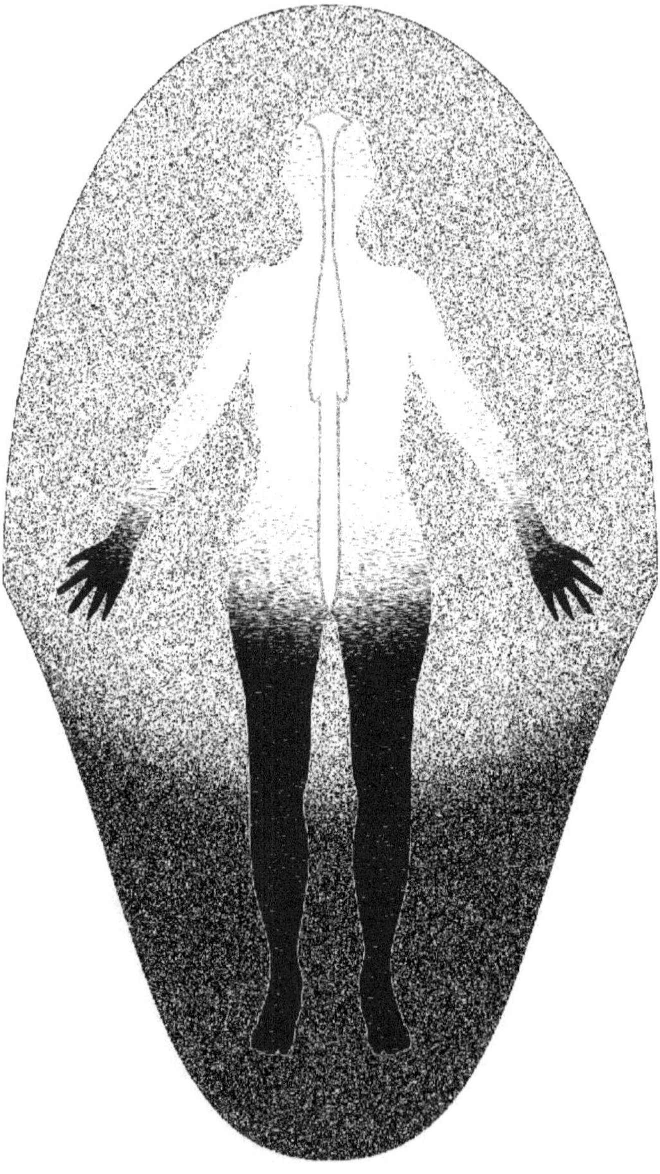

In the material creation, with a psychic body, the perceiver, the individual self, is itself the pure extent of its own consciousness. That is its form. However it functions based on what is perceived; thus it is influenced not to realize itself by itself, but to absorb the perceptions. These perceptions occur when it is linked to a sensing mechanism. The spirit derives a correct or erroneous notion by sensual influence. By that it transmigrates from one situation to another and is implicated.

Application:

Even though the perceiver is the pure extent of its consciousness, its conviction, once formed in any way, is patterned by what it perceived. The extent of its consciousness or the range of its aura is further extended by selected or forced energy alliances through which the entity identifies with numerous moods and prejudices. Yoga, according to Patañjali, *means withdrawal of one's attention, or decreasing the extended range of consciousness. This indicates that there would be no mistaken identity or coloration of the core-self.*

Verse 21

तदर्थ एव दृश्यस्यात्मा ॥ २१ ॥

tadarthaḥ eva dṛśyasya ātmā

tad = tat – that; arthaḥ – purpose; eva – only; dṛśyasya – of what is seen; ātmā – individual spirit.

The individual spirit, who is involved in what is seen, exists here for that purpose only.

Analysis:

As it is, as we experience it in ourselves, and as we hear from others, this existence is meant for experiencing either ourselves as we are or ourselves as we are connected to various other sensing mechanisms. In short, a person's existence is reduced to perceiving this or that in the material world.

Application:

The individual spirit who is involved in what is seen, may either accept the experience presented to him and react to it as urged, or he may sidestep the experiencing mechanism and move in the direction of liberation. The active-reactive profile of a living entity is finally adjusted when it realizes its tenuous position in material nature. When it figures that its buoyancy is affected by the various environmental pressures it encounters in material nature, it longs to gain the upper hand.

Verse 22

कृतार्थं प्रति नष्टमप्यनष्टं तदन्यसाधारणत्वात्॥ २२॥

kṛtārthaṁ prati naṣṭam api
anaṣṭaṁ tadanya sādhāraṇatvāt

kṛt – fulfilled done; ārthaṁ – purpose; prati – toward; naṣṭam – destroyed, non-existent, non-effective; api – although, but; anaṣṭaṁ – not finished, still existing, effective; tat – that; anya – others; sādhāraṇatvāt – common, normal, universal.

It is not effective for one to whom its purpose is fulfilled, but it has a common effect on the others.

Analysis:

The material world loses its effectiveness on a realized yogin. For him its purpose is fulfilled. It no longer operates on him. He no longer reacts to it as others do. For the others, however, it remains in effect. The others agree on its potency and place stress on it. They accept the convictions derived from it and proceed with the social way.

In a sense this statement by *Patañjali* refutes the idea of mass liberation. Here the liberation is individual and only for those who retracted their spiritual energy from linkage into the subtle mundane sensing energy.

Others will remain in the material world because its effects bind their attention.

Śrī Krishna in the *Bhagavad Gītā* did not profess mass liberation of many living entities, neither by an act of faith nor by belief or confidence. He too singled out individuals for liberation:

manuṣyāṇāṃ sahasreṣu kaścid yatati siddhaye
yatatām api siddhānāṃ kaścin māṃ vetti tattvataḥ

Someone, in thousands of human beings, strives for psychological perfection. Of those who endeavor, even of those who are perfected, someone knows Me in truth. *(Gītā 7.3)*

Application:

These life experiences have little impact on one to whom its purpose is fulfilled but it has a common effect on others and keeps them occupied and enthralled. A living entity can remain stymied in material nature for billions of creative cycles. The conditioning and its resultant bewilderment is infinite.

Verse 23

स्वस्वामिशक्त्योः स्वरूपोपलब्धिहेतुः संयोगः ॥ २३ ॥

sva svāmiśaktyoḥ svarūpa upalabdhi hetuḥ saṁyogaḥ

sva – own nature, own psyche; svāmi – the master, the individual self; saktyoḥ – of the potency of the two; svarūpa – essential form; upalabdhi – obtaining experience; hetuḥ – cause, reason; saṁyogaḥ – conjunction.

There is a reason for the conjunction of the individual self and its psychological energies. It is for obtaining the experience of its essential form.

Analysis:

This states indirectly that the living entity who has a psychological make-up can only realize his essential or spiritual nature, by first coming in contact with the subtle material nature and then differentiating himself from that mundane power.

The conjunction *(saṁyoga)* is enforced because no limited being has the power to join itself with material nature or to disconnect itself from it. This is why *Patañjali* acknowledged that special person who taught even the ancient yogis.

kleśa karma vipāka āśayaiḥ
aparāmṛṣṭaḥ puruṣaviśeṣaḥ Īśvaraḥ
tatra niratiśayaṁ sarvajñabījam
sa eṣaḥ pūrveṣām api guruḥ kālena anavacchedāt

He, this particular person, being unconditioned by time, is the guru even of the ancient teachers, the authorities from before.

The Supreme Lord is that special person who is not affected by troubles, actions, development or by subconscious motivations.

There, in Him, is found the unsurpassed origin of all knowledge. (Yoga Sūtra 1:24 - 26)

The ultimate purpose of the conjunction is for the limited beings to objectively realize their spiritual selves, apart from and distinct from the subtle material nature which they accept initially as their personal psychologies.

The individual self is supposed to be the master of its psychological powers, but initially it is overtaken, influenced and dominated by them. Thus it must endeavor to gain autonomy.

Application:

Even though the conjunction of the individual spirit and its psychological energy is condemned, still its ultimate purpose is justified when the person attains liberation. Then it is appreciated that material nature afforded the objective experience of the core-self through blending and then contrasting with the self. It is all about objectivity. The aspect that was lacking in the soul's psyche, in its primordial state, was objectivity. It had a full stock of subjectivity initially. As a raw material, it was a subjective reality.

Its fusion into material nature forced objectivity on it. Its effort to banish that purview by removing the ego is a failed effort only. It does not have the power to remove the sense of identity.

Verse 24

तस्य हेतुरविद्या ॥ २४ ॥

tasya hetuḥ avidyā

tasya – of it; hetuḥ – cause; avidyā – spiritual ignorance.

The cause of the conjunction is spiritual ignorance.

Analysis:

Besides the fact that there is a forced conjunction between the individual limited spirits and the mundane sensing energies, there is also an underlying reason for this, which is innate spiritual ignorance of the limited beings. They did not understand themselves initially. The Supreme Being may be blamed for putting the limited beings in peril by forcing them into conjunction with the mundane psychology, but the reason for His action is stated in this verse; being the spiritual ignorance of His limited dependents.

As far as the Supreme Being was concerned, the only way to free us from that ignorance was to put us in conjunction with the mundane psychology. From that position we may derive disgust *(nirvedaḥ)* with that energy and then through introspection study ourselves and our linkage with it and with His assistance, work for emancipation.

The blame placed on the Supreme Being is lifted as soon as we understand that initially, we were with an innate and primeval spiritual ignorance. The contrast between us and the mundane energy is the only aspect that motivates self-realization.

Application:

Always keep in mind that the inability to know the difference between one's spirit and its sensing tools is the very cause of their conjunction in the first place. Kriyā *yoga is designed to remove that inability. Recognition means the identification of an object. From that comes assessment about its value. If there is no recognition the object might imperil the observer.*

Verse 25

तद्भावात्संयोगाभावो हानं तद्दृशेः कैवल्यम्॥ २५॥

tad abhāvāt saṁyogā abhāvaḥ
hānaṁ taddṛśeḥ kaivalyam

tad = tat – that spiritual ignorance; abhāvāt – resulting from the elimination; saṁyogā – conjunction; abhāvaḥ – disappearance, elimination; hānaṁ – withdrawal, escape; tad = tat – that; dṛśeḥ – of the perceiver; kaivalyam – total separation from the mundane psychology.

The elimination of the conjunction which results from the elimination of that spiritual ignorance is the withdrawal that is the total separation of the perceiver from the mundane psychology.

Analysis:

Yogis should study this verse to get *Patañjali*'s definition of *kaivalyam.* This term previously signified various forms of liberation, according to the spiritual sect which advocated it. However, to understand *Patañjali,* we must stick to his meaning. Clearly in context, *kaivalya* is defined in this verse in contrast to *saṁyogā* or conjunction between the individual spirit and his subtle mundane psychology *(sva).* This psychology is hinted at, in the second verse of chapter one, as operational functions:

yogaḥ cittavṛtti nirodhaḥ

> The skill of yoga demonstrated by the conscious non-operation of the vibrational modes of the mento-emotional energy. (Yoga Sūtra 1:2)

There is no mention of *kaivalyam* being union with God or oneness with God. It does not imply that one has become God or that one has merged into the Absolute Truth. *Patañjali,* in context, spoke of complete isolation of the individual limited spirit from its psychological sensing mechanisms which are derived from material nature. He spoke of the individual limited spirit situating itself and realizing itself as its essential spiritual nature.

draṣṭā dṛśimātraḥ śuddhaḥ api pratyayānupaśyaḥ
The perceiver is the pure extent of consciousness but its conviction is patterned by what it perceives. *(Yoga Sūtra 2:20)*

Application:

One must practice the kriyā *discipline because it affords a detachment whereby the perceiver is separated from its sensing tools. That objectivity is necessary for self-realization and knowing the ways and means of the spiritual self.*

Verse 26

विवेकख्यातिरविप्लवा हानोपायः ॥२६॥

vivekakhyātiḥ aviplavā hānopāyaḥ

viveka – discrimination; khyātiḥ – insight; aviplavā – unbroken, continuous; hānopāyaḥ = hana – avoidance + upāyaḥ – means, method.

The method for avoiding that spiritual ignorance is the establishment of continuous discriminative insight.

Analysis:

Vivekakhyātiḥ is discriminative insight, gained through higher yoga practice or naturally occurring as a result of actively using a yoga *siddha* form or a spiritual body. It is neither book knowledge nor concepts derived from authoritative teachers. Most persons require yoga to develop this, even though a rare few may possess this naturally.

Spiritual ignorance *(avidyā)* which is the ignorance of the difference between one's spiritual energy and its linkage or mixture with mundane psychology, is only removed by the development of the discriminative insight.

Application:

The unification with the sensing tools is to be avoided. If achieved, one develops the discriminative insight, which affords one freedom from identity with the urges of the mind and emotions. This evolves into visual spiritual perception of the spiritual environments where the divine entities reside.

Verse 27

तस्य सप्तधा प्रान्तभूमिः प्रज्ञा ॥ २७॥

tasya saptadhā prāntabhūmiḥ prajñā

tasya – of his; saptadhā – seven fold; prānta – boundary or edge + bhūmiḥ – territory, range (prāntabhūmiḥ – stage); prajñā – insight.

Concerning the development of discriminative insight, there are seven stages.

Analysis:

Śrī Patañjali clarified that in developing the discriminative insight, one moves through seven stages. It does not happen overnight. It develops in increments.

Application:

There are seven stages of progress when developing the discriminative insight, which gives one the ability to differentiate between the self and its sensing tools. If there is no confidence in slow progression, if there is no encouragement to persist, yoga practice will peter out due to lack of attaining fantastic results. To be successful one must guard against this.

Verse 28

योगाङ्गानुष्ठानादशुद्धिक्षये ज्ञानदीप्तिराविवेकख्यातेः ॥ २८॥

yogāṅgānuṣṭhānāt aśuddhikṣaye jñānadīptiḥ āvivekakhyāteḥ

yogāṅgānuṣṭhānāt = yoga – yoga process + aṅga – part + anuṣṭhānāt – from consistent practice; aśuddhiḥ – impurities; kśaye – on the elimination; jñānadīptiḥ – radiant organ of perception; āvivekakhyāteḥ = a – till, until, up to + viveka – discrimination + khyāteḥ – insight.

From the consistent practice of the parts of the yoga process, on the elimination of the impurity, the radiant organ of perception becomes manifest, until there is steady discriminative insight.

Analysis:

There is really no shortcut around steady practice and persistent attention day after day. From this, the impurities gradually diminish, until they fade altogether. Then the intellect of perception in the subtle body becomes radiant. It emits a light and sees supernaturally and spiritually. This is the *jñāna dīpaḥ* or *jñānadīptiḥ*. It is also called *jñānachakşuh*. When there is consistent practice in using this vision in *dhyāna* and *samādhi* yoga, then there is steady discriminative insight for the yogi, but not otherwise.

Application:

The radiant organ of perception becomes available to one who has consistently practiced the kriyā *yoga process. It is experienced when there is elimination of psychological impurities. This organ is in the head of the subtle body. It is a subtle object which is distinct from the core-self and the sense of identity.*

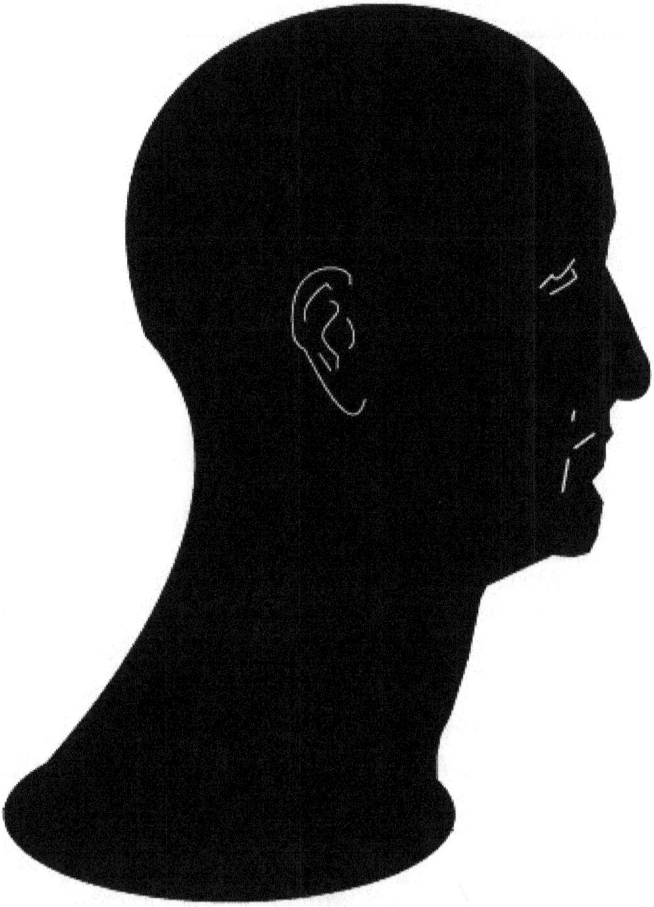

blank mental condition

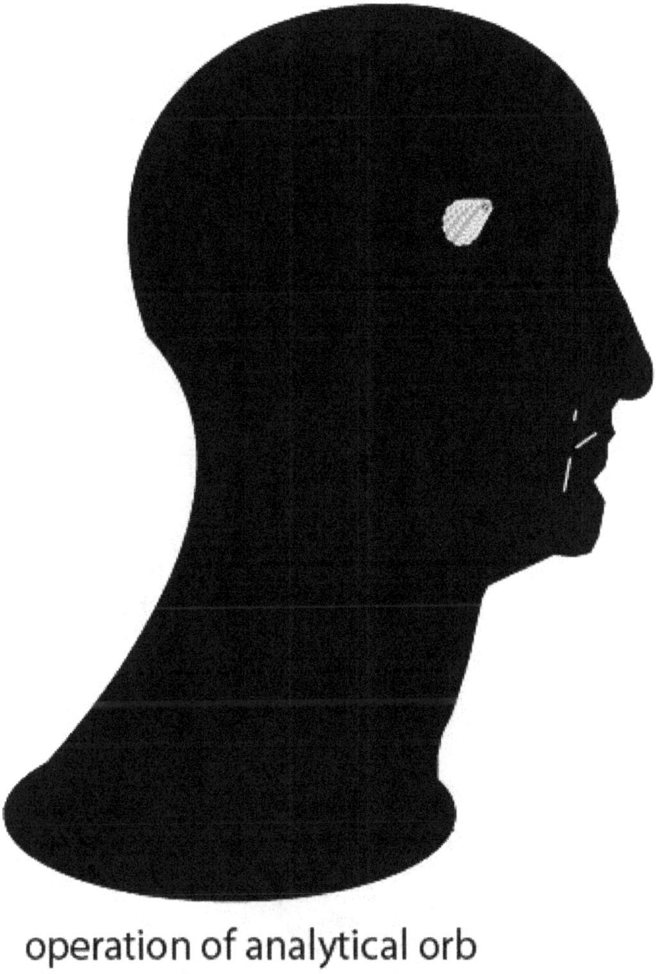

operation of analytical orb
creation of images and ideas

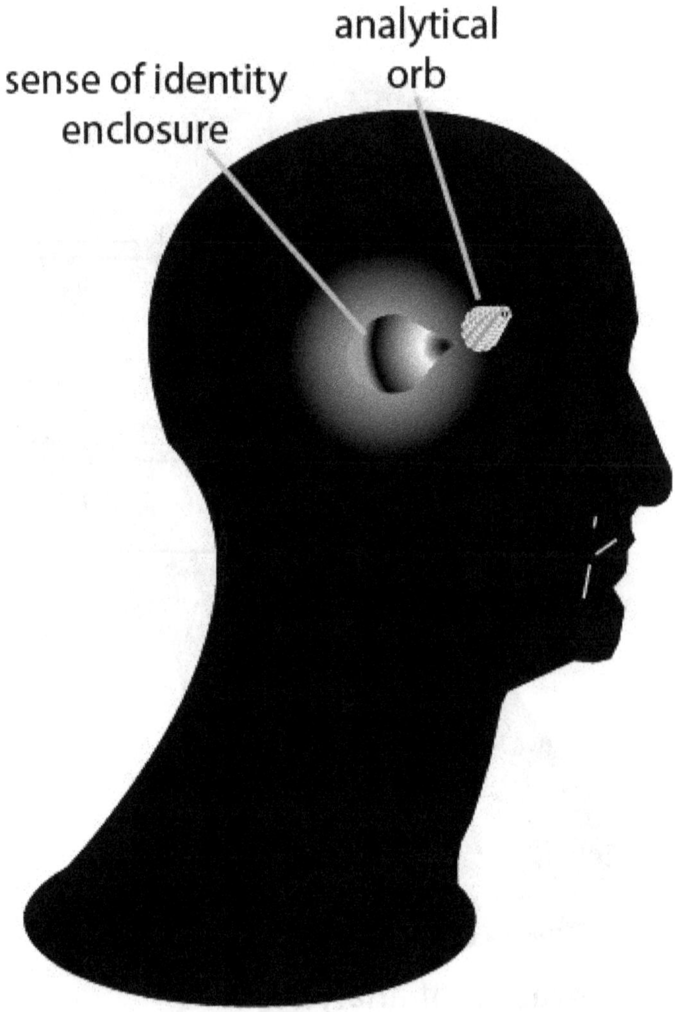

attentive I-self enclosed by sense of identity,
helplessly focused on analytical orb

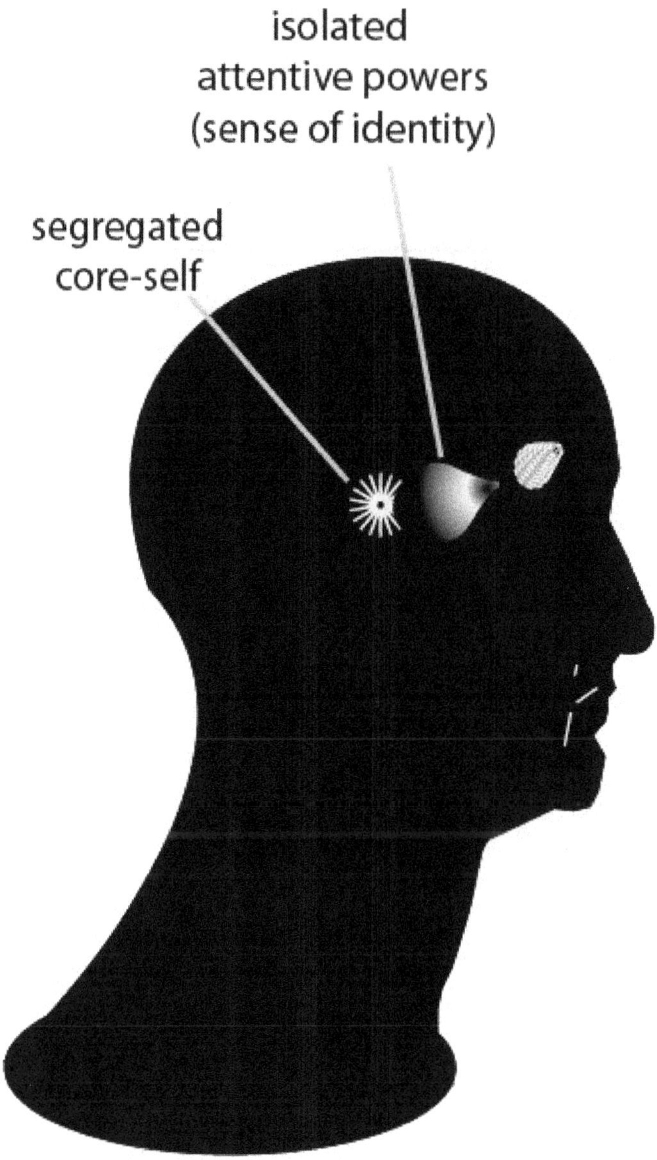

core-self freed
from identity dominance

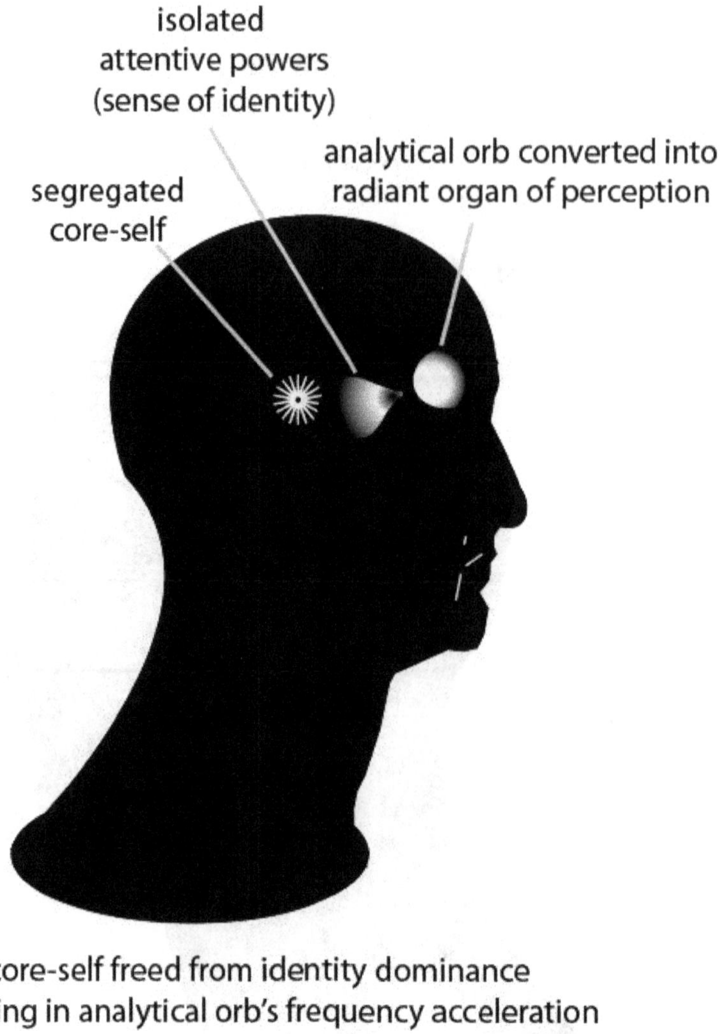

One does not identify the organ in the neophyte stages. It is perceived only in advanced meditation. Initially, the sight of it is momentary only. By persistence in samãdhi *practice permanent objective perception of it is gained.*

Verse 29

यमनियमासनप्राणायामप्रत्याहारधारणाध्यानसमाधयोऽष्टावङ्गानि ॥ २९ ॥

yama niyama āsana prāṇāyāma pratyāhāra dhāraṇā dhyāna samādhayaḥ aṣṭau aṅgāni

yama – moral restraints; niyama – recommended behaviors; āsana – body postures; prāṇāyāma – breath infusion; pratyāhar – sensual energy withdrawal; dhāraṇā – linking of the attention to higher concentration forces or persons; dhyāna – effortless linkage of the attention to higher concentration forces or persons; samādhayaḥ – continuous effortless linkage of the attention to higher concentration forces or persons; aṣṭau – eight; aṅgāni – parts of a thing.

Moral restraints, recommended behaviors, body posture, breath infusion, sensual energy withdrawal, linking of the attention to higher concentration forces or persons, effortless linkage of the attention to higher concentration forces or persons, continuous effortless linkage of the attention to higher concentration forces or persons are the eight parts of the yoga system.

Analysis:

Śrī Gorakṣnāth in his writings gave six parts to yoga, leaving out the preliminary parts of *yama* moral restraints, and *niyama* recommended behaviors. This is because those two are preliminary. A person who has not integrated those must instill them in himself as he practices the advanced portions. I experienced many students who are not masterful at the preliminary stages. They should master these as they proceed or they will discover that their lack of skill in cultural dealings causes impediments. According to the advisories and warnings issued by Krishna to Arjuna in the *Bhagavad Gītā*, a person who does not have an exemption from cultural activities, cannot succeed fully in yoga. Actually the sooner that one can realize this, the better and more advanced one will be. If one does not cooperate with the central person in the Universal Form, with Krishna, it will be impossible to achieve *samādhi*.

Gorakṣnāth did not want the *haṭha* yogis to waste time and energy in the moral field, in trying to perfect righteous living, but nevertheless, if one does not work his way cautiously through the cultural world, one will fail at yoga. We should accept that *Gorakṣnāth* was a birth taken by *Śrī Skanda Kūmara*, the celibate son of Lord Shiva. As such the yoga guru never advocated married life but that does not mean that it has no value. It has all value if we require other human bodies. The moral restraints and recommended behaviors keep us on the good side of Dharma, the supernatural person who sponsors righteous life style.

Application:

Restraining from vices and sensual addictions, becoming habituated to a disciplined life which accelerates yoga, doing bodily postures which enhance health, performing breath infusion, removing one's attention from the things pertaining to this existence, shifting one's attention to higher concentration forces or persons, holding one's attention there long enough for it to become habituated to the higher forces or persons, and experiencing the resultant fusion of the attention into the higher dimension encountered, are the eight parts of the yoga system. This is the ascending order of progress. One may learn or apply these haphazardly but in the advanced stage it becomes necessary to recognize and implement this series.

Verse 30

अहिंसासत्यास्तेयब्रह्मचर्यापरिग्रहा यमाः ॥ ३० ॥

ahiṁsā satya asteya
brahmacarya aparigrahāḥ yamāḥ

ahiṁsā – non-violence; satya – realism; asteya – non-stealing; brahmacarya – sexual non-expressiveness which results in the perception of spirituality; aparigrahāḥ – non-possessiveness; yamāḥ – moral restraints.

Non-violence, realism, non-stealing, sexual non-expressiveness which results in the perception of spirituality (brahman) and non-possessiveness are the moral restraints.

Analysis:

Some authorities list other moral restraints, but these given by *Śrī Patañjali* cover the whole spectrum. These qualities should be cultivated if they are not innate to one's character.

Ahiṁsā is the attitude of genuine harmlessness towards other creatures, not just human beings. Of course, the human form of life is comparatively more valuable than other species, but a yogi should know that creatures in other life forms must fulfill lower gratifications before they are permanently transformed to higher forms. Their lives should not be underrated. A yogi should not assume a master-of-the-species attitude. He should not harm any other creature willfully. He should situate himself circumstantially so that occasions for killing do not arise.

According to Lord *Mahāvīra* and other *Tīrthankaras* in the Jain disciplic succession, we have no business killing other creatures. A yogin should be non-violent. If one finds that he has a violent nature or that a part of his psyche takes pleasure in harming or in seeing others in difficulty, then he should work to purify that part. Each yogin has to realize defects and work to remove them by the relevant techniques.

Satya or realism includes truthfulness, but for the yogin it is more than conventional honesty. It has to do with developing the deep insight described by *Śrī Patañjali* in the previous verse as *jñāna-dīptiḥ* and as *vivekakhyātiḥ*. This gives one deep insight into reality, even to perceive past lives and to properly interpret the *saṁskār* subconscious impressions which are buried deep in memory and which surface from time to time.

Asteya or non-stealing is a must for a yogin. The tendency for stealing is innate in the subtle body. A yogin has to work with the self to eliminate it. This requires vigilance.

Brahmacarya has a conventional meaning as celibacy but it is more than that. It is an active or dynamic celibacy which is assisted by yoga practice and which results in the perception of spiritual reality. This means mastership of celibacy yoga, so that, even in an adult body, the sexual urge is sublimated and does not arise to motivate the psyche. A celibate ascetic should not have sexual intercourse unless he or she desires to have a child. Ideally, one should only have as many intercourses as there are children produced from the body. This is the ideal behavior. Failing in this a yogin has to work with the psyche to improve its sexual outlook, so that eventually its sexual needs are eliminated by the practice of celibacy yoga and *kuṇḍalinī* yoga. Without attaining celibacy one cannot become liberated. The energy of the subtle body will not be efficiently used if sexual expression continues through it. Thus one will not realize the subtle mundane existence which is compulsory for spiritual seekers.

Aparigrahāḥ or non-possessiveness deals with understanding that whatever we encounter in the gross or subtle existence is the property of more powerful beings. The only real possession we have is the task of our purification. The critical nature within us which usually seeks external expression should be directed backward into the psyche. This redirected critical force improves our condition by the application of corrective tendencies.

Overall these moral restraints are necessary for a yogi, but he does not master these initially, even though they are listed as the first stage of yoga. He masters a little and then continues to gain more control of his nature as he advances and increasingly sees how subtle the defects are and how specific he must be to root them out.

Application:

*The **moral restraints** consist of the following:*

***Non-violence:** The avoidance of violence towards other life forms, the avoidance of psychological violence towards other spiritual entities, the practice of a calm, detached mood as professed by Sri Krishna in the Bhagavad Gītā, if one is duty bound to discipline or apply violence to anyone.*

***Realism:** The practice of studying the situations carefully before acting or reacting to them. It is the practice of assessing the defects of one's intellect to gage its reliability in perceiving truth. It is relieving oneself of the need for a favorable or palatable truth.*

***Non-stealing:** Curing oneself of the natural urge to steal by carefully observing and monitoring the psychological mechanism of stealing which is innate to nature.*

***Sexual non-expressiveness which results in the perception of spirituality (brahman):** Becoming detached from expressive sexuality and from normal exhibitions and demonstrations of sexuality either as a male or female. Investing the energy usually used in sexuality for the perception of spirituality.*

***Non-possessiveness:** Carefully studying the sense of possession; suppressing it effectively while studying methods of its eradication and spiritually supportive uses.*

Verse 31

जातिदेशकालसमयानवच्छिन्नाः सार्वभौमा महाव्रतम्॥ ३१ ॥

jāti deśa kāla samaya anavacchinnāḥ
sārvabhaumāḥ mahāvratam

jāti – status; deśa – location; kāla – time; samaya – condition; anavacchinnāḥ – not restricted by, not adjusted by; sārvabhaumāḥ – relating to all standard stages, being standard; mahāvratam – great commitment.

Those moral restraints are not to be adjusted by the status, location, time or condition. They, being the great commitment, are related to all stages of yoga.

Analysis:

Sārvabhaumā means relating to all the earth. However *bhaumā*, as a synonym, also means stage or foreground, as explained in verse 27 with the term *prāntabhūmiḥ*. In the latter stages of yoga, the first stages maintain relevance. The yogi never reaches a stage where he can completely ignore moral restraints.

Śrī Patañjali accredited those moral restraints as the great commitment (*mahāvrata*).

Application:

Even though one may be pressured to adjust the moral restraints, one should strive to sidestep the causes and justifications for deviation. The pressures come on from the status, location, time or condition. Since the moral restraints are applicable in all stages of yoga, they are a great commitment for every ascetic. Since providence will take offence and short-circuit the liberating efforts of a yogi, one cannot be successful if one neglects the restraints.

Verse 32

शौचसन्तोषतपःस्वाध्यायेश्वरप्रणिधानानि नियमाः ॥ ३२ ॥

śauca santoṣa tapaḥ svādhyāya
īśvarapraṇidhānāni niyamāḥ

śauca – purification; santoṣa – contentment; tapaḥ – austerity; svādhyāya – study of the psyche; īśvara – Supreme Lord; praṇidhānāni – profound religious meditation; niyamāḥ – recommended behaviors.

Purification, contentment, austerity and profound religious meditation on the Supreme Lord are the recommended behaviors.

Analysis:

Many religious leaders ridicule *Patañjali* because he classified profound religious meditation to the Supreme Lord as part of an elementary stage in yoga practice, but just as the first stage remains relevant throughout the practices (*Sārvabhaumā* verse 31), so also every other stage remains in place, and is improved upon as the yogi moves to higher levels.

According to some critics, *Patañjali* hawked too much about yoga and neglected the *bhakti* or *bhakti*-yoga, giving it an insignificant place in the layout of spiritual disciplines. However if one checks the *Bhagavad Gītā* carefully, one will discover that Śrī Krishna, who declared Himself as the Supreme Lord, gave high precedence to yoga.

The other aspect of *Śrī Patañjali*'s treatment of devotion to God, is understood when we consider the term *praṇidhānāni*. He spoke of profound religious meditation. This is a mystic process of internal focus upon the Supreme Lord to reach the Divinity in a totally different dimension. But why, one may ask, did *Patañjali* not place this as the foremost aspect of yoga practice? The reason is simple: One cannot perfect this unless one first masters yoga. The skill to do this comes only by perfecting the austerities.

In the *Bhagavad Gītā*, the purpose of yoga is defined by *Śrī* Krishna in the following terms:

tatraikāgraṃ manaḥ kṛtvā yata-cittendriya-kriyāḥ
upaviśyāsane yuñjyād yogam ātma-viśuddhaye

> ... being there, seated in a posture, having the mind focused, the person who controls his thinking and sensual energy, should practice the yoga discipline for self-purification. (Gītā 6:12)

Śrī Krishna also explained that a yogi should commit to cultural activities for the sake of psychic purification:

kāyena manasā buddhyā kevalair indriyair api
yoginaḥ karma kurvanti saṅgam tyaktvātma-śuddhaye

> With the body, mind and intelligence, or even with the senses alone, the yogis, having discarded attachment, perform cultural acts for self-purification. (Gītā 5:11)

Patañjali does not contradict *Śrī* Krishna. In fact he reinforces what Krishna said.

Application:

The ***recommended behaviors*** *are as follows:*

Purification: *Psychic cleansing which is achieved by mastery of kundalini yoga for purifying the subtle body and its energies.*

Contentment: *This is the practice of detachment from desire for mundane life. One must find an effective way of changing one's nature to eradicate the desire for mundane experiences.*

Austerity: *This refers to the practice of* kriyā *yoga under the guidance of a more advanced yogi. These austerities should suppress unwanted desires to the point of eliminating them. Such desires are those which cause extroversion and which discourage the quest for liberation.*

Profound meditation on the Supreme Lord: *One can meditate on the Person God if one has a functional relationship with Him. Over all, this is impractical for most practitioners since they either have an imaginary relationship with a preferred deity or a very meager connection. To be realistic one has to develop a relationship with a person who is more advanced in the spiritual path laid out by Patañjali.*

Verse 33

वितर्कबाधने प्रतिपक्षभावनम्॥ ३३॥

vitarkabādhane pratipakṣabhāvanam

vitarka – doubt, argument; bādhane – in annoyance or disturbance; pratipakṣa – what is opposite or contrary; bhāvanam – manifesting, imagining, conceiving, considering.

In the case of the annoyance produced by doubts, one should conceive of what is opposite.

Analysis:

When there are any doubts regarding the moral restraints and the recommended behaviors, a yogi should counteract that state of mind by conceiving of the opposite. In other words, sometimes a yogi is pressured by the same status, location, time or condition mentioned in verse 31. Then he may cast aside the five great commitments, feeling that he is allowed to do so because of a particular status he is awarded by providence, or because of being in a certain location, or through the time of an occurrence, or because he was pressured by certain conditions. However, *Patañjali* objects and states that the yogi should not give-in but should hold on to the principles by considering and contemplating the five great commitments with greater force.

If a yogi complies with this instruction, his course into higher yoga would be accelerated, otherwise he will be stalled in lower stages for a long time. Sometimes a yogi gets an idea to do something which jeopardizes his practice. He may feel compelled to comply with a pressure of providence which is forced into his mind. Usually, such a situation will pass on even if the yogi does not satisfy the urge, but if he is rash, he will act in the wrong way and forestall practice. Thus *Patañjali* asks that we consider the contrary anytime we get an urge to act against the moral principles.

Sometimes in the astral world and in parallel dimensions a yogi is circumstantially positioned for breaking moral rules, but when he gets back into the material body and recalls the incident, he regrets or thinks that for some reason he was unable to use discrimination. *Patañjali* mentioned this discriminative insight before under the terms of *vivekakhyātiḥ*. Unless this develops to the extent that it is ingrained, the yogi will break the moral restraints whenever his discriminative insight vanishes or is weakened.

Application:

When doubts about yoga arise, one should ignore the ideas and intensify practice. Evidence for extra-sensory perception is present around us twenty-four hours per day. Being aware of that requires shifting one's attention for this level of existence to what is unseen. This requires confidence, since the unseen is an abstraction initially.

Verse 34

वितर्का हिंसादयः कृतकारितानुमोदिता लोभक्रोधमोहपूर्वका मृदुमध्याधिमात्रा

दुःखाज्ञानानन्तफला इति प्रतिपक्षभावनम्॥ ३४ ॥

vitarkaḥ hiṁsādayaḥ kṛta kārita anumoditāḥ lobha krodha moha pūrvakaḥ mṛdu madhya adhimātraḥ duḥkha ajñāna anantaphalāḥ iti pratipakṣabhāvanam

vitarkaḥ – doubts; hiṁsa – violence; ādayaḥ – and related matters; kṛta – done; kārita – cause to be done; anumoditāḥ – endorsed, approved; lobha – greed; krodha – anger; moha – delusion; pūrvakaḥ – caused by, proceeded by; mṛdu – minor; madhya – mediocre; adhimātraḥ – substantial; duḥkha – distress; ajñāna – spiritual ignorance; ananta – endless; phalāḥ – results; iti – thus; pratipakṣa – opposite type; bhāvanam – considerations.

Doubts which produce violence and related actions, which are performed, caused to be done or endorsed, and which are caused by greed, anger and delusion, even if minor, mediocre or substantial, cause endless distress and spiritual ignorance as the results. Therefore, one should consider the opposite features.

Analysis:

Violence and related actions run contrary to the moral restraints of non-violence, realism, non-stealing, sexual non-expressiveness and non-possessiveness. Any ideas which run contrary to morality and which seem to justify such immoral acts are to be abandoned. If a yogin finds that he does not have the power to abandon immoral acts, then he should think deeply of the benefit of morality. This may give him the required detachment and invoke in him sufficient patience so that he restrains from vices until the impulsions pass out of his mind or lose their impulsive force.

If a moral code is to be broken at a certain time, it will be done by someone somehow, but if the energy or motivation for that act finds the yogi to be an unwilling subject, it will move away from him and influence some other person to act. A yogi should understand this. A yogi may be tricked again and again by those compulsions to do immoral acts but eventually, he will begin to develop a resistance to those forceful motivations which cause him to deviate. Arjuna questioned *Śrī* Krishna about this in the *Bhagavad Gītā*:

balād iva niyojitaḥ arjuna uvāca atha kena prayukto 'yaṃ
pāpaṃ carati pūruṣaḥ anicchann api vārṣṇeya

Arjuna said: Then explain, O family man of the Vrishnis, by what is a person forced to commit an evil even unwillingly, just as if one was compelled to do so? *(Gītā 3.36)*

Application:

One may doubt that one can exist without committing some minimal violence. For instance, even if one refrains from eating animal flesh, one will have to eat something else, vegetables or fruits for example. And in that case there will be violence against trees, insects and microbes. Still one should minimize such violence and hold faith that ultimately it can be removed by transfer to another dimension where the violence will be absent. If one does not succeed at yoga practice, the implication is that one will be condemned to material existence, with endless distress and continued misidentification with the mundane energy in any of its gross or subtle formations.

Verse 35

अहिंसाप्रतिष्ठायां तत्सन्निधौ वैरत्यागः ॥ ३५ ॥

ahiṁsāpratiṣṭhāyāṁ tatsannidhau vairatyāgaḥ

ahiṁsā – non-violence; pratiṣṭhāyāṁ – on being firmly established; tat – his; sannidhau – presence, vicinity; vaira – hostility; tyāgaḥ – abandonment.

On being firmly established in non-violence, the abandonment of hostility occurs in his presence.

Analysis:

This charm over the violent nature of others is sometimes exhibited by great yogins. Sometimes it even manifests in the life of a student yogin. It begins in human society where people who are normally hostile to each other exhibit undue kindness even to enemies, when they are in the presence of a yogin.

The force of the non-violent nature of the yogi may disarm and temporarily disintegrate the hostile nature of others. Sometimes this is shown when a fish-eating human being is in the presence of a great yogin. The fish-eater feels as if he can eat nothing besides vegetables or fruits. But the animal nature is again manifested when the person gets out of the range of the yogin. At the same time a great yogin may have no effect on a cannibal, or flesh-eater. The lower tendencies may be so strong as to resist saintly influence or it may be that the yogin assumes a reticent demeanor seeking not to adjust the life style of others.

Application:

When a yogi is firmly established in non-violence, it is exhibited by his lifestyle. Then even hostile creatures abandon their aggressive stance in his presence. But all the same, some creatures become nervous and aggravated when he is near. Those who specialize in exploiting others become stressed in his presence and may react by expressing prejudices towards him.

Verse 36

सत्यप्रतिष्ठायां क्रियाफलाश्रयत्वम्॥ ३६ ॥

satyapratiṣṭhāyāṁ kriyāphalāśrayatvam

satya – realism; pratiṣṭhāyāṁ – on being established; kriyā – actions; phalāḥ – results; āśryatvam – what serves as a support for something else.

On being established in realism, his actions serve as a basis for results.

Analysis:

It may be contested that in all cases, a person's action serves as the basis of the results he will be afforded by providence, either for good or bad, according to what was committed. However the yogi is more conscious of actions and potential results than others. This is because of mystic perception in the truths of how this world operates. An enlightened yogi's actions, particularly his mystic actions, are consistent with realism.

In these verses instead of using the term *tiṣṭha*, *Patañjali* uses *pratiṣṭhā* which means to be firmly established, as opposed to initially or haphazardly established. This comes after sufficient practice. In the case of the divine beings, it is part of their superior performance.

Application:

When a yogi is established in realism, his actions serve as a basis for selfless results. He is not easily frustrated because he acts in accordance with reality, is subordinate to it, respects it and rarely makes unrealistic plans in attempts to contravene it.

Verse 37

अस्तेयप्रतिष्ठायां सर्वरत्नोपस्थानम्॥ ३७॥

asteyapratiṣṭhāyāṁ sarvaratnopasthānam

asteya – non-stealing; pratiṣṭhāyāṁ – on firmly establishing; sarva – all; ratna – gems, precious things; upasthānam – approaching, waiting upon.

On being firmly established in non-stealing, all precious things wait to serve a yogin.

Analysis:

Usually, a yogin is unconcerned about precious things. His mind is fixed on the most precious thing, which is spiritual elevation. Thus many opportunities for exploitation come to a yogin but he does not take advantage of them. People often wonder why a great yogi wastes his life away, and why he does not exploit all the people and resources which are in a position to be used by him. The answer is that a yogi is too preoccupied with yoga practice. A great yogin is easily discovered if one searches for the person around whom, all sorts of wealth manifest but is not used, the person who is indifferent to it, seemingly stupid, seemingly not realizing the worth in valuables and in the cheap labor which could be derived from others.

Application:

When the yogi has subdued the stealing tendency in human nature, material existence endeavors to serve him. Thus it seems that all precious things become available to him. And still he has a lack of interest in exploitation and making a profit.

Verse 38

ब्रह्मचर्यप्रतिष्ठायां वीर्यलाभः ॥ ३८॥

brahmacaryapratiṣṭhāyāṁ vīryalābhaḥ

brahmacarya – sexual non-expressiveness which results in the perception of spirituality; pratiṣṭhāyāṁ – being firmly established; vīrya – vigor; lābhaḥ – what is gained.

On being firmly established in the sexual non-expressiveness which results in the perception of spirituality, vigor is gained.

Analysis:

This means dynamic celibacy established by virtue of yoga practice in terms of *āsana* postures and *prāṇāyāma* breath nutrition methods which will be mentioned forthwith by *Patañjali.*

This is the *ūrdhvaretā* stage where the yogi masters *kuṇḍalinī* yoga and celibacy yoga.

Application:

When the yogi has practiced effective methods of sex activity reduction and elimination, his vigor to perform yoga proportionately increases. Thus his perception of spirituality is actuated.

Verse 39

अपरिग्रहस्थैर्ये जन्मकथन्तासम्बोधः ॥ ३९ ॥

aparigrahasthairye janmakathaṁtā saṁbodhaḥ

aparigraha – non-possessiveness; sthairye – in the consistent; janma – birth; kathaṁtā – how, the reason for; saṁbodhaḥ – full or correct perception regarding something.

The reason for and the correct perception of one's birth is known when there is consistent non-possessiveness.

Analysis:

When a yogi has mastered the quality of non-possessiveness in relation to this gross level of reality, his energy of appreciation shifts to the subtle plane. Thus he perceives the reason for the birth he recently took. If he develops that clairvoyant skill, he comes to understand why others took up a certain body. He can know his past lives and that of others. However, if upon realizing that he has this skill, he becomes attracted to popularity and wants to be endearing and beloved, he might abuse himself. Then, the skill will gradually leave him as he becomes habituated to appropriating fame in the material world.

Application:

Due to the development of non-possessiveness, the yogi intuits the causes of birth. By mystic skill he reviews actions from past lives which caused him to take the present body. He makes adjustments to avoid the same mistaken course when transmigrating.

Verse 40

शौचात्स्वाङ्गजुगुप्सा परैरसंसर्गः ॥ ४० ॥

śaucāt svāṅgajugupsā paraiḥ asaṁsargaḥ

śaucāt – from purification; svāṅga = sva – oneself + aṅga – limbs; jugupsā – aversion, disgust; parair = pariaḥ – with others; asaṁsargaḥ – non-association, lack of desire to associate.

From purification comes a disgust for one's own body and a lack of desire to associate with others.

Analysis:

True purification comes after long and hard yoga austerities. The student yogi, once he purified the psyche, develops disgust for the same material body through which he worked hard to purify. This happens because the material body and the subtle form interspaced into it, have an innate tendency to absorb the pollutions which pull an ascetic down from yoga practice. As soon as a student yogi stops practice, he regresses. Even though the material body is an asset, it also remains as a liability so long as it exists. Worse still, is the subtle body, because, until one can shed it and take a yoga siddha form, one is in danger of being degraded. The subtle body is worse than the gross form when it comes to adaptation and acceptance of vices.

A yogi develops a lack of desire to associate with others, except for his advanced teachers. Otherwise, a yogi always runs the risks of degradation, due to susceptibility to the habits of others. Unfortunately, people may think that a yogi hates or avoids them. Actually a yogi has no time to hate anyone because he has to attend to practice and the energy which would be used to relate favorably and unfavorably to others is needed to accelerate progress. As a matter of course, he develops a desire not to associate with others. It is a result of higher yoga practice.

Application:

From purification of the subtle body comes disgust for one's own gross form and lack of desire to associate sexually with others.

Verse 41

सत्त्वशुद्धिसौमनस्यैकाग्र्येन्द्रियजयात्मदर्शनयोग्यत्वानि च॥४१॥

sattvaśuddhi saumanasya ekāgra indriyajaya ātmadarśana yogyatvāni ca

sattva – being, nature, psyche; śuddhi – purification; saumanasya – concerning benevolence; ekāgra – ability to link the attention to one concentration force or person; indriya – sensual energy; jaya – conquest; ātma – spirit; darśana – sight, vision; yogyatvāni – being fit for yoga or abstract meditation; ca – and.

Purification of the psyche results in benevolence, the ability to link the attention to one concentration force or person, conquest of the sensual energy, vision of the spirit and fitness for abstract meditation.

Analysis:

Purification of the psyche *(sattva-śuddhi)* is possible only after celibacy yoga is mastered. Then the student yogi develops benevolence towards everyone. This is a type of detachment, but in its social application it functions as benevolence or good will towards one and all.

This student yogi develops the ability to link his mind to one concentration force in the *dhāraṇā* sixth stage of yoga practice. He masters the sensual energy by perfecting the *pratyāhār* fifth stage, and is able to begin the *dhyāna* seventh stage, to have the vision of the spirit and a fitness for abstract meditation. This is not impersonal meditation as some profess, but rather meditation on levels above both this physical world and the lower astral regions.

Application:

Purification of the subtle energy results in a great reduction in emotional needs. From that stability one finds it easy to link the attention to one concentration force or person. After much practice one acquires conquest of the sensual energy. One gets vision of the spirit and becomes fit for abstract meditation.

Verse 42

सन्तोषादनुत्तमसुखलाभः ॥४२॥

saṅtoṣāt anuttamaḥ sukhalābhaḥ

saṅtoṣāt – from contentment; anuttamaḥ – supreme, the very best; sukha – happiness; lābhaḥ – obtained.

From contentment, the very best in happiness is obtained.

Analysis:

This is a calm type of happiness devoid of the excitations which come from the pursuit of cravings and vices. A yogi appreciates this contentment that others dislike because it lacks excitement.

Application:

With the reduction of sensual life in this world, with a developed resistance to desires, one gains contentment. From that, the very best in happiness is obtained.

Verse 43

कायेन्द्रियसिद्धिरशुद्धिक्षयात्तपसः ॥४३॥

kāya indriya siddhiḥ aśuddhikṣayāt tapasaḥ

kāya – body; indriya – sensual energy; siddhiḥ – skill, perfection; aśuddhi – impurity; kṣayāt – from the elimination; tapasaḥ – austerity.

Austerity, resulting in the elimination of impurity, produces perfection of the body and sensual energy.

Analysis:

This is the basis of results gained in the grueling austerities of *āsana* and *prāṇāyāma*, the third and fourth stages of yoga practice. When the impurities in the subtle body are removed, one gains skill in controlling the gross and subtle bodies as well as the sensual energy housed in them. This is mastered in *kuṇḍalinī* yoga, celibacy yoga and purity-of-the-psyche yoga (*sattvaśuddhi* verse 41), *(ātmaśuddha Bhagavad Gītā 6:12)*.

Tapasaḥ means austerity. One may ask which austerity? This question is answered in the term *aśuddhikṣayāt*, which means the austerities which result in the elimination of *kṣayāt* or impurities.

Application:

Kriya yoga austerities which are highlighted by mystic actions in and with the subtle body, do result in elimination of emotional impurities. That gives perfection of the subtle form in which the troublesome, vice-seeking sensual energy is housed.

Verse 44

स्वाध्यायादिष्टदेवतासम्प्रयोगः ॥४४॥

svādhyāyāt iṣṭadevatā saṁprayogaḥ

svādhyāyāt – from study of the psyche; iṣṭadevatā – cherished divine being; saṁprayogaḥ – intimate contact.

From study of the psyche comes intimate contact with the cherished divine being.

Analysis:

Patañjali has not named the *iṣṭadevatā*, the cherished divine personality. That person might be different for other ascetics. Many divine beings serve as cherished Lords of the limited entities.

However, when the yogi achieves complete purity of the psyche, he gets a divine vision through which he meets the cherished deity face to face and can relate with that divinity.

Application:

An in-depth mystic research into the nature of the subtle body causes the yogi to make contact with more advanced mystics. This leads to communication with divine beings, and eventually he gets in touch with the cherished divine beings, one of whom is the Supreme Lord.

Verse 45

समाधिसिद्धिरीश्वरप्रणिधानात्॥ ४५॥

samādhisiddhiḥ īśvarapraṇidhānāt

samādhi – continuous effortless linkage of the attention to a higher concentration force or person; siddhiḥ – perfection, skill; īśvara – supreme lord; praṇidhānāt – from the profound religious meditation.

From the profound religious meditation upon the Supreme Lord comes the perfection of continuous effortless linkage of the attention to that Divinity.

Analysis:

Now all accusations against *Śrī Patañjali* regarding his alleged ideas of impersonalist and atheism are totally refuted. *Śrī Patañjali Mahāmuni* was undoubtedly a theist of the first order. *Śrī* B.K.S. Iyengar in his translation and commentary on the *sūtras*, explained that *Patañjali* was an incarnation of Lord *Ādiśeṣa*, the divine serpentine bedstead of Lord *Viṣṇu*. *Patañjali's* mother was named *Goṇikā*.

Application:

From the profound religious meditation upon the Supreme Lord or upon any of the divine beings, comes a full time communion with that divinity.

Verse 46

स्थिरसुखमासनम्॥ ४६॥

sthira sukham āsanam

sthira – steady; sukham – comfortable; āsanan – bodily posture.

The posture should be steady and comfortable.

Analysis:

The yoga *āsana* for meditation should be one that is steady and comfortable. Ideally, one should sit for meditation in the lotus posture, the *padmāsana*, if that posture is unsteady and uncomfortable, one should practice to improve it. During meditation one should use a posture that keeps the body steady and the mind relaxed. As one practices more and more, the difficult postures become easier and easier to perform.

Application:

A steady and comfortable posture is achieved after much practice.

Verse 47

प्रयत्नशैथिल्यानन्तसमापत्तिभ्याम् ॥ ४७ ॥

prayatna śaithilya ananta samāpattibhyām

prayatna – effort; śaithilya – relaxation; ananta – endless, infinite; samāpattibhyām – meeting, encounter.

It results in relaxation of effort and meeting with the infinite.

Analysis:

Āsana is perfected when it becomes steady and comfortable, so much so that the yogin relaxes his efforts to hold the body in the posture. With ease, he shifts his attention to link it with the infinite.

Application:

When mastered, it results in relaxation of the effort to subdue the body and make it serve the spiritual aims. That assists in the quest for meeting with the infinite.

Verse 48

ततो द्वन्द्वानभिघातः ॥ ४८ ॥

tataḥ dvandvāḥ anabhighātaḥ

tataḥ – then; dvandvāḥ – the dualities of happiness and distress, heat and cold; anabhighātaḥ – no shrinking, no attacking, no botheration.

From then on, there are no botherations from the dualities like happiness and distress or heat and cold.

Analysis:

When there is perfect posture of body in which the yogin attains continuous effortless linkage of his attention to a higher concentration force, or divine person, then the botherations of the mento-emotional energy which concerns happiness and distress cease for him. These continue in the lives of the student yogins who are on a lower level of practice. They should master themselves through consistent effort.

Application:

Once the body is mastered, comfortable or uncomfortable climate and pleasant or unpleasant emotions, no longer bother the person. By repeatedly moving the attention to the spiritual side of existence, the yogi succeeds in reorienting himself to abstraction. But later after much practice, this abstract void situation becomes a dimension which is teeming with spiritual objects.

Verse 49

तस्मिन्सति श्वासप्रश्वासयोर्गतिविच्छेदः प्राणायामः ॥४९॥

tasmin satiśvāsa praśvāsayoḥ
gativicchedaḥ prāṇāyāmaḥ

tasmin – on this; sati – being accomplished; śvāsa – inhalation; praśvāsayoḥ – of the exhalation; gati – the flow; vicchedaḥ – the separation; prāṇāyāmḥ – breath regulation.

Once this is accomplished, breath regulation, which is the separation of the flow of inhalation and exhalation, is attained.

Analysis:

The *prāṇāyāma* cannot be mastered properly until one has perfected postures or *āsanas* but preliminary *prāṇāyāma* can be learned beforehand. The stages of yoga are learned one by one or even haphazardly according to one's destiny regarding availability of knowledgeable teachers. One cannot focus properly on the vital force until one has mastered a suitable posture. This is the point but one can become familiar with the various *prāṇāyāmas* beforehand.

A yogin has to learn how to separate the flow of breath, so that the inhalation is distinct from the exhalation, so that there is a pause between these. This is why the word *vicchedaḥ* was used. It means separation, cleavage, or gap. Generally, mammals breathe in and out without pause because their breath is not complete or sufficient. It is usually shallow. The exhalation is rushed out to speed up the next intake of air. When one reconditions the lung apparatus, so that the intake is complete, this rush for exhalations in order to inhale again, ceases. The separation of the intake and out-breath becomes evident, along with the benefits of that for meditation.

Application:

Once this is accomplished, the body's anxiety for air is greatly decreased, and there are pauses between the flow in inhalation and exhalation. This experience occurs just before, during and after samādhi *states. The rate of heart beat drops, the breathing system relaxes. Sometimes the lungs appear to have stopped their rhythm contraction and expansion.*

Verse 50

वाह्याभ्यन्तरस्तम्भवृत्तिः देशकालसङ्ख्याभिः परिदृष्टो दीर्घसूक्ष्मः ॥५०॥

bāhya ābhyantara stambha vṛttiḥ deśa kāla
saṁkhyābhiḥ paridṛṣṭah dīrgha sūkṣmaḥ

bāhya – external; ābhyantara – internal; stambha – restrained, suppressed, restrictive; vṛttiḥ – activity, movement operation; deśa – place; kāla – time; saṁkhyābhiḥ – with numbering accounting; paridṛṣṭah – measured, regulated; dīrgha – prolonged; sūkṣmaḥ – subtle, hardly noticeable.

It has internal, external and restrictive operations, which are regulated according to the place, time and accounting, being prolonged or hardly noticed.

Analysis:

Ideally, *prāṇāyāma* is learned from a teacher who practiced to proficiency. Such teachers are hard to find. The first accomplishment of a student yogi is to learn how to purify the *nāḍīs* in the subtle form. When that is achieved, he will discover other *prāṇāyāmas* automatically by the grace of the force of *prāṇa* and by the awakening of the *kuṇḍalinī* chakra.

Prāṇāyāma teachers usually stress a count for alternate breathing in the ratio of 1:4:2, meaning that one should inhale through one nostril for one count, then retain the air for four proportionate counts and then exhale all air through the other nostril during two counts, such that if one starts inhaling through the right nostril alone, one will hold the air, then expel it through the left nostril. Then begin the cycle by inhaling through the left nostril, holding and expelling the air through the right nostril. Eventually one should increase the duration, so that the time for a count increases. This is done without straining the lungs. If the *nāḍīs* are not fully charged before one begins, and if one is not a celibate yogi, one will not be successful with this practice. There are many preliminary practices required for success in yoga. One would be fortunate if one could learn these from an accomplished teacher.

Application:

Breathing has internal, external and restrictive operations, which are regulated according to the place, time and accounting, being prolonged or hardly noticed. A change in lifestyle affects this. Breath infusement gives one an inside view of the pathways used by the life force for energy distribution. It increases one's grip on the kuṇḍalinī. *It reduces the energy requirements of the physical body which results in more dream recall, astral projection and frequency of dimensional switching.*

Verse 51

वाह्याभ्यन्तरविषयाक्षेपी चतुर्थः ॥५१॥

bāhya ābhyantara viṣaya ākṣepī caturthaḥ

bāhya – external; ābhyantara – internal; viṣaya – objective; ākṣepī – transcending; caturthaḥ – the fourth.

That which transcends the objective, external and internal breath regulation is the fourth type of breath infusement techniques.

Analysis:

In the previous *sūtra, Śrī Patañjali* listed three types of operations, relating to internal, external and restrictive operations of the breath. Then he gave a fourth operation to transcend the objective of the three preliminary operations.

Application:

A more advanced condition is realized which has nothing to do with physical breathing. This is the energy consumption of the subtle body. That regulation of the subtle energy or prāṇa *is the fourth type of* prāṇāyāma *energy intake.*

Verse 52

ततः क्षीयते प्रकाशावरणम्॥५२॥

tataḥ kṣīyate prakāśa āvaraṇam

tataḥ – thence, from that; kṣīyate – is dissipated; prakāśa – light; āvaraṇam – covering, mental darkness.

From that is dissipated, the mental darkness which veils the light,

Analysis:

After much practice and mastership of advanced *prāṇāyāma* the dark mind-space is cleared. An illuminating light *(prakāśa)* is perceived.

Application:

When a yogi shifts his attention to the subtle plane of consciousness, the darkness within the mind becomes dissipated, resulting in perception of light in real subtle objects.

Verse 53

धारणासु च योग्यता मनसः ॥५३॥

dhāraṇāsu ca yogyatā manasaḥ

dhāraṇāsu – for linking the attention to a higher concentration force or person; ca – and; yogyatā – being conducive for abstract meditation; manasaḥ – of the mind.

and from that, is attained the state of the mind for linking the attention to a higher concentration force or person.

Analysis:

Dhāraṇā practice requires a preliminary mastership in certain aspects of *prāṇa* energy control. This is why when someone sits to meditate without first doing *prāṇāyāma*, he cannot be successful even though he may imagine himself in peace, happiness and light. One has to make the mind fit for yoga practice *(yogyatā manasaḥ)*. The mind will prevent the attention from linking to a higher concentration force or person if the mind itself is not surcharged with a higher grade of pranic energy. It will be unable to make a higher linkage, except now and again, by a fluke, haphazardly. For consistent practice one must do the *āsana postures* with *prāṇāyāma* breath infusion daily before meditation practice.

Application:

The establishment of always being able to link one's attention to a higher concentration force or person, is manifested after consistent practice in association with accomplished yogis. This is relief in the quest for relocating to a spiritual environment.

Verse 54

स्वविषयासम्प्रयोगे चित्तस्य स्वरूपानुकार इवेन्द्रियाणां प्रत्याहारः ॥५४॥

svaviṣaya asaṁprayoge cittasya svarūpāanukāraḥ iva indriyāṇāṁ pratyāhāraḥ

sva – their own; viṣaya – objects of perception; asaṁprayoge – in not contacting; cittasya – of the mento-emotional energy; svarūpa – own form; anukāraḥ – imitation, patterning, assuming; iva – as if, as it were; indriyāṇāṁ – senses; pratyāhāraḥ – withdrawal of sensual energy and its focus on the mind.

The withdrawal of the senses is, as it was, their assumption of the form of mento-emotional energy when not contacting their own objects of perception.

Analysis:

In his word-for-word meanings, *Śrī* B.K.S. Iyengar gave the root word for *pratyāhārah*. The basic parts of that Sanskrit word are as follows:

prati + aṅg + hṛ – to draw towards the opposite.

When the mento-emotional energy, the *citta*, is outward bound, it is called sensual energy or *indriyāni*. But when it is inward bound it is called *citta* or emotional force. A yogin has to master that *citta* energy and reorient it so that he alters its outward bound habit.

Application:

The self should learn how to subsist on the bare sensual energy by itself without its usage of procuring objects. This is called pratāyhār *or sensual energy withdrawal. After mastering this, the yogin notices that the withdrawal of the senses is their assumption of the form of unformed psychological energy which is quiescent when it is not contacting the objects of perception.*

Verse 55

ततः परमा वश्यतेन्द्रियाणाम्॥५५॥

tataḥ paramā vaśyatā indriyāṇām

tataḥ – then, from that accomplishment; paramā – highest, greatest; vaśyatā – subdued, subjugation, control; indriyāṇām – of the sense.

From that accomplishment comes the highest degree of control of the senses.

Analysis:

Pratyāhār practice, when mastered, gives the student yogin the qualification to practice higher yoga for adjustments on the mystic plane.

Application:

From that accomplishment comes the highest degree of control of the senses because they are powered by the inner sensual energy which a human being identifies as his emotions and mental force. When the senses pursue objects in the external world, they acquire resistance to the core-self. This energy is experienced as sensual compulsion, such that even if the person does not require the sense object pursued, he or she is forced to endeavor for it. When the senses are withdrawn or barred association with an object the authority of the core-self increases and the senses remain restricted internally. On some occasions, the senses express a reluctance to accommodate the core-self. It expresses this as a depressed state of mind. A yogi should tolerate this.

Chapter 3
Vibhūti Pāda:
Glory Displayed

Verse 1

देशबन्धश्चित्तस्य धारणा ॥ १ ॥

deśa bandhaḥ cittasya dhāraṇā

deśa – location; bandhaḥ – confinement, restriction; cittasya – of the mento-emotional energy; dhāraṇā – linking of the attention to a concentration force or person.

Linking of the attention to a concentration force or person, involves a restricted location in the mento-emotional energy.

Analysis:

For higher meditation, everything required for practice is within the mental and emotional energy fields. This is the psychological environment from which a yogin can break out of this dimension to enter other parallel worlds, which are either subtle, supernatural or spiritual. It is from within the mento-emotional energy that one breaks out of this world. The paradox is that the very same mental and emotional energy, which causes us to become attached to this world, can also in turn, inspire liberation. The gate for exiting this world is in the same mento-emotional energy *(cittasya).*

Many people feel that a yogi enters into his own psyche, develops it, feels as powerful as God and then becomes perfect. Little do they understand that from within his psyche, a yogi finds entry into parallel worlds. From particular locations, *deśa*, or confining locations *(deśa bandhah)*, a yogi finds doorways and peep holes that give him access to other worlds, places that he might be transferred after permanently leaving the physical body.

Application:

The yogi must be so familiar with the realm of mind and emotions, that he recognizes where thoughts, ideas, images and memories arise. Their particular location in the mind environment and emotional atmosphere should be known. Then he may practice the sixth stage of yoga, which is linking of the attention to a concentration force or person through a restricted location in the mento-emotional space. One begins in familiar territory which means tracking and cataloging the various locations in the mind and their functions. The appearance of a mental image, symbol or sound should be observed as a place where such and such occurs and one should suspect that there is a subtle organ at that place in which these impressions arise.

Eventually one will see the hidden subtle object which creates the impressions. This would mean two things:

a. development of supernatural perception

b. perception of a super-subtle sensing mechanism

Each sense has a super-subtle sense counterpart which would be revealed to a yogi in due course.

Verse 2

तत्र प्रत्ययैकतानता ध्यानम्॥ २ ॥

tatra pratyayaḥ ekatānatā dhyānam

tatra – there, in that location; pratyayaḥ – conviction or belief as mental content, instinctive interest; ekatānatā – one continuous threadlike flow of attention = eka – one + tānatā – thread of fiber; dhyānam – effortless linking of the attention to a higher concentration force or person.

When in that location, there is one continuous threadlike flow of one's instinctive interest, that is the effortless linking of the attention to a higher concentration force or person.

Analysis:

The key term in this verse is *pratyayaḥ*. Shivram Apte in his Sanskrit English dictionary gave the following meanings: conviction, settled belief, trust, faith, conception, idea, and notion. Together, these mean instinctive interest. When that *(pratyayaḥ)* flows in a continuous threadlike motion at the place of focus, then it is the *dhyāna*, seventh stage of yoga practice.

The *rāj* yogi I.K. Taimni gave stretching or streaming unbrokenly as one, as the meaning for *ekatānatā*. A student yogi would do well by carefully studying the Sanskrit of this verse, because it is not sufficient to say that *dhāraṇā* is concentration or that *dhyāna* is contemplation or meditation. Such definitions are vague.

Application:

In the seventh stage of yoga, the next stage, that of dhyāna, *the yogi experiences that there is a continuous threadlike flow of his instinctive interest to the selected location in the mind or emotions. This is the effortless linkage of the attention to a higher concentration force or person. This stage is attained after many hours of practice, when the mento-emotional energy exhausts its potential for entertaining the core-*

self with images, mental sounds and outbursts of subtle potent impressions.

Most neophytes rarely reach this stage, because the mento-emotional energy maintains the onslaughter of presenting impressions which guide the self back into the world of social responsibilities.

Verse 3

तदेवार्थमात्रनिर्भासं स्वरूपशून्यमिव समाधिः ॥ ३ ॥

tadeva arthamātranirbhāsaṁ
svarūpaśūnyam iva samādhiḥ

tadeva = tat – that + eva – only, alone; artha – purpose objective; mātra – only, merely; nirbhāsaṁ – illuminating; svarūpa – own form; śūnyam – empty, void, lacking; iva – as if; samādhiḥ – continuous effortless linking of the attention to a higher concentration force or person.

That same effortless linkage of the attention when experienced as illumination of the higher concentration force or person, while the yogi feels as if devoid of himself, is* samādhi *or continuous effortless linkage of his attention to the special person, object, or force.

Analysis:

The word *śūnyam* or void occurs in reference to the *svarūpa* or form of the yogi, and only in the sense that while he is in contact with the transcendental force, object or person of his interest, he is so connected that his own form seems as if absent and his awareness is so indentified with the transcendence that he is aware of nothing else..

The Sanskrit article *iva* means 'as if.' When there is continued effortless linkage of the attention to a higher concentration force, object or person, the yogi's attention is completely or almost completely saturated by that higher reality, so it feels as if he is not there *(śūnyam iva)* and that only the higher reality is present with illumination *(nirbhasam).* This gives him a thorough insight into transcendental objects or persons.

Application:

When, however, that sense of effortless linkage of the attention joins continually to a particular location in the mind or emotions or outside into a higher dimension, it is the highest stage of yoga, that of samādhi. *It may be a link to a greater yogi, a divinity or a bliss energy. This is experienced as illumination by the higher concentration force or person while the yogi feels as if devoid of his conditioned self.*

It is all about location. The core-self transits from the location of the subtle energy into super-subtle and beyond. It leaves behind certain sense facilities and resumes these when it transits back to the lower level. He understands from this, that transit to another existential territory implies assumption of new senses which are suitable to that habitat.

Verse 4

त्रयमेकत्र संयमः ॥४॥

trayam ekatra saṁyamaḥ

trayam – three; ekatra – in one place, all taken together as one practice; saṁyamah – complete restraint.

The three as one practice are the complete restraint.

Analysis:

In *Bhagavad Gītā*, *samyama* is mentioned in chapter four.

śrotrādīnī 'ndriyāni anye saṁyamāgniṣu juhvati
śabdādīn viṣayān anye indriyāgniṣu juhvati
sarvāṇī 'ndriya karmāṇi prāṇakarmāṇi capare
ātmasaṁyama yogāgnau juhvati jñānadīpite

Other yogis offer hearing and other sensual powers into the fiery power of restraint. Some offer sound and other sensual pursuits into the fiery sensual power.

Some ascetics subject the sensual actions and the breath function to self-restraint by fiery yoga austerities, which are illuminated by experience. (4.26, 27)

Sam means very, quite, greatly, thoroughly, very much, all, whole, complete. *Yamah* means restraint, control.

It is obvious that we must interpret the word in the context of a particular writer's use. *Śrī* Krishna's use of the term is similar to what *Śrī Patañjali*'s, but *Patañjali* is specific in saying that *samyama* is the combining of the three practices of higher yoga into one discipline. When *dhāraṇā*, *dhyāna* and *samādhi* are made into one technique, that is called *samyamah* in *Śrī Patañjali's* vocabulary.

From that perspective, there would be only 6 stages to yoga, namely *yama, niyama, āsana, prāṇāyāma, pratyāhār*, and *samyamah* as a combined stage. This actually happens when one masters *dhyāna* yoga. Sometimes in *dhyāna*, one slips back to the *dhāraṇā* stage and sometimes it progresses automatically to *samādhi*. Thus *Śrī Patañjali* is correct in bridging the three higher stages. When there is success in this, the mento-emotional energy is completely restrained from its involvement in this world and in the lower subtle world.

Application:

The three higher stages of yoga, when practiced in sequence, are considered as the complete restraint; then the sixth stage directly progresses into the seventh and seventh into the eighth and final stage. As a yogi advances he spends less and less time cultivating lower stages but on occasion he does regress. He finds himself in a lower stage and is required to work his way upwards again. With patience, without resentment, he resumes that lower practice, does it for as long as necessary to resume the higher stage.

Verse 5

तज्जयात्प्रज्ञालोकः ॥५॥

tajjayāt prajñālokaḥ

taj = tad = tat – that; jayāt – from the mastery; prajñā – insight; ālokaḥ – illuminating.

From the mastery of that complete restraint of the mento-emotional energy, one develops the illuminating insight.

Analysis:

This illuminating insight is not a phenomenon in the mind or mere insight or intuition. It is rather the illuminated intellect in action, peering into parallel dimensions and spiritual atmospheres. With that illuminating insight, one sees visually into other worlds through one's intellect and also directly through a vision which is formed by one's attention.

Application:

By regular practice of the three sequential higher stages, one gains mastery over the mental and emotional urges, and then the illuminating insight becomes available for usage. This has little to do with mergence or oneness of everything. It is related to spiritual beings in a spiritual environment with spiritual objects.

Verse 6

तस्य भूमिषु विनियोगः ॥ ६ ॥

tasya bhūmiṣu viniyogaḥ

tasya – of it, of this; bhūmiṣu – in stages; viniyogaḥ – application, employment, practice.

The practice of this complete restraint occurs in stages.

Analysis:

Complete restraint after mastering the three higher states of yoga does not happen instantaneously, except for those yogis who practiced considerably in solitude. All others attain *samyama* or complete restraint of the mental and emotional energy by stages while attempting to reach the culmination of the process, which is *samādhi*. A student yogi who has a grasp on the *dhāraṇā* practice does that. Then he graduates to *dhyāna* and then to *samādhi*. Even after he reaches *samādhi*, he must sometimes begin at *dhāraṇā* and waits in the psyche for a progression to *dhyāna* and then on to *samādhi*. Sometimes for one reason or other, he struggles with the *dhāraṇā* stages and goes no further. Sometimes he progresses on the *dhyāna* and goes no further. At other times, he may attain *samādhi*. This is why *Patañjali* has alerted the student yogis that its practice occurs in stages.

Application:

This development occurs in stages. In fact for some yogis, they spend hours meditating and barely reach this stage. Some feel that they will be in this state at the time of death and thereafter, but they are mistaken.

The only thing that disappears at death is the physical body and the responsibilities which were assigned to it. Every psychological aspect, goes with the person at the time of death and no radical change becomes manifest merely by the absence of the physical form.

All psychic aspects increase at death both what is desirable and undesirable. Thus a yogi has to attain samādhi *before leaving the body, not after its death.*

Verse 7

त्रयमन्तरङ्गं पूर्वेभ्यः ॥ ७ ॥

trayam antaraṅgaṁ pūrvebhyaḥ

trayam – three; antaraṅgaṁ = antar – internal, psychological, concerning the thinking and feeling organs + aṅgaṁ – part; pūrvebhyaḥ – in reference to the preliminary stages mentioned before.

In reference to the preliminary stages of yoga, these three higher states concern the psychological organs.

Analysis:

Dhāraṇā, *dhyāna* and *samādhi* concern the psychological organs. These concern mystic practice as assisted by the physical and social practices which involve *yama, niyama, āsana, prāṇāyāma* and *pratyāhāra*. In the five preliminary stages there are mainly physical actions, but in the three higher stages, it is mostly mystic actions to control, observe and operate psychological organs in the subtle body.

Application:

This higher yoga concerns voluntary control over the psychological organs in the mind and the creative urges in the emotions. If one thinks that the objective is to reach a void, one will condemn the self to the spiritual blindness and may never perceive the supernatural and spiritual (antar) *organs* (aṅgam).

Verse 8

तद्पि बहिरङ्गं निर्बीजस्य॥८॥

tadapi bahiraṅgaṁ nirbījasya

tadapi = that = api – even; bahiraṅga = bahir – external + aṅgaṁ – part; nirbījasya – not motivated by the mento-emotional energy.

But even that initial mastership of the three higher stages of yoga, is external in reference to meditation, which is not motivated by the mento-emotional energy.

Analysis:

Initially, a student works for yoga success on the basis of disgust with the subtle and gross material energies. It is due to the impressions lodged in his mental and emotional energies. Thus in a sense he cannot strive without that basis. As *Patañjali* told us, the purpose of that energy is to give experience in the world and also conversely motivate us to strive for liberation.

prakāśa kriyā sthiti śīlaṁ bhūtendriyātmakaṁ
bhogāpavargārthaṁ dṛśyam

What is perceived is of the nature of the mundane elements and the sense organs and is formed in clear perception, action or stability. Its purpose is to give experience or to allow liberation. (Yoga Sūtra 2:18)

While initially the student yogi practices *samyama* or complete restraint from lower motivations, later on, he progresses on the basis of forces, objects and persons he encounters in the spiritual atmosphere. These latter motivations are free from flaws. These are termed seedless or lacking urges from this side of existence.

Application:

But even that initial mastership of the three higher stages of yoga is external in reference to meditation which is not motivated by the mental and emotional energy. Therefore one should strive to reach the advanced stages. However this does not imply nor suggest that the lower stages should be neglected. If one does not get a good foundation in the elementary stages, one will not integrate into the advanced levels.

Verse 9

व्युत्थाननिरोधसंस्कारयोरभिभवप्रादुर्भावौ निरोधक्षणचित्तान्वयो निरोधपरिणामः ॥९॥

vyutthāna nirodha saṁskārayoḥ
abhibhava prādurbhāvau nirodhakṣaṇa
cittānvayaḥ nirodhapariṇāmaḥ

vyutthāna – expression; nirodha – suppression; saṁskārayoḥ – of the mento-emotional impressions; abhibhava – disappearance; prādurbhāvau – and manifestation; nirodha – restraint, cessation; kṣaṇa – momentarily; citta – mento-emotional energy; ānvayaḥ – connection; nirodha – restraint; pariṇāmaḥ – transforming effects.

When the connection with the mento-emotional energy momentarily ceases during the manifestation and disappearance phases when there is expression or suppression of the impressions, that is the restraint of the transforming mento-emotional energy.

Analysis:

Many yogis who become masters of *kriyā* yoga do not take detailed notes of the preliminary and advanced practices. Because those yogis are to be liberated, they do not see the need to keep a record for review. Fortunately, *Patañjali* saw the need. This is a detailed study of his practices.

A student yogi should note what is emotional and what is mental. He should note that the two energies are interchangeable under certain psychological circumstances. Even when the mental energy holds to its own integrity, showing a distinction between itself and the emotions, the two energies still communicate with each other. Beyond that, a student should note how impressions arise and subside. Anyone who has done concentration, contemplation or meditation knows very well that the impressions come and go of their own accord. In this case, *Patañjali* spoke of the interval *(kṣaṇa)* between the expression of an idea in the mind and the suppression of that very same notion. At first this sounds simple, but let us take a closer look.

When an idea arises in the mind, depending on its value to the emotions, it may be expanded or it may be dissipated immediately. If it is expanded, what really takes place? If expanded, the idea ceases for a split second. The memory in conjunction with the imagination creates another idea which is associative to the one which disappeared. *Patañjali* wants us to focus on that split second cessation *(nirodhakṣaṇa)*. He wants us to extend that split second to a much longer period. If we could keep the mind in that state, we would enter into *samādhi*.

Of course such a feat is easier said than done. Sometimes effortlessly, the mind remains for five or ten seconds in that blank state. Expert yogis hold the mind in that state for minutes and some for hours at a time. This is their accomplishment of *samādhi*. One will find that if one can hold the mind there, the imagination faculty will change into an actual illuminating sight, an eye capable of spiritual vision. With the help of Lord Krishna, Arjuna had some experiences of this at *Kurukṣetra*. When again Arjuna wanted that insight, *Śrī* Krishna, with mild disappointment, declined. He said, in the *Anu-Gītā*, that He could not again impart it to Arjuna because it involved a mystic skill which Krishna expressed at *Kurukṣetra* for a specific purpose.

By careful study of this verse, one understands what is required for yoga success, which is the prolonging of the momentary blankness which occurs in the mind between the expression within it of one idea and another. The whole problem with meditation has to do with this.

For success, a yogi must be prepared to spend years if necessary noticing that momentary blankness and practicing to hold the mind there. Initially, it will seem impossible to stop the mind there, but by regular and sustained practice, the period for holding that state is extended.

Application:

It may be asked: What is the description of the mind and emotions when the creative urges cease? The answer is: The mind energy and emotional feelings periodically assume, of their own accord, a stillness wherein there is no activity. This happens just after an idea or image subsides and just before another one begins. The interim period may be long or momentary. When this happens impulsively, a yogi has no control over it, but he should still observe it and focus sharply on the blank interval. He should carefully note the location where the idea or image subsides. He should attach his attention to that place in the mind or emotion environment. When practicing however, he should, with attention, suppress any emerging idea or image and hold his mind or emotion in that blank state so that no other idea or image expresses itself.

Obviously it takes consistent practice. The momentary lull between the end of one mental impression and the initiation of another one, is a very special place and vibration, which the yogi should observe and then transit into. He should achieve existential residence in that space for long periods of time.

Verse 10

तस्य प्रशान्तवाहिता संस्कारात्॥ १०॥

tasya praśāntavāhita saṁskārāt

tasya – of this; praśānta – spiritual peace; vāhita – flow; saṁskārāt – from the impressions derived.

Concerning this practice of restraint, the impressions derived cause a flow of spiritual peace.

Analysis:

When the yogi repeatedly practices to keep the mind in a condition of restraining, causing the transformations of the mento-emotional energy to cease, then his memory is accredited with quieting impressions which remind him again and again about the uninterrupted flow of spiritual peace.

Application:

When a yogi first gets a foothold on this mastership, he notices a decrease of the various impulsive objectives of the mind and emotions and an increase in the blank duration which occurs between the emergence and the dissolution of ideas. This brings on a peace the yogi greatly appreciates. His attraction to this peace acts as a magnet to attract him again and again to samādhi *practice. If he had no contact with anything divine beyond this peace, he may proclaim this to be the ultimate objective and his spiritual quest may end here.*

The harassment which he suffered from material existence and the responsibilities which he was tagged with, decrease drastically after he makes firm contact with this bliss consciousness.

Verse 11

सर्वार्थतैकाग्रतयोः क्षयोद्यौ चित्तस्य समाधिपरिणामः ॥ ११ ॥

sarvārthatā ekāgratayoḥ kṣaya udayau cittasya samādhipariṇāmaḥ

sarvārthatā – varying objective; ekāgratayoḥ – of the one aspect before the attention; kṣaya – decrease; udayau – and increase; cittasya – of the mento-emotional energy; samādhi – the continuous effortless linkage of the attention to the higher concentration force, object or person; pariṇāmaḥ – transforming effects, change.

The decrease of varying objectives in the mento-emotional energy and the increase of the one aspect within it are the changes noticed in the practice of continuous effortless linking of the attention to higher concentration forces, objects or persons.

Analysis:

We are reminded that the *samādhi* stage will come after long practice. It will come gradually over time of practicing *samyama*, as *Patañjali* defined, being the practice of *dhāraṇā* which progresses into *dhyāna*, which then changes into *samādhi*.

As one tries to practice *samādhi*, one will find that there is a decrease in the mind's many objectives and an increase of its tendency for one focus as dictated by the practice. This one focus is not a focus on a deity but rather it is the focus mentioned in verse 9 of this chapter, which is the restraint of the transformation of the mento-emotional energy.

It has nothing to do with any object or any person, divine or ordinary. It is a battle within the psychology of the yogi, for control of the psyche.

When the yogin notices that his mind's habits change so that it desires more of that peace, then he knows he made progress. This is not a void in this world or in the subtle domain but rather a void in his own psyche, whereby his memory does not discharge ideas which burst in the mind environment into impressions which trigger other impressions and thoughts and which torment the yogi and frustrate his efforts for psyche control.

Application:

When one learns how to use the attention to suppress any emerging idea or image, and to hold the mind and emotions in that blank state, that mastership causes a flow of spiritual peace. Impressions from that restraining activity do enter the memory. Those records aid and support the yogi, giving him more and more power over the impulsive creative urges. The memories which previously haunted and taunted the yogi, now act in his favor and supports the spiritual quest. The antagonistic energy in the mento-emotional energy dissipates, leaving the yogi without a psychological opponent.

Verse 12

ततः पुनः शान्तोदितौ तुल्यप्रत्ययौ चित्तस्यैकाग्रतापरिणामः ॥ १२ ॥

tataḥ punaḥśānta uditau tulya pratyayau
cittasya ekāgratāpariṇāmaḥ

tataḥ – then; punaḥ – again; santoditau = śānta – tranquilized, settled, subsided + uditau – and agitated, emerging; tulya – similar; pratyayaḥu – conviction or belief as mental content, instinctive interest; cittasya – of the mento-emotional energy; ekāgratā – of what is in front of one aspect before the attention; pariṇāmaḥ – transforming effects, change.

Then again, when the mind's content is the same as it was when it is subsiding and when it is emerging, that is the transformation callcd "having one aspect in front of or before the attention".

Analysis:

This condition of mind is related to everything which was described in this chapter so far. As the yogin gets to the stage where his mind content is no longer dominated by memories, he is able to keep his attention in a quiescent state, (*praśānta vāhita* verse 10). However, this is maintained only by keeping the expressive and depressive energies of the mind out of contact with the memory.

At any time, when the attention is allowed to contact the memory, either by accident or as induced or deliberately, the mind content will be altered to accommodate various images and sounds (*sarvārthatā*, verse 11). That is counter-productive, causing regret for the yogi, since it puts him at odds with his objective, which is to cease such mental operations completely.

The subsiding and emerging nature of the mind cannot be changed but a yogi can get relief by his assumption of a focus into other dimensions and by freezing the mind through *prāṇāyāma* practice. Nonetheless, as soon as possible, the mind will resume its previous state. This is, in a sense, disgusting. It causes the yogin to feel that somehow he has to abandon the mind.

It is not easy to have a single aspect in front of the attention. By nature the mind seeks to change its position by an in-and-out, rising-and-falling, creating-and-disintegrating function. This is the natural condition of a mind. This is why it is necessary to do *prāṇāyāma*. By infusing the breath and by surcharging the mind with a high charge of subtle energy *(prāṇa),* it slows down or abandons lower diversions altogether. But then again as soon as the higher pressure charge dissipates, the mind returns to its normal gyrations, except in the case of those yogins who developed a yoga siddha body. Skeptics therefore argue that yoga is a waste of time. They feel no one can overcome the gyrating nature of the mind.

For the mind content to be the same when the mento-emotional energy is moving to create images or to disintegrate the same and for the mind to remain consistently blank like this for some time, the yogin has to master the *dhāraṇā*, sixth stage of yoga practice, whereby he can link the mind to a transcendental force and at the same time hold on to or look through his attention energy.

The technique used for this is the one where the yogi keeps his attention locked to the subtle sound which comes in from the *cit ākāśa*. Usually that is heard in the vicinity of the right ear. As a yogi hears this, he also focuses on diffused light in front of him *(ekagrata).* There is no visual object before his attention at this time. He merely listens to the naad sound in vicinity of the right ear, while looking forward through his attention which makes slight contact with the mento-emotional energy *(citta).* When his looking action relaxes of its own accord, he may see a diffused light before him.

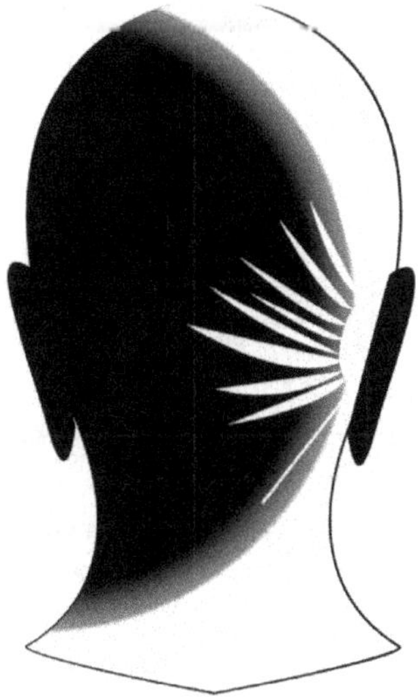

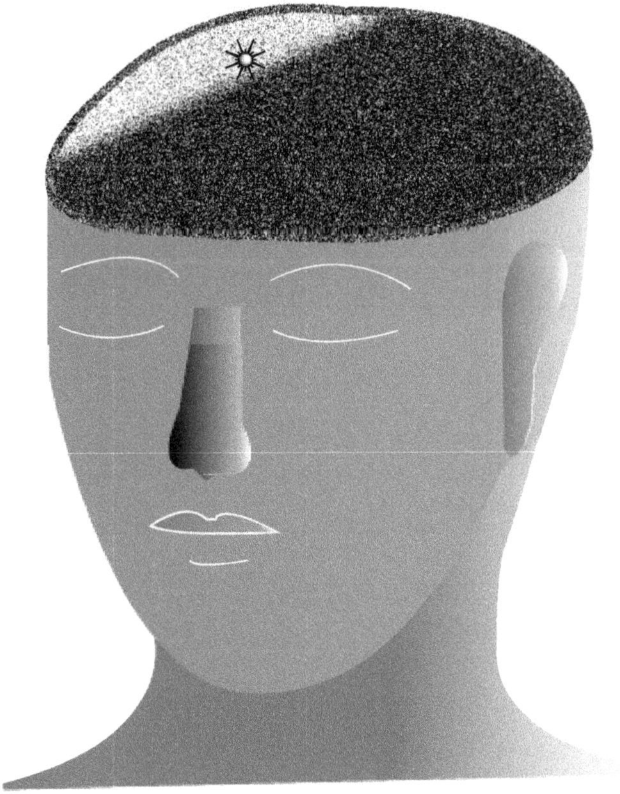

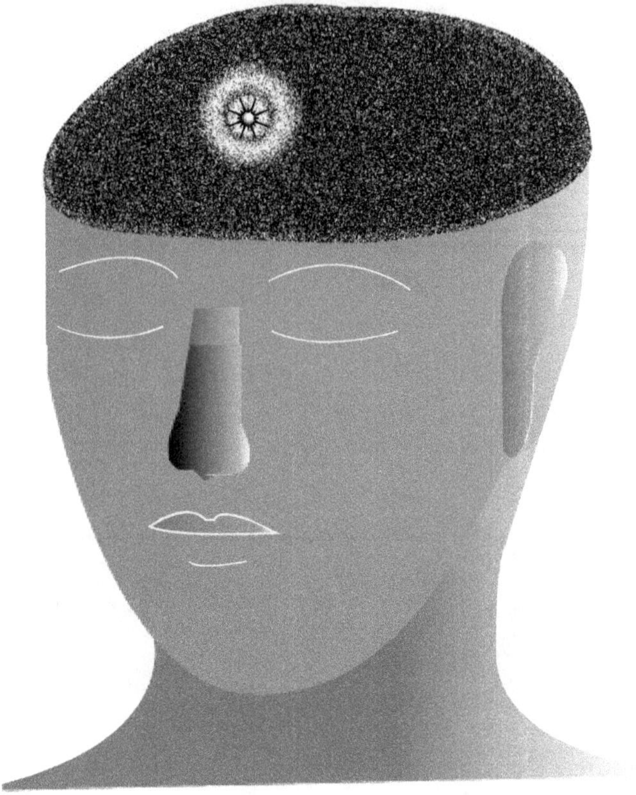

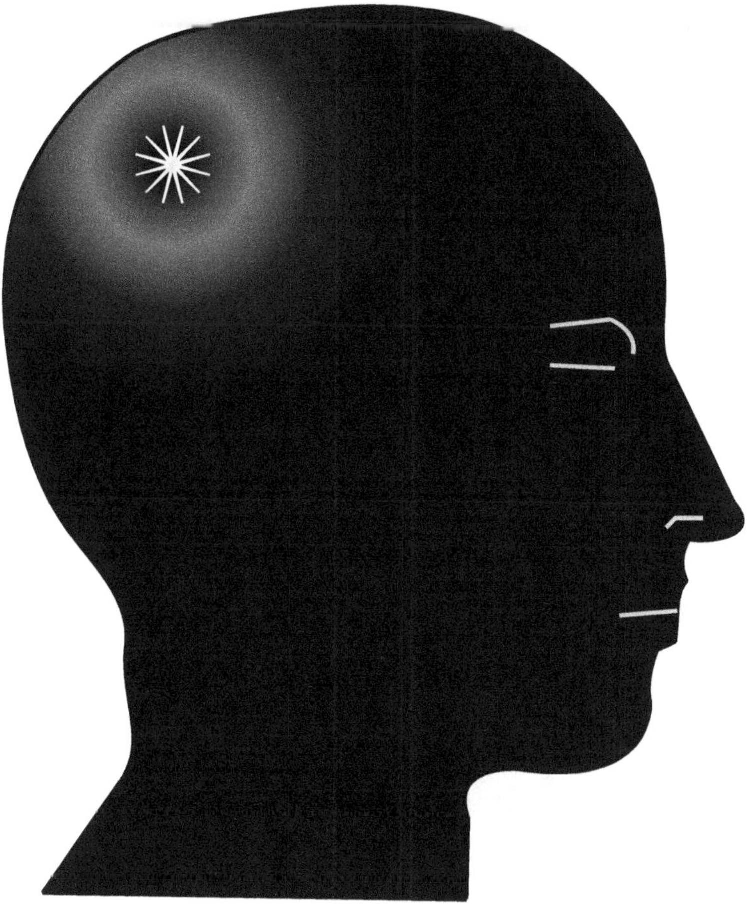

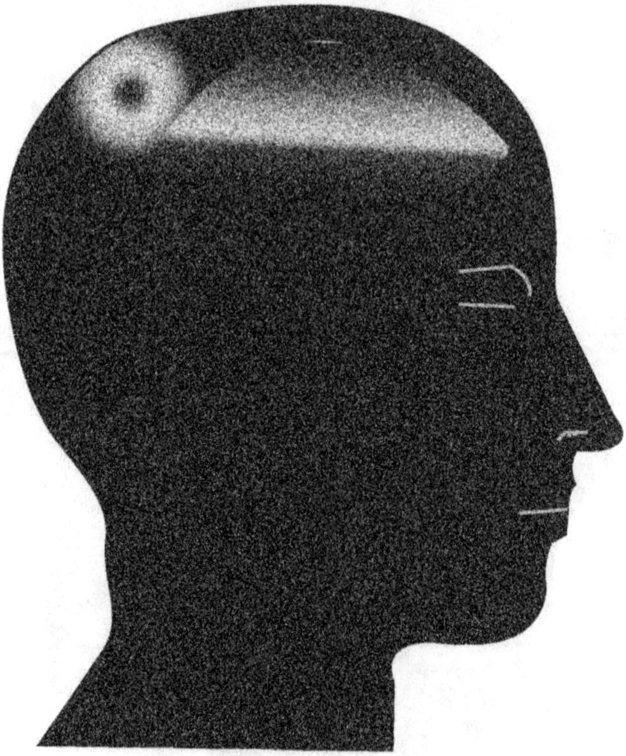

Patañjali already mentioned that diffusion as subtle light. That was in Verse 52 of the last chapter.

tataḥ kṣīyate prakāśa āvaraṇam

From that is dissipated, the mental darkness which veils the light. (Yoga Sūtra 2.52)

The diffused light which is actually light mixed with cloudy energy or misty force, will be separated such that the misty force or cloudy energy will disappear, leaving only light. When a yogi attains this practice, it is understood that he mastered the seventh stage of yoga called *dhyāna*.

Some people think that this practice includes imagining a deity, a supernatural or spiritual being, or imagining a subtle primal force, but that is incorrect. The yogi only needs to get his supernatural and spiritual visions to be operative. Then he sees everything in the *cit ākāśa*, the sky of consciousness. He does not need to imagine super-subtle or divine objects.

Application:

The blankness of the mind and emotions is the desired objective for that initial samādhi *practice, even though perception will develop later in it. A yogi has to hold out in that blankness if he is to obtain transcendental sensual perception.*

The gyrating behavior of the mind ceases when the yogi can grasp and remain in the interval between the subsiding of an idea and the ever-enlarging creation of a new impression.

Verse 13

एतेन भूतेन्द्रियेषु धर्मलक्षणावस्थापरिणामा व्याख्याताः ॥ १३ ॥

etena bhūtendriyeṣu dharma lakṣaṇa avasthā pariṇāmāḥ vyākhyātāḥ

etena – by this; bhūta – the various states of matter; indriyeṣu – by the sensual energy; dharma – quality; lakṣaṇa – shape, characteristic; avasthā – condition; pariṇāmāḥ – changes, transformation; vyākhyātāḥ – is described.

By this description of the changes, quality and shape, the two changing conditions of the states of matter, as well as of the sensual energy, were described.

Analysis:

The whole subtle and gross material energy is effectively dealt with in this yoga practice, in the efforts of the yogi to subdue his psyche. The whole controlling effort entails the development of a complete disinterest in the gross and subtle material energy, called *bhūtendriya* in this verse. Our response to the mundane energy is our downfall. When we learn how to control that response and how to eventually cease responding altogether, we gain the control which we so desperately seek.

Application:

By this practice one gets personal experience of the quality, shape, changing conditions of the various states of matter and the sensual energy. Thus the mental and emotional provinces are clarified and are no longer a confusing or vague environment. One is no longer confused about it.

Verse14

शान्तोदिताव्यपदेश्यधर्मानुपाती धर्मी ॥ १४ ॥

śānta udita avyapadeśya dharma anupātī dharmī

śānta – collapsed; udita - emergent; avyapadeśya – what is not to be defined, what is latent; dharma – law, sustaining force; anupātī – reach full retrogression; dharmī – most basic condition.

When the collapsed, emergent and latent forces reach full retrograde, that is the most basic condition.

Analysis:

Most commentators attribute *dharma* as the *prakṛti* energy, or the most subtle form of material nature. This is correct. However, when *dharma* is specifically mentioned with yoga, it refers to the most basic condition. A yogi strives to achieve complete detachment and independence from this energy. Once he gets down to its most basic condition, or to the ultimate substratum of material nature, he can examine it with supernatural vision and make decisions for not responding to it anymore. Once he sees the course of its progression into manifestation and retrogression out of manifestation, he will neither be afraid of it nor attracted to it. Essentially it served its purpose for him and he subsequently becomes liberated quickly and definitely.

Obviously we harbor some desire to be in touch with material energy. Thus it is necessary that we understand the attraction to it and eliminate our fondness for it or remove whatever influenced us to embrace it.

Application:

When the emerging, manifesting, collapsing or not-yet-manifested ideas, images or emotions push back into the mental or emotional energy, and when that energy has a blankness or quiescence, that is the most basic condition for samādhi *practice.*

Verse 15

क्रमान्यत्वं परिणामान्यत्वे हेतुः ॥ १५ ॥

krama anyatvaṁ pariṇāma anyatve hetuḥ

krama – sequence; anyatvaṁ – otherness, difference; pariṇāma – transformation change; anyatve – in difference; hetuḥ – cause.

The cause of a difference in the transformation is the difference in the sequential changes.

Analysis:

A student yogi may become preoccupied with the variety of changing scenes that occur when the mento-emotional energy *(citta)* goes through its operations. This preoccupation can be overcome by help from a senior yogin, such that he will no longer follow the sequential changes but will instead observe the operations of the energy. The content of the operations is not important. If he focuses on operations and not content, he will acquire supreme detachment and get leverage over the transformations which occur in the mind and emotions, and which keep him from achieving the supernatural and spiritual insights.

Some student yogins, like infants, become spell-bound by the imagination faculty and its bewildering images and discuss how to curb it with their teachers. They make little progress in higher yoga. This fascination with the differences in the various transformations is caused only by differences in the sequential changes and not from anything substantial or meaningful. It is not the content of the mind *(pratyayaḥ),* or the conviction or moody appetite of the mind that is relevant but rather the way the mind operates.

A person entering a film theater usually becomes enthralled with the images on the screen. This is an amateur's reaction. He should be interested in the projector which causes the movie to be shown and the mind of the director who created the images. This is more important than the content of the various movies. When a student yogi gets this understanding, he becomes freed. So long as one is attracted primarily to the mind content, one will not adhere to the instructions for higher yoga, but will instead, complain about the disciplines just as how a child cries if his parent takes him out of a movie theater before a film is finished.

The parent wants to show the child the projection apparatus and the operator of the mechanism, but the child finds the projection room to be boring and less stimulating than the film. He feels that it is not interactive with him. Likewise the student yogi usually fights tooth and nail with advanced teachers who come down from *siddhaloka* to free them.

The difference in the sequential change of ideas and images in the mind occur because of how the memory and imagination interact with the information which comes in a compressed form from the senses from the subtle and gross world. This admixture is bewildering. Advanced yogis advise us to forgo them altogether. Their policy is that instead of looking at those impressions, we should just avoid them all together. This avoidance disempowers the attractions and frees us from their hypnotic glare.

The analogy of the boy in the movie house would help in this case. The more he stays out of the movie house, the more detached and disinterested he may become. The more he goes to it, the more his nature reacts in response to it and the more attached and interested he becomes. His interest is abused, and needlessly exploited by fiction. This is why in India, there was a period of history where many leading yogis condemned human consumption of name and forms. If we become repeatedly enthralled with names of things and with the forms of things, it will cause us to become increasingly fascinated with this world and that will push us away from liberation.

According to the sequence of the various film slides, the movie shows in particular ways which may invoke our interest, either to cause happiness, distress or indifference, and according to how the memory, imagination, reasoning and sensual intake interact, we become fascinated with the differences in the transformation within our minds and emotions. Thus the important thing is to understand how the mind operates regardless of its content.

Unfortunately, this is easier said than done. When one becomes determined to follow this advice, he discovers that somehow he is enthralled by the content of the mind. That itself entraps him. At least that is how a student yogin will feel. At this point, he should study the operation of the entrapment mechanism.

The boy in our analogy must study how the movie building was constructed with a small door for entry on a back street and a large attractive door for entry on a main street. The very construction of the place is bewildering and causes one to go into the theater through the front door, which leads into the gallery where the movie is showing. Once the boy understands this he can avoid that door and find his way to the small door on the back street which leads to the projection room where he will be able to study something that is of vital importance to him, which is the way the projection apparatus operates.

Sometimes a student yogi repeatedly finds himself in front of a series of images projected by the imagination faculty or released from the memory or from the sensual organs which collect information. Before he can realize it, or be objective to it, he finds himself looking at, analyzing, and interacting with these images. This procedure, though impulsive must be stopped by the student yogin.

Application:

But when there is expression of ideas, images or emotional feelings, these are usually different because of the sequential changes in the emotional energy. One has to go through a transformation as one transits to other dimensions, but that change is not the same as the evolutionary adaptations one is pushed through in material existence. A yogi notices the difference.

Verse 16

परिणामत्रयसंयमादतीतानागतज्ञानम्॥ १६ ॥

pariṇāmatraya saṁyamāt atīta anāgatajñānam

pariṇāma – transformation change; traya – threefold; saṁyamāt – from the complete restraint of the mento-emotional energy; atīta – past; anāgata – future; jñānam – information.

From the complete restraint of the mento-emotional energy in terms of the three-fold transformations within it, the yogi gets information about the past and future.

Analysis:

These verses regarding the perfectional skills or *siddhis* gained by certain practices, caused *Patañjali* to be criticized by those religious leaders who feel that the *siddhi* perfectional powers are a distraction either from liberation or from attaining love of God. However, the accusation is ungrounded because *Patañjali* very realistically informs about the course of development, alerting us to what lies ahead. The perfectional skills cannot be avoided by anyone who advances in spiritual disciplines. We need training in how not to be charmed by these powers of the lower and higher subtle bodies.

Everything about the past, in microscopic and atomic impressions, is in our individual memories and in the cosmic memory pool. Any of this information can be retrieved by the Supreme Being.

śrī-bhagavān uvāca
bahūni me vyatītānijanmāni tava cārjuna
tāny aham veda sarvānina tvam vettha parantapa

The Blessed Lord said: Many of My births transpired, and yours, Arjuna. I recall them all. You do not remember, O scorcher of the enemies. *(Bhagavad Gītā 4.5)*

Everything about the future is potentially present in the existence right now. The parameters which will cause the formation of the future are present. The Supreme Being can look at it and accurately gage the probabilities.

One should not interpret this verse to mean that a yogi can know everything. If he applies himself sufficiently, he can enter into the cosmic memory and decipher some impressions. First of all, he must be allowed to do that. This allowance is not always granted to a yogi by the Supreme Being. However a yogi does not need permission of the Supreme Being to enter his own limited memory bank. His ability to do that relies on expertise in the complete restraint of the mento-emotional energy.

A great yogin, *Śrīla* Yogeshwarananda deciphered the cosmic parameters which control what will happen in the future of this universe. Therefore it is possible but only a rare yogin can do this. The complete conquest of the mento-emotional energy is a feat reserved for a few great yogis like him. The important achievement is to get the memory under control. When this is done one can study the relationship between one's limited memory and the cosmic reservoir of past impressions.

Some people feel that if a yogi reaches a stage of knowledge about the past and future, he would be omniscient, but that is an exaggeration. Such information will not affect the course of history or change the probability, or affect how the Supreme Being relates to the limited personalities. Its value is in the potency to convince the yogi to make an exit from these gross and subtle mundane histories. Still, that is not all, because a yogin has to acquire permission to do that. That permission must be gained from the Supreme Being, who might not grant it to a particular yogin.

Application:

When the yogi repeatedly pushes back the images or emotions into the mental and emotional energy, he gains access to the deeper layers of the memory, even to those from previous lives in previous material worlds. He gains perception of those future possibilities which would be based on past impressions, but he sees a way out of the bottleneck of destiny.

Verse 17

शब्दार्थप्रत्ययानामितरेतराध्यासात्सङ्करस्तत्प्रविभागसंयमात्सर्वभूतरुतज्ञानम्॥ १७॥

śabda artha pratyayānām itaretarādhyāsāt
saṅkaraḥ tatpravibhāga saṁyamāt
sarvabhūta rutajñānam

śabda – sound; artha – meaning; pratyayānām – pertaining to the mind content, convictions, idea; itaretara = itara + itara = one for the other; adhyāsāt – resulting from the super-imposition; saṅkaraḥ – intermixture; tat – their; pravibhāga – differentiation, sorting, classification, mental clarity; saṁyamāt – from the complete restraint of the mento-emotional energy; sarva – all; bhūta – creature; ruta – sound, cry, yell, language; jñānam – information, knowledge.

From the complete restraint of the mento-emotional energy in relation to mental clarity, regarding the intermixture resulting from the superimposing one for the other, of sound, its meaning

and the related mentality, knowledge about the language of all creatures is gained.

Analysis:

When a student yogin simplifies his mentality by sorting its various parts, and when he detaches his imagination faculty from its involuntary connection to the memory, as well as when he consistently retracts the sensual energies from the gross and lower subtle worlds, he gains a certain mental clarity, by which his intellect instantaneously sorts the sound, its inherent meaning and the related idea which was made by any other creature.

Application:

The yogi removes himself from biases which relate to sound, and when he can steady his attention on that alone, getting beyond words, sounds and their formation, he makes contact with the object being described by any creature. Thus different languages do not confuse his perception.

On the physical level, language, letter representation of language and pictorials of objects are required for communications. There is a higher plane where even photo art has no place because communication is direct always.

Verse 18

संस्कारसाक्षात्करणात्पूर्वजातिज्ञानम्॥ १८॥

saṁskāra sākṣātkaraṇāt pūrvajātijñānam

saṁskāra – the subtle impressions stored in memory; sākṣātkaraṇāt – from causing to be visibly present, direct intuitive perception; pūrva – before, previous; jāti – status, life; jñānam – knowledge.

From direct intuitive perception of the subtle impressions stored in the memory, the yogi gains knowledge of previous lives.

Analysis:

A yogi may know his past life or that of others. He can intuit into the memory impressions and retrieve the compressed information, which is then translated by his purified intellect.

Application:

The yogi gains knowledge of his previous lives by developing direct intuitive perception of the subtle impressions stored in his own or another's memory.

Verse 19

प्रत्ययस्य परचित्तज्ञानम्॥ १९॥

pratyayasya paracittajñānam

pratyayasya – of the mind content; para – of others; citta – of the mento-emotional energy; jñānam – information.

A yogi can know the contents of the mental and emotional energy in the minds of others.

Analysis:

Even though a student yogi might experience this, he must check the purity of his intellect to be sure that his intuition has interpreted accurately. He should not inform others that he has this ability. Unless he gets directions from an advanced yogi, he should not disclose to others anything about the intuitions.

Generally, a yogi should not interfere with the lives of others, for he should be aware of divine supervision of the supernatural persons like Krishna and Shiva.

Application:

Though he can know the mental or emotional content of a person, he should not seek to use that skill. Unless he is advised to do so by a senior yogi, he should not exercise that perception. He should not reveal to others that he has that capacity. A yogi who does not adhere to these restrictions will be drawn back into the social affairs on the physical level. Feeling appreciated there, he will amass a following and become distant from higher entities.

Verse 20

न च तत्सालम्बनं तस्याविषयीभूतत्वात्॥ २०॥

na ca tat sālambanaṁ tasya aviṣayī bhūtatvāt

na – not; ca – and; tat – that; sālambanaṁ – leaning on, resting on, support; tasya – of that; aviṣayī – not an object of anything, imperceptible; bhūtatvāt – the actual object.

And he does not check a factor which is the support of that content, for it is not the actual object in question.

Analysis:

This explains the accuracy of the intuitional powers of an advanced yogin.

Application:

The tendency of the memory and imagination is to check, recheck, create and recreate opinions and conclusions. An advanced yogi eliminates this because it hampers higher yoga. Thus he does not allow the mind to project one idea after another in an endless sequence which entertains or keeps one occupied with less control over the emotions.

Verse 21

कायरूपसंयमात्तद्ग्राह्यशक्तिस्तम्भे चक्षुःप्रकाशासम्प्रयोगेऽन्तर्धानम्॥ २१ ॥

kāya rūpa saṁyamāt tadgrāhyaśakti
stambhe cakṣuḥ prakāśa asaṁprayoge 'ntardhānam

kāya – body; rūpa – form; saṁyamāt – from the complete restraint of the mento-emotional energy; tad – that; grāhya – appropriating, grasping, sensual perceptiveness; śakti – power, potency, energy; stambhe – on the suspension; cakṣuḥ – vision; prakāśa – light; asaṁprayoge – on not contacting; 'ntardhānam = antardhānam – invisibility.

From the complete restraint of the mento-emotional energy in relation to the shape of the body, on the suspension of the receptive energy, there is no contact between light and vision, which results in invisibility.

Analysis:

The mento-emotional energy emanates a psychic light called an aura. If this aura is restrained or if it loses its expressiveness, the particular form cannot be seen by another. A yogi may also suspend this energy from operating. In that case, others who send out psychic feelers to find him, discover to their dismay that he is missing. Sometimes when this happens, the persons who seek to locate that yogi know that he is in the vicinity. They become annoyed and attribute the lack of contact to his mystic power and anti-social tendency.

The lack of contact *(samprayoga)* between the light and vision deals with the light coming from the yogi's form and the vision beam which emanates from the person who searches psychically or physically for him. Sometimes a yogi can sit right next to a person and that person cannot realize that the yogi is by his side. One of my gurus, a certain Rishi Singh Gherwal was hired by the British Government to find himself. Being employed as a spy to find a spy he remained in the services of the British for many years. He was a *mahāyogi* but was unknown because of humility and resistance to popularity.

Application:

When the receptive energy of the subtle body is curbed, the yogi develops a resistance to social contact. This causes him to have some invisibility. When a yogi sidesteps from social involvement, his antisocial stance is observed by others, who rate him as a useless good-for-nothing. This harassment may bother and even fatigue the yogin. Some yogis find it hard to tolerate this disapproval from other human beings and to please others, for peace' sake, they cease practice and buckle down in the rag tag social world.

Other yogis who are more repelled from human interaction and who remember the reverses of such a life, bear on with the insults and force themselves against the tide of social opinion. Eventually these fighters reach a stage where even their bitterest critics appreciate them and volunteer to shelter them from inconveniences.

Verse 22

एतेन शब्दादि अन्तर्धानम् उक्तम्

etena śabdādi antardhānam uktam

etena – by this; śabdādi = śabda – sound + ādi – and the related sensual pursuits; antardhānam – invisibility, non-perceptibility; uktam – described.

By this method, sound and the related sensual pursuits, may be restrained, which results in the related non-perceptibility.

Analysis:

A yogi may use a mystic process to cause imperceptibility in any or all aspects of sensual energy, so that he may not be detected by others. But this should only be done for the sake of yoga progression. If a yogi uses these mystic skills for other reasons, it will distract from yoga practice and cause a lapse in progression.

Sometimes people transmit thoughts to attract a yogi. They do this by thinking. These thoughts originate from their psyches just like radio waves from a transmitter. These thoughts are usually meant to engage a yogi in cultural activities which do not accelerate, but rather, decelerate practice. Thus a yogi has to protect progression by de-energizing those transmissions. The methods for this vary according to the level of practice.

Just as a yogi might sit next to someone on a bus or train and travel many miles, without the person recognizing him, even though he is the very person whom that searcher seeks, so a yogi might stay out of reach of the others even though he might be near physically. Conversely a person may know a yogi so well that even if he is located in another universe, thoughts reach him instantly.

Application:

This imperceptibility may be applied to the other sensual perceptions. A yogi, who has superior guidance, does not focus on developing each extra-sensory perception. They develop spontaneously. He may use any or all of them to accelerate progress and to sidestep impediments.

Verse 23

सोपक्रमं निरुपक्रमं च कर्म तत्संयमादपरान्तज्ञानमरिष्टेभ्यो वा॥२३॥

sopakramaṁ nirupakramaṁ ca karma
tatsaṁyamāt aparāntajñānam ariṣṭebhyaḥ vā

sopakramaṁ – set about, undertaken, already operative; nirupakramaṁ – dormant, destined; ca – and; karma – cultural activities; tat - that; saṁyamād = saṁyamāt – from the complete restraint of the mento-emotional energy; aparānta – of the other end, of death entry into the hereafter; jñānam – knowledge; ariṣṭebhyaḥ – from portents; vā – or.

Complete restraint of the mento-emotional energy in relation to current and destined cultural activities results in knowledge of entry into the hereafter. Or, the same result is gained by the complete restraint in relation to portents.

Analysis:

Both current and future cultural activities are the result of destiny, which is a combination of several forces. These destined energies work now. They worked in the past. They will work in the future. By restraining the mento-emotional energy in relation to the confusing impressions which we absorb, and the ones which are stored in memory, we may derive intuitive or direct supernatural perceptions of the subtle world to ascertain when it would be necessary for any of us to leave a material body. By this process, a yogi can leave his body and enter other dimensions of the hereafter where other civilizations transpire.

Each person who is about to leave his or her body experiences portents. Most cannot properly interpret the indications. With clarity, a yogi can accurately gage those signs and messages.

Application:

By applying his attention to current or destined cultural activities, when no other ideas, images or memories occur in the mind, the yogi gains insight into the hereafter. He may apply attention to supernatural occurrences which facilitate the perception of other dimensions.

Verse 24

मैत्र्यादिषु बलानि ॥ २४ ॥

maitryādiṣu balāni

maitrī – friendliness; ādiṣu – and by related qualities; balāni – powers.

By complete restraint of the mento-emotional energy in relation to friendliness, he develops that very same power.

Analysis:

When the yogi detaches himself from the cultural prejudices which were cultivated in this and in some past lives, he develops universal friendliness without bias from the subconscious memory or predisposition. However, being aware of these predispositions in his memory, he can know what friendly or antagonistic relationships he had with others in past lives.

Application:

By applying his attention to friendliness within his nature and in the subtle cosmic environment, he develops universal benevolence.

Verse 25

बलेषु हस्तिबलादीनि ॥ २५ ॥

baleṣu hasti balādīni

baleṣu – by strength; hasti – elephant; bala – strength; ādīni – and the same for other aspects.

By complete restraint of the mento-emotional energy in relation to strength, the yogin acquires strength of an elephant. The same applies to other aspects.

Analysis:

A yogi acquires certain mystic perfections during practice. These cannot be avoided. A yogi should stick to his objectives as recommended by advanced teachers. Then he is not distracted by supernatural power, but simply observes its development and notes the various faculties of the subtle and super-subtle bodies.

Application:

By applying his attention to strength, personally or generally, he acquires the power of an elephant. This type of application is effective in other aspects.

Verse 26

प्रवृत्त्यालोकन्यासात्सूक्ष्मव्यवहितविप्रकृष्टज्ञानम्॥ २६ ॥

pravṛitti āloka nyāsāt sūkṣma
vyavahita viprakṛṣṭajñānam

pravṛttyālokanyāsāt = pravṛtti – destined activity, the force of cultural activity + āloka – supernatural insight + nyāsāt – from placing or applying; sūkṣma – subtle; vyavahita – concealed; viprakṛṣṭa – remote; jñānam – knowledge.

From the application of supernatural insight to the force producing cultural activities, a yogi gets information about what is subtle, concealed and remote from him.

Analysis:

Sometimes it is necessary to side-step destiny and see what will happen if one takes one kind of action or if one stays in a particular dimension or world. Then a yogi might apply supernatural vision to peer into the future, so that he can make a decision to remain in one dimension or transfer into another. A yogi can only discover what he is allowed through the grace of the Supreme Being, but that allowance is very wide. He may get special insight from Lord Shiva or from some other divine being.

Application:

When after much practice, a yogi develops the supernatural insight he would, of course, apply it to the force which produces cultural activities. Thus he gets information about what is subtle, concealed and remote from him. Cultural activities are the bane of spiritual life. It is the attraction of material existence even for spirits who move about in microscopic forms like bacteria, fungus and viruses.

A yogi has to get to the bottom of this if he is to transcend this existence.

Verse 27

भुवनज्ञानं सूर्ये संयमात्॥ २७॥

bhuvanajñānaṁ sūrye saṁyamāt

bhuvana – the solar system; jñāna – knowledge; sūrye – on the sun-god or the sun planet; saṁyamāt – from the complete restraint of the mento-emotional energy.

From the complete restraint of the mento-emotional energy in relation to the sun god or the sun planet, knowledge of the solar system is gained.

Analysis:

If a yogi ponders the jurisdictional influences of the sun-god or sun planet, he may find out if he applies his spiritual sight to the spiritual, supernatural, or gross influences of the sunlight. The sun god's influence abounds physically, supernaturally, and spiritually. This is why *Śrī* Krishna described the paths used by proficient yogis at the time of death.

yatra kāle tv anāvṛttim āvṛttiṁ caiva yoginaḥ
prayātā yānti taṁ kālaṁ vakṣyāmi bharatarṣabha
agniḥ jyotiḥ ahaḥ śuklaḥ ṣaṇmāsā uttarāyaṇam
tatra prayātā gacchanti brahma brahmavido janāḥ
dhūmo rātriḥ tathā kṛṣṇaḥ ṣaṇmāsā dakṣiṇāyanam
tatra cāndramasaṁ jyotiḥ yogī prāpya nivartate
śuklakṛṣṇe gatī hyete jagataḥ śāśvate mate
ekayā yāti anāvṛttim anyayāvartate punaḥ

O bullish man of the Bharata family, I will tell you of the departure for the yogis who do or do not return.

The summer season, the bright atmosphere, the daytime, the bright moonlight, the six months when the sun appears to move north; if at that time, they depart the body, those people who know the spiritual dimension, go to the spiritual location.

The smoky, misty or hazy season, as well as in the night-time, the dark-moon time, the six months when the sun appears to move south; if the yogi departs at that time, he attains moonlight, after which he is born again.

The night and the dark times are two paths which are considered to be perpetually available for the universe. It is considered so by the authorities. By one, a person goes away not to return; by the other, he comes back again. (*Bhagavad Gītā* 8.23 – 26)

Application:

He may apply his supernatural insight to the sun god or the sun planet. Thus knowledge about the solar system is gained. He may get opportunities to transit in a body of light to the sun planet where divine beings like Jesus Christ reside, and where even fruits grow on trees which are made of light, and there are buildings made of light.

Verse 28

चन्द्रे ताराव्यूहज्ञानम्॥ २८॥

candre tārāvyūhajñānam

candre – on the moon or moon-god; tārā – stars; vyūha – system; jñānam – knowledge.

By complete restraint of the mento-emotional energy, in reference to the moon or moon-god, the yogi gets knowledge about the system of stars.

Analysis:

This refers to a yogi who has an interest in going beyond the jurisdiction of the solar god. To relieve himself of reliance on this person, a yogi must get permission for transference to another zone. A yogi needs permission both to leave this realm as well as to enter any other.

A yogi's desire for something is no guarantee that he will acquire it. It depends on if he is permitted and if he qualifies by the required austerities. Yogis, who are spiritually linked to a local deity like the sun-god or moon-god, cannot relinquish that connection conveniently, even though they may get permission for a change of services or for relocation to another zone that is controlled by the same deity.

Application:

From an application to the moon or moon-god, he gets knowledge about the system of stars. Modern astronomers deny a relationship between the moon and stars. They say that the stars are suns which are light-years away from the earth. However a yogi has to link from the moonlight to starlight if he is to astrally travel to the stars. This does not contradict the evidence of modern astronomy.

Verse 29

ध्रुवे तद्गतिज्ञानम्॥ २९ ॥

dhruve tadgatijñānam

dhruve – on the Pole Star; tat – that; gati – course of heavenly planets and stars; jñānam – knowledge.

By the complete restraint of the mento-emotional energy in relation to the Pole Star, a yogi can know of the course of planets and stars.

Analysis:

Some yogis develop interest in the planets and stars and inquire about them to satisfy curiosity. Other yogis have serious interest in it and hope to migrate from this planet to other superior places. They check on the other zones before leaving their bodies, to be sure that their conceptions of these places match the actual situations there. Such yogis use their higher astral bodies to move from sphere to sphere checking the various living conditions in the other celestial places.

Application:

By application to the Pole Star he can know of the course of the planets and stars. The attraction a yogi has for a distant locale may be insufficient to override his residence in this domain. Mere desire and even accumulation of transit power may not cause the fulfillment of a yogi's desire to transit to another solar system or galaxy.

Verse 30

नाभिचक्रे कायव्यूहज्ञानम्॥ ३० ॥

nābhicakre kāyavyūhajñānam

nābhi – navel; cakre – on the energy gyrating center; kāya – body; vyūha – arrangement, lay out; jñānam – knowledge.

By complete restraint of the mento-emotional energy in relation to the focusing on the navel energy-gyrating center, the yogi gets knowledge about the layout of his body.

Analysis:

It is necessary in the course of *kuṇḍalinī* yoga to energize the energy gyrating centers or chakras. These are located on the spinal column of the subtle body. This corresponds to the central nervous system in the gross form. The navel chakra extends to the front of the body, to the solar plexus region. In the case of student yogis, it may also point downward. In advanced celibate yogis it points upwards.

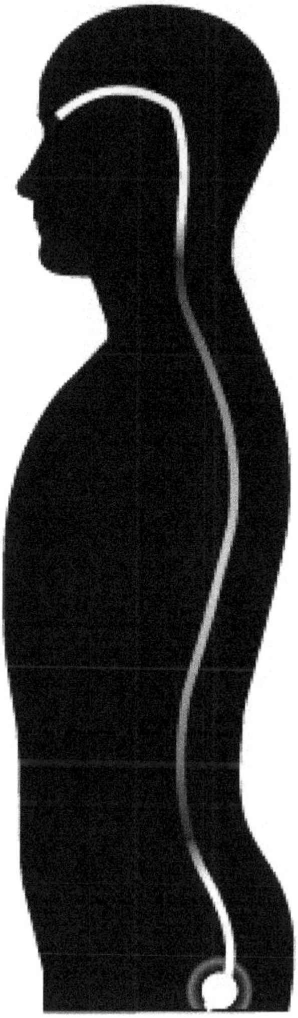

Kundalini Spinal Passage
base to brow chakra

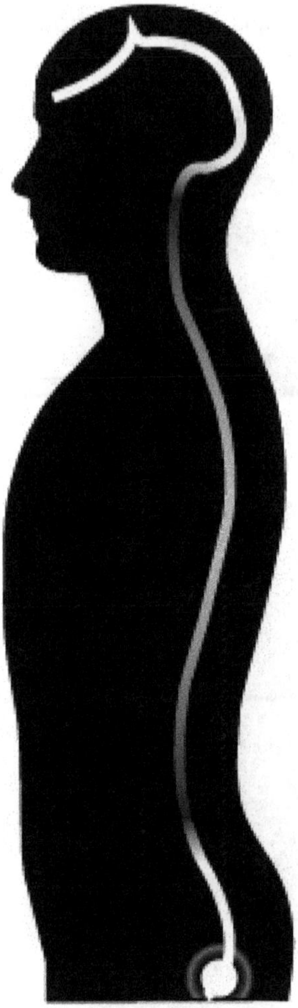

Kundalini Spinal Passage
base to back of head
to crown to brow chakra

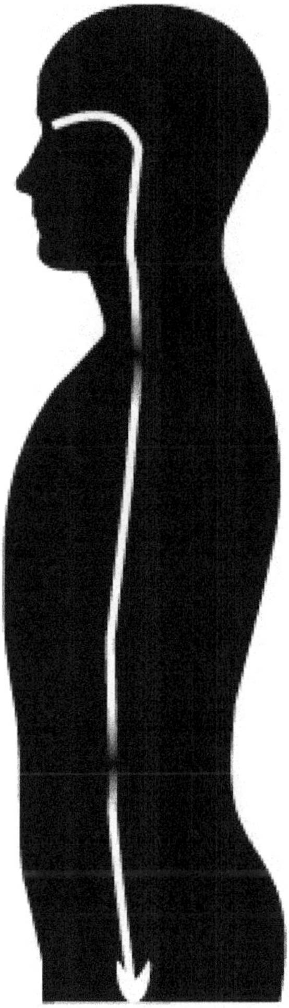

Kundalini Middle Passage
subtle sexual reservoir
to crown chakra

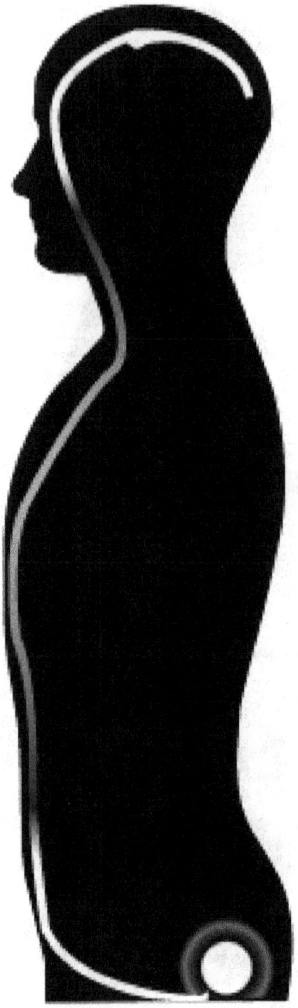

Kundalini Frontal Passage:
base to navel to brow chakra
brow chakra to crown to back of head

A yogin may enter the navel chakra of his body or that of others, from the front of the body, from the navel, where the umbilical cord was connected while that body developed in the womb of its mother. From there a yogi can see the entire layout of the body, including its lifespan, its potential for disease and its maximum capacity for helping the soul in the quest for liberation.

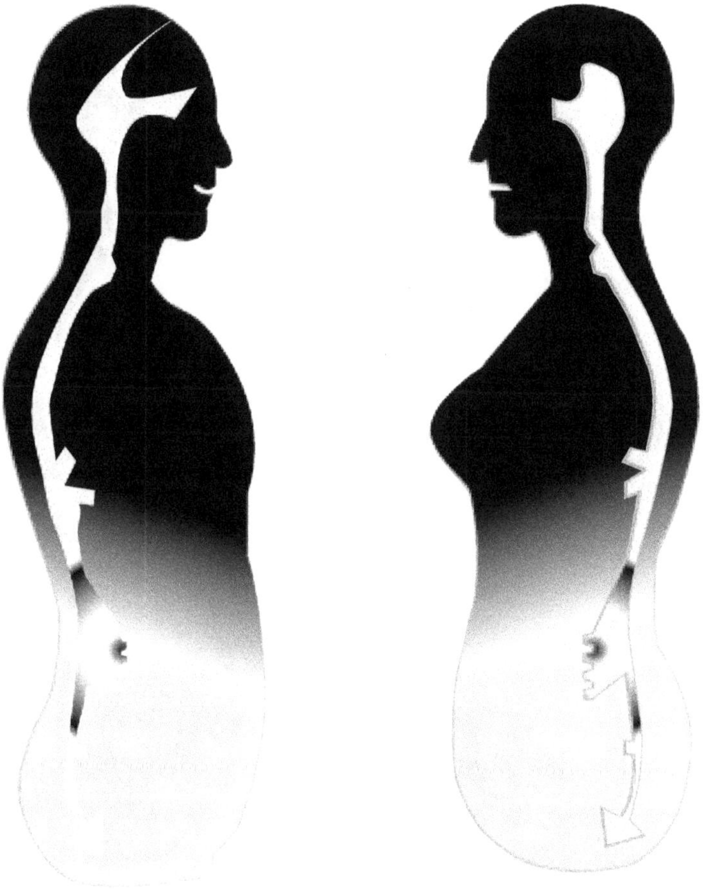

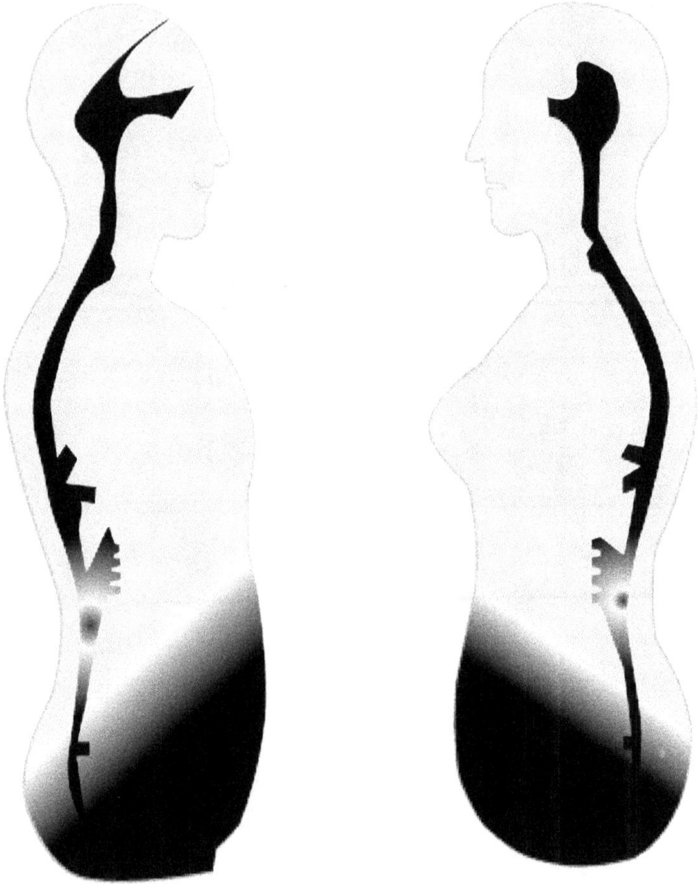

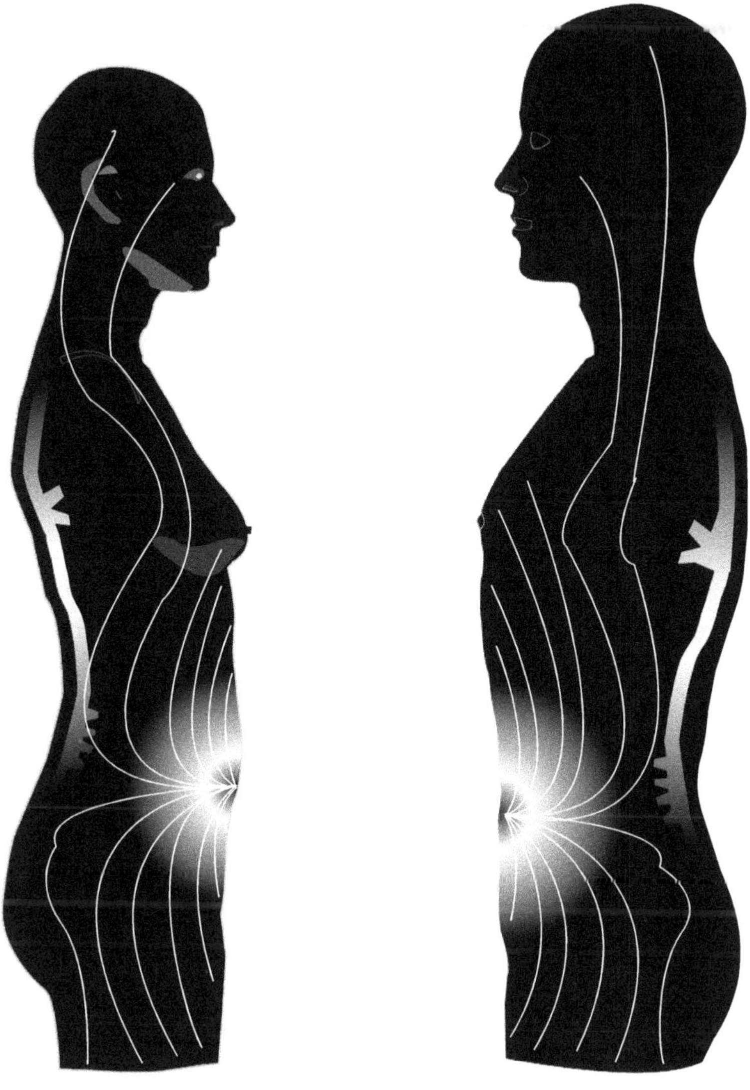

In some cases, a person cannot be liberated in the present body. When a yogi sees this he does not encourage liberation, but directs that person to earn more conducive birth opportunities. In yogic terminology the navel chakra is called *maṇipuraka*. It is the third major chakra when counting these from the bottom of the spine. By completing the course of *haṭha* yoga, a yogi curbs this chakra.

Application:

By supernaturally focusing on the navel energy-gyrating center, the yogi gets knowledge about the layout of the subtle body. This information and experience is had by the embryos, but they cannot utilize it.

Verse 31

कण्ठकूपे क्षुत्पिपासानिवृत्तिः ॥ ३१ ॥

kaṇṭhakūpe kṣutpipāsā nivṛttiḥ

kaṇṭha – throat; kūpe – on the gullet; kṣut – hunger; pipāsā – thirst; nivṛttiḥ – cessation, suppression.

By the complete restraint of the mento-emotional energy in focusing on the gullet, a yogi causes the suppression of hunger and thirst.

Analysis:

The practice of suppressing hunger and thirst is part of *haṭha* yoga. The purpose is for the life force to cease independent activities. A *haṭha* yogi endeavors to bring the life force under control, not to stop it from functioning but to cease its independent activities which are counter-productive to the aims of yoga. Thus, a yogi surcharges and subsequently purifies the energy gyrating centers (chakras) one by one, beginning at the base of the spine.

Some people feel that they can use *rāja* yoga to purify the chakras from the top downwards, from the brow or crown chakra. Actually this cannot be done, except in a person's imagination. One has to do *kuṇḍalinī* yoga by a vigorous practice like *bhastrika prāṇāyāma*. By charging the body with *prāṇa* and pushing it down into the passages which are filled with *apāna*, one causes purification from the base chakra upwards. It takes a certain amount of practice relative to the extent of impurities.

A yogi does cause his hunger and thirst to be suppressed initially when he sets out to control those urges. After sustained practice, his subtle body changes and the urges for solid and liquid food go away. Concurrently, the throat chakra undergoes change.

Of course a yogi can be degraded, because whatever low habits or vices he acquired in the past, he can again take up in the future if he is careless, or if he is transferred into a body where only those aspects are available.

Application:

By focusing on the gullet, he causes the suppression of appetite.

Verse 32

कूर्मनाड्यां स्थैर्यम्॥ ३२॥

kūrmanāḍyāṃ sthairyam

kūrma – tortoise, a particular subtle nerve; nāḍyāṁ – on the nadi or subtle nerve; sthairyam – steadiness.

By the complete restraint of the mento-emotional energy in focusing on the kurma nāḍi subtle nerve, a yogi acquires steadiness of his psyche.

Analysis:

This addresses one's readiness to enter *samādhi*, which is continuous effortless linkage of one's attention to a higher concentration force, object or person. Unless one can keep the body in a steady pose, preferably the *padmāsana* lotus posture, and also have the bodily urges like hunger quelled completely, one cannot enter *samādhi*.

The *kurmanāḍi* is located below the gullet. Given the location, if one has not stilled the gross and subtle nerves in this area, one will not be able to enter *samādhi*. When those nerves are stilled, the life force gives up its effort to protect and overly maintain the lower part of the body, below the neck. Unless the life force can be relieved from its basic survival duties, it does not allow the person to enter *samādhi*.

Application:

By focusing on the kurmanāḍi *nerve which runs from below the gullet down the inner center of the subtle body, he acquires steadiness of the psyche. This subtle channel allows the yogi to gain exemption from sexual intercourse. He is able to re-route the energy distribution so that sexual focus is eliminated.*

Verse 33

मूर्धज्योतिषि सिद्धदर्शनम्॥ ३३॥

mūrdhajyotiṣi siddhadarśanam

mūrdha – the head; jyotisi – on the shining light; siddha – the perfected being; darśanam – the view of.

By the complete restraint of the mento-emotional energy as it is focused on the shining light in the head of the subtle body, a yogi gets views of the perfected beings.

Analysis:

Mūrdhajyotiṣi is known otherwise as *jñānadīpa* or *jñānadīptih* or *jñānachakṣu*. It is a light seen in the front central area of the subtle head. This light is the energized intellect. In its normal stage in a human being, it is dark and cloudy, like a filament of a light bulb which gets insufficient current. The insufficient current warms the filament but does not cause it to glow noticeably. When the yogi masters *prāṇāyāma* and perfects himself in the disciplines of *kuṇḍalinī* and celibacy yoga, his intellect gets sufficiently charged. It glows with shining light *(jyotiṣi),* otherwise it remains dull but is felt as the centre of the mind, as the ability to understand, analyze, plan and draw conclusions.

When a yogi develops to the extent that his intellect glows in the subtle head, he perceives the perfected beings, the siddhas like *Śrī Bābāji Mahasaya*, *Śrī Gorakṣanāth*, and other *mahāyogins*. Sometimes fortunately he sees Shiva at Kailash in another dimension. Once a yogin sees the siddhas, it is understood that he is blessed. If he accelerates the practice further, he will develop a yoga siddha body. He can take advice and get rare *kriyā* yoga techniques from the supernatural beings he perceives. Such a yogin does not rely on physical contact with a yoga guru. Hence he does not need a guru who uses a physical form. He takes initiation either physically or subtly from superior entities.

Application:

By focusing on the shining light in the subtle head, he gets views of the perfected beings.

Verse 34

प्रातिभाद्वा सर्वम्॥ ३४॥

prātibhād vā sarvam

prātibhād = prātibhāt – resulting from samyama on the shining organ of divination; vā – or; sarvam – everything, all reality.

By complete restraint of the mento-emotional energy, while focusing on the shining organ of divination in the head of the subtle body, the yogin is able to know all reality.

Analysis:

This *prātibha* is the *brahmarandra* development in the head of the subtle body of a yogi. At first a yogi develops this top part of the subtle body known as the *brahmarandra*. *Śrī Patañjali* used the term, *prātibha* which literally means relating to divination or genius. A yogi who has developed his *brahmarandra* is said to be liberated even while using a gross body. Provided he gains approval from higher authorities like Shiva or Krishna such a yogi can select which of the dimensions he would live in after he sheds the material body.

Application:

By focusing on the shining organ of divination in the head of the subtle form, he gets the ability to know all reality. The brahmarandra operates by entering supernatural forms which are invisible to persons using physical bodies. A yogi experiences a vision which can perceive bodies which are made of light frequencies.

Verse 35

हृदये चित्तसंवित्॥ ३५॥

hṛdaye cittasaṁvit

hṛdaye – on the samyam on the causal body; citta – mento-emotional energy; saṁvit – thorough insight.

By the complete restraint of the mento-emotional energy as it is focused on the causal body in the vicinity of the chest, the yogi gets thorough insight into the causes of the mental and emotional energy.

Analysis:

For all these practices, one should have mastered the *samyama* procedure described before by *Śrī Patañjali* as a development from *dhāraṇā* to *dhyāna* to *samādhi*. Once this is mastered, one can apply the practices described. Stated differently one who masters *samādhi* can use *samādhi* for more progression.

A person whose mind is jumpy, whose emotions are reactive and who is still bound to the cultural affairs of this world, cannot develop *samādhi*. It is that simple. In fact such a person cannot go beyond attempts at *dhāraṇā*, which is effortful linkage of the attention to a higher concentration force, object or person. This is because the mento-emotional energy will remain unstable, locking and unlocking various ideas and images which emerge from the memory, enter through sensual perception or develop in the darkish non-glowing intellect.

Until the mento-emotional energy is established by a complete *pratyāhāra* sensual withdrawal procedure, the attention will not be freed to focus on the void which occurs at a split second interval between locking and unlocking of the mento-emotional energy. All these factors must be properly mastered before one can get to the *dhyāna* effortless linkage of the attention to higher concentration force, object or person. And when that is mastered by regular practice, then one can practice *samādhi* which is the continuous effortless linkage of the same.

Application:

By focusing on the causal body in the vicinity of the chest, a yogin gets thorough insight into the cause of the mental and emotional energies, because these energies were sourced in the causal body which is in the central chest of the subtle form. This refers to its location only. It is a super-subtle energy which is interspaced in the subtle form, just as that form is superimposed in the gross body.

Verse 36

सत्त्वपुरुषयोरत्यन्तासङ्कीर्णयोः प्रत्ययाविशेषो भोगः

परार्थत्वात्स्वार्थसंयमात्पुरुषज्ञानम्॥ ३६॥

sattva puruṣayoḥ atyantāsaṁkīrṇayoḥ pratyayaḥ aviśeṣaḥ bhogaḥ parārthatvāt svārthasaṁyamāt puruṣajñānam

sattva – intelligence energy of material nature; puruṣayoḥ – of the individual spirit; atyanta – excessively, extremely, very; asaṁkīrṇayoḥ – of what is distinct or separate; pratyayaḥ – mental content, awareness within the psyche; aviśeṣaḥ – not distinct, inability to distinguish; bhogaḥ – experience; parārthatvāt – what is apart from another thing; svārtha – one own, self interest; saṁyamāt – from the complete restraint of the mento-emotional energy; puruṣa – individual spirit; jñānam – knowledge.

Experience results from the inability to distinguish between the individual spirit and the intelligence energy of material nature, even though they are very distinct. By complete restraint of the mento-emotional energy while focusing on self-interest distinct from the other interest, a yogi gets knowledge of the individual spirit.

Analysis:

To understand this verse we must go back to chapter 2, verses 20 – 25 as follows:

draṣṭā dṛśimātraḥ śuddhaḥ api pratyayānupaśyaḥ
tadarthaḥ eva dṛśyasya ātma
kṛtārthaṁ prati naṣṭam api
anaṣṭaṁ tadanya sādhāraṇatvāt
sva svāmiśaktyoḥ svarūpa upalabdhi hetuḥ saṁyogaḥ

tasya hetuḥ avidyā
tad abhāvāt saṁyogā abhāvaḥ
hānaṁ taddṛśeḥ kaivalyam

The perceiver is the pure extent of his consciousness but his conviction is patterned by what is perceived.

The individual spirit who is involved in what is seen exists here for that purpose only.

It is not effective for one to whom its purpose is fulfilled but it has a common effect on the others.

There is a reason for the conjunction of the individual self and his psychological energies. It is for obtaining the experience of his own form.

The cause of the conjunction is spiritual ignorance.

The elimination of the conjunction which results from the elimination of that spiritual ignorance is the withdrawal that is the total separation of the perceiver from the mundane psychology.

This verse, which defines experience as a byproduct of the inability to distinguish between the individual spirit and the intelligent energy of material nature, is the heart of the matter of self-realization. In this precise declaration, *Patañjali* condemns our experiences *(bhogas)* in material nature.

They come to us because of an inability to distinguish between our spirits and the intelligent energy of material nature. The implication is this: If we could distinguish between our spirits and the intelligence energy of material nature, then we would not have to take the course of experience *(bhogah)* through material nature, through the various species of life, in and out of the various subtle and gross dimensions, which are produced in and are formed of subtle and gross material nature.

Focusing on the spirit itself apart from the other interests of material nature provides a way out. *Patañjali* earmarked not just material nature but its *sattva* features or its highest, most sensitive, and intelligent energy.

Application:

Experience in the material world results from the inability to distinguish between the individual spirit and the intelligence energy of material nature, even though they are very distinct. By complete restraint of the mental and emotional energies while focusing on self-interest distinct from the other concerns, a yogi acquires knowledge of the individual spirit. This is called self-realization. It has to be integrated into one's lifestyle. It should affect one's relationship to social situations.

Verse 37

ततः प्रातिभश्रावणवेदनादर्शास्वादवार्ता जायन्ते ॥ ३७ ॥

tataḥ prātibha śrāvaṇa vedana
ādarśa āsvāda vārtāḥ jāyante

tataḥ – thence, therefore, from that focus; prātibha – the shining organ of divination; śrāvaṇa – hearing; vedana – touching; ādarśa – sight; āsvāda – taste; vārtāḥ – smell; jāyante – is produced.

From that focus is produced smelling, tasting, seeing, touching and hearing, through the shining organ of divination.

Analysis:

Now all of a sudden, *Śrī Patañjali* continues with a promising statement about yoga development. One should review sūtra 36 of this chapter. It is vital that one understands the implication of it, which is *nirvāṇa* or the blowing out of the subtle and gross material existence.

From complete restraint of the mental and emotional energy and the focusing on the self-interest of the spirit, leaving aside completely the interests of material nature, the yogi applies his organ of divination, his developed *brahmarandra*, to all sensual pursuits. Then, instead of sensing through the mento-emotional energy *(citta),* he senses directly through spiritual detection. This was addressed before:

draṣṭṛdṛśyayoḥ saṁyogo heyahetuḥ

> The cause which is to be avoided is the indiscriminate association of the observer and what is perceived. *(Yoga Sūtra 2.17)*

The idea that the individual spirit will merge into the absolute and will then be without senses is not given in *Patañjali's sūtras*, even though many yogis and yogi philosophers advocate that conclusion.

Application:

From that focus is produced supernatural smelling, tasting, seeing, touching and hearing, through the shining organ of divination. All types of sensing take place in a spiritual body. Individuality is not wiped out but it is not encumbered by awkward responsibilities either.

Verse 38

ते समाधावुपसर्गा व्युत्थाने सिद्धयः ॥ ३८ ॥

te samādhau upasargāḥ vyutthāne siddhayaḥ

te – they, those abilities; samādhau – in samādhi continuous effortless linkage of the attention to a higher concentration force, object or person; upasargāḥ – impediments; vyutthāne – in expressing, going outwards, rising up; siddhayaḥ – mystic perfectional skills.

Those divination skills are obstacles in the practice of continuous effortless linkage of the attention to a higher concentration force, object or person. But in expressing, they are considered as mystic perfectional skills.

Analysis:

A yogi's practice stalls when he is distracted by new perfectional skills which manifest as he progresses. Those who feel a necessity to exploit such skills, are diverted from practice and become involved in social life as before. They may become premature gurus teaching an incomplete or distorted yoga process.

Application:

The divination skills may prove to be obstacles in advanced yoga practice. Yet to worldly people, they are considered as spectacular powers. The invitation which a yogi gets to use mystic power may be loaded with bad motives. It may come from whimsical urges in the psyche of living beings who are in a lower state. If a yogi succumbs, the display of supernatural powers will ruin his relationship with superiors and cause him to lose spiritual progress.

Verse 39

बन्धकारणशैथिल्यात्प्रचारसंवेदनाच्च चित्तस्य परशरीरावेशः ॥ ३९ ॥

bandhakāraṇa śaithilyāt pracāra
saṁvedanāt ca cittasya paraśarīrāveśaḥ

bandha – bondage; kāraṇa – cause; śaithilyāt – due to relaxation, collapse; pracāra – channel flow; saṁvedanāt – from knowing; ca – and; cittasya – of the mento-emotional energies; para – another; śarīra – body; āveśaḥ – entrance, penetration.

The entrance into another body is possible by slackening the cause of bondage and by knowing the channels of the mento-emotional energy.

Analysis:

The slackening of the cause of bondage is done by a yogi, when he reaches the causal level mentioned in verse 35. From the causal plane, he is able to slacken the cause of having to take the current body. Then he leaves that body temporarily while it stays in hibernation in *samādhi*. He enters the forms of others. A spiritual master may also do this after his body dies. He enters into the forms of his disciples on earth and speaks to small or large audiences, giving instructions. This prevents him from having to take a new material form. In that way he remains in the astral world for many years, avoiding physical rebirth.

A word of caution:

Some great yogis like *Śrī Ādi Śaṅkarācārya* and *Mahāyogin Śrī Matsyendranāth* entered the bodies of others, while their disciples maintained their gross forms. They did this for special purposes. Over all, a student yogi should not endeavor for this *paraśarīrāveśaḥ siddhi* since it is very risky. It is said that recently in our era, T. Lobsang Rampa who was a Tibetan mystic yogi in the past life, entered into an Englishman's body after the said occupant agreed to contribute his form in exchange for some merits of Rampa. Generally such a course is not recommended for a student yogin.

If one gets in the causal plane and stays long enough one may develop an ability to adjust one's resultant reactions which are left in a particular dimension and which would forestall liberation. Thus one may do so and not have to exhibit the *paraśarīrāveśaḥ siddhi*.

If one enters the form of another, one has to go through the channels of that person's mento-emotional energy. That entails adopting part of the person's disposition and assuming some of the person's responsibilities. That is dangerous since one may forget one's cultural identity and may begin to feel as if one is the other person. *Śrī Matsyendranāth*, even though he was a *siddha* at the time, was rescued by his most advanced disciple, the *mahāyogin Śrī Gorakṣnāth*. *Matsyendranāth* entered the body of another person and forgot his identity after adopting the stranger's psyche. In the case of *Śrī Ādi Śaṅkarācārya*, he did not forget himself, but the queen of the King's body whom he adopted, wanted to kill *Śaṅkara's* yogi body. She wanted him to stay as her husband and not return to his body. These examples warn of the dangers in adopting the body of another.

It is interesting that a great yogin as *Śrī Ādi Śaṅkara* had to enter the almost near-dead body of a king, just to experience sexual intercourse with a female, because a yogi can have such experiences on the astral planes near to this world or he may enter a parallel world and get such experiences. It is unnecessary to enter any other person's physical body for this reason. We must conclude therefore that destiny corrupts a yogin at specific stages, in order to tempt him to take certain dangerous and risky actions.

Śrī Ādi Śaṅkarācārya is rated as an incarnation of Lord Shiva. From what I learned in association with *siddhas* in the higher astral world, he is *Skanda Kūmara*, the celibate son of Shiva. Due to insubordination to *Devī*, Lord Shiva's wife, he had this difficulty in that incarnation. If one plans to be celibate, one should not expect much help from *Devī,* Goddess *Durgā*, but all the same, she is in a position to disrupt one's advancement.

Application:

The entrance into another's body is possible by slackening the cause of bondage to cultural activities and by knowing the channels which the mental and emotional energies use to entertain and dominate the self. This status is attained through mastership of kuṇḍalinī śakti. *Since* kuṇḍalinī *is the system which operates and sponsors transmigration, the core-self cannot move from form to form in various species, except by being hosted by* kuṇḍalinī. *One serious mistake of spiritual seekers is to neglect the study and mastership of this life force.*

Verse 40

उदानजयाज्जलपङ्ककण्टकादिष्वसङ्ग उत्क्रान्तिश्च ॥४०॥

udānajayāt jala paṅka kaṇṭakādiṣu asaṇgaḥ utkrāntiḥ ca

udāna – air which rises from the throat and enters the head; jayāt – from the conquest of; jala – water; paṅka – mud; kaṇṭaka – thorns; ādiṣi – and similar aspects; asaṅgaḥ – non contact; utkrāntiḥ – rising above; ca – and.

By mastery over the air which rises from the throat into the head, a yogi can rise over or not have contact with water, mud or sharp objects.

Analysis:

Udāna vāyu is the air which rises from the throat area to the top of the head. In *kuṇḍalinī* yoga a yogi controls this air, when he forces the *apāna* air, the lowest most polluted air in the body, up and out of the body through the spinal column. Sometimes for convenience sake, one is able to miraculously cross water, mud or sharp objects, even though one may not willfully exhibit such perfectional power, as demonstrated by many great yogis and by Lord Jesus Christ.

Certain animals have the natural power since their spirits use forms which are able to suppress and regulate the *udāna vāyu*. Of course, a yogi's exhibition of that siddhi is something different. The expression of miracles, even though it helps a yogi on occasion, can cause impediments under other conditions. These exhibitions are not recommended. *Śrī Patañjali* lists these not to encourage usage but to alert student yogis of the benchmarks of yoga practice.

Application:

By mastery over the air which rises from the throat into the head of the subtle body, a yogi can cause his gross form to rise over or not have contact with water, mud or sharp objects. He may safely use this ability to form conclusions about the mobility of certain subtle forms. Or he may use this for convenience without displaying it to others.

Verse 41

समानजयाज्ज्वलनम्॥४१॥

samānajayāt jvalanam

samāna – digestive energy; jayāt – conquest; jvalanam – shining, burning, blazing, with firey glow.

By conquest of the* samāna *digestive force, a yogi's psyche blazes or shines with a fiery glow.

Analysis:

Conquest of the *samāna* digestive force comes by the practice of *kuṇḍalinī* yoga which entails various *āsanas* combined with *prāṇāyāma*, especially *bhastrika prāṇāyāma*. By that, a yogi gets control over diet. He purifies the navel region of the body. This sets the stage for purification of the sexual functions which opens a gate for the yogi to attack the *mūlādhār* anal region. After this is achieved in the downward course, it must be achieved in the upward course, as the *prāṇa* is pushed down and forces the *apāna* energy to move upwards through a subtle tubing called the *suśumnā nāḍi*. When a yogi on the upward purification course, purifies his navel region, he experiences frontal *kuṇḍalinī*. He achieves conquest over the *samāna* digestive fire. His subtle body then appears with an orange tinted fiery glow.

Application:

By conquest of the digestive force in the gross body, a yogi's subtle form blazes or shines with a fiery glow. This is perceived physically as health and vitality.

Verse 42

श्रोत्राकाशयोः सम्बन्धसंयमाद्दिव्यं श्रोत्रम्॥४२॥

śrotra ākāśayoḥ saṁbandha saṁyamāt divyaṁ śrotram

śrotra – hearing sense; ākāśayoḥ – of space; saṁbandha – relationship; saṁyamāt – from the complete restraint of the mento-emotional energy; divyaṁ – divine, supernatural; śrotram – hearing sense.

By the complete restraint of the mento-emotional energy, while focusing on the hearing sense and space, a yogin develops supernatural and divine hearing.

Analysis:

Each yogi masters a particular mystic skill based on the force of practice, the association while progressing and the cultural background from many previous lives. As a result, particular skills attract one's attention. However, if one has the association of Shiva and other *mahāyogis*, one will not invest time in using the mystic skills but will stay focused on the objective of psyche purification; something from which one could quickly gain spiritual perfection.

Application:

By special focus on the hearing sense and space, a yogin develops supernatural and divine hearing. He should not alert others of this. Clairaudience is a useful power for causing a yogi to sidestep resentment.

Verse 43

कायाकाशयोः सम्बन्धसंयमाल्लघुतूलसमापत्तेश्चाकाशगमनम्॥४३॥

kāya ākāśayoḥ saṁbandha saṁyamāt laghutūlasamāpatteḥ ca ākāśagamanam

kāya – body; ākāśayoḥ – of the sky, atmosphere; saṁbandha – relation; saṁyamāt – from the complete restraint of the mento-emotional energy; laghu – light; tūla – cotton fluff; samāpatteḥ – of meeting, of linking; ca – and; ākāśa – atmosphere; gamanam – going through, passing through.

By the complete restraint of the mento-emotional energy, while linking the mind to the relationship between the body and the sky and linking the attention to being as light as cotton fluff, a yogi acquires the ability to pass through the atmosphere.

Analysis:

This does not necessarily mean levitation of the physical body. It can mean usage of the subtle body. Since every user of a physical body, already has a subtle form which can pass through the atmosphere with ease, it is not necessary to focus on making the physical body as buoyant as a cotton fluff which can defy gravity and float easily in the air. In addition, a yogi who can see or hear from afar would not require that his gross body be moved from one place to another merely to see in that other place.

Application:

By linking the mind to the relationship between the body and the sky and linking the attention to being as light as cotton fluff, a yogi acquires the ability to objectively pass his subtle form through the atmosphere. In some rare cases, a yogi's physical body floats. Such occurrences have nothing to do with displays to the public. If a yogi decides to exhibits miracles, he takes a downward course.

Verse 44

बहिरकल्पिता वृत्तिर्महाविदेहा ततः प्रकाशावरणक्षयः ॥४४॥

bahiḥ akalpitā vṛttiḥ mahāvidehā tataḥ
prakāśa āvaraṇakṣayaḥ

bahiḥ – outside, external; akalpitā – not manufactured, not artificial, not formed; vṛttiḥ – operation; mahā – great; videhā – bodiless state; tataḥ – thence, from that, resulting from that; prakāśa – light; āvaraṇa – covering, mental darkens; kṣayaḥ – dissipation, removal.

By the complete restraint of the mento-emotional energy which is external, which is not formed, a yogi achieves the great bodiless state. From that the great mental darkness which veils the light, is dissipated.

Analysis:

The great bodiless state, *mahāvidehā*, is a special accomplishment of great yogis, who go beyond the causal plane but who do not get an exception to leave this solar system. Either by choice or because they fail to obtain the exemption for whatever reason, they remain in the unformed, untapped pure mental energy which was not parceled out to individual spirits. They remain free of involvements. Such yogins hardly interact in the cultural world which is so important to a human being. For those great yogis the mental darkness which human beings consistently experience, does not exist. They have moved beyond the subtle negative influences of material nature.

Application:

By restraining his response to the mental and emotional energy, which is universal, a yogi achieves the great bodiless state. From that, the great mental darkness which veils subtle light is dissipated. After hours and hours of meditation, after repeatedly adjusting a faulty lifestyle, a yogi's mind remains illuminated. The great mental darkness vanishes.

Verse 45

स्थूलस्वरूपसूक्ष्मान्वयार्थवत्त्वसंयमाद्भूतजयः ॥४५॥

sthūla svarūpa sūkṣma anvaya arthavatva saṁyamāt bhūtajayaḥ

stūla – gross form; svarūpa – real nature; sūkṣma – subtle; anvaya – following, connection, distribution; arthavatava – purpose, value; saṁyamāt – from the complete restraint of the mento-emotional energy; bhūta – states of matter; jayaḥ – conquest.

By the complete restraint of the mento-emotional energy, while linking the attention to the gross forms, real nature, subtle distribution and value of states of matter, a yogi gets conquest over them.

Analysis:

Some yogins are diverted from progression by too much research into the material nature. However, for them those diversions are necessary, until they accomplish their objectives or reach stages of greater resistance. The main asset of a yogi is to keep in touch with more advanced ascetics so that even if the student yogin becomes fascinated or stalled, his advanced teachers can guide him away from degradation.

Application:

By restraining his mind and emotions, while linking the attention to gross forms, real nature, subtle distribution and super-subtle states of matter, a yogi gets conquest over them, but only in reference to his individual existential rights. A yogi does not all of a sudden become God or even become a god. His power does increase but only in reference to what he should be responsible for in the first place.

Verse 46

ततोऽणिमादिप्रादुर्भावः कायसम्पत्तद्धर्मानभिघातश्च ॥४६॥

tataḥ aṇimādi prādurbhāvaḥ kāyasaṁpat taddharma anabhighātaḥ ca

tataḥ – thence, from that; aṇandi = aṇima – minuteness + ādi – and the related mystic skills; prādurbhāvaḥ – coming into existence, manifesting; kāya – subtle body; saṁpat – wealth, prosperity, perfection; tad – tat = of that; dharma – attributes, functions; anabhighātaḥ – non-obstruction; ca – and.

From minuteness and other related mystic skills, come the perfection of the subtle body and the non-obstruction of its functions.

Analysis:

Non-obstruction of the functions of the subtle body pertains to its application to varying levels. The subtle form does not have one uniform expression on every plane. Each dimension taxes or frees it to perform in certain ways. On the lower planes, the *kuṇḍalinī* life force delivers a low charge to operate the subtle body. That entails certain inborn restrictions which confine the form to a gross body and the related limitations. On the higher plane, the life force delivers a high charge. That opens vistas of sensual magic which are not even dreamt of on the lower levels.

When the yogi develops the mystic skills, he finds that the subtle body is perfected to such a degree that the *nāḍis*, subtle tubes, within it carry a subtle fluid which is as crystal clear as pure water. From certain dimensions this appears to be liquid light traveling through the subtle body. Some of this purity filters into the gross body and the yogi is said to perform miracles.

The obstructions experienced by a common man, and those fascinations that occupy a neophyte are removed from the perfected soul, because his subtle form is purified. The way of operation of the subtle body is obstructed by impurities which arise from attachments to the material energy. When a yogi completes the *pratyāhār* fifth stage of yoga and when he ceases interactions with the *citta* mento-emotional energy, thus retiring his intellect from involvements and calculations regarding cultural activities, he reaches the required level of purity.

Application:

From the assumption of minuteness and other related mystic skills, come the perfection of the subtle body and the non-obstruction of its functions. The curiosity of a living being develops into a full blown disease in the subtle body. Thus one has to curb this tendency by fulfilling it to a greater degree. Many lower life forms were assumed merely by trying to satisfy the urge of curiosity and this is supported by one's sense for excitement.

In the last stages, just before achieving liberation, a yogi comes to terms with excitement and curiosity. These essential drives serve their ultimate purpose, at last, when he sees the dimensional scope of material existence and the supernatural persons and energies which function in and through it.

Verse 47

रूपलावण्यबलवज्रसंहननत्वानि कायसम्पत्॥४७॥

rūpa lāvaṇya bala vajra saṁhananatvāni kāyasaṁpat

rūpa – beautiful form; lāvaṇya – charm; bala – mystic force; vajra – diamond-like, infallible; saṁhananatvāni – definiteness, hardness; kāya – subtle body; saṁpat – perfection.

Beautiful form, charm, mystic force, and diamond-like definition come from perfection of the subtle body.

Analysis:

Most commentators interpret *kāya* as the physical body. However, in advanced yoga practice, *kāya* is the subtle body, the temporary but long lasting body which the yogin must perfect before he can attain liberation.

When the subtle body is upgraded by the practice of *kuṇḍalinī* yoga, it attains beauty of form, mystic force and diamond-like definition. It embodies clarity. Its colors become free from cloudiness and vagueness. It moves into the higher pranic force. It is experienced as a *sattva guṇa* body, a form of the most refined subtle matter.

Application:

Beautiful form, charm, mystic force and diamond-like definition come from energizing the subtle body. This is attained by mastership of kuṇḍalinī *yoga.*

Verse 48

ग्रहणस्वरूपास्मितान्वयार्थवत्त्वसंयमादिन्द्रियजयः ॥४८॥

grahaṇa svarūpa asmitā anvaya arthavattva saṁyamāt indriyajayaḥ

grahaṇa – sensual grasping; svarūpa – own form; asmitā – identification; anvaya – connection, association; arthavatva – value, worth; saṁyamāt – from the continuous effortless linkage of the attention; indriyajayaḥ – the mastery of the sensual energy by psychological control.

From the continuous effortless linkage of the attention to sensual grasping, to the form of the sensual energy, to its identifying powers, to its connection instinct and to its actual worth, a yogi acquires conquest over his relationship with it.

Analysis:

It is important to understand and to accept for oneself, that these achievements occur after prolonged practice. Those who feel they can achieve these overnight will definitely be frustrated. Yoga practice matures and remains firm only after long practice, and not just for one life but through a succession of lives, until the practice becomes an instinct.

A yogin must study the sensual energy. He must also take hints from the way others use their sensual powers. It takes time to accomplish this. The sensual energy is subtle and moves at a rapid rate to execute its functions. It is mostly involuntary, which means that it operates on its own. This makes it difficult to track. However, after long practice, a yogin secures a foothold in these achievements described by *Patañjali*. One must study how the sensual energy appropriates or grasps subtle phenomena. This is indicated by the term *anvaya*. One must study how the energy connects with and associates with various types of subtle and gross objects. One must know the form of the sensual energy, its *svarūpa*. This is its form when it does not assume the identity of other objects. One should understand its nature for identification as well as its worth to the self. When all this is achieved, then the yogi gains mastery over his relationship to that sensual force.

Application:

From supernatural linkage to sensual grasping, to the form of the sensual energy, to its identifying powers, to its connection instinct and to its actual worth, a yogi acquires conquest over his relation with the sensual energy. This pertains to his reach beyond the psyche. Purification is done while using a material body. Its main function is to displace lower psychic energy with a higher grade. Initially there is no concern with the external environment. When one achieves psychic purity, one perceives the pure worlds with divine inhabitants. Then one realizes that such experience occurred because one's subtle form has a matching purity.

Verse 49

ततो मनोजवित्वं विकरणभावः प्रधानजयश्च॥ ४९॥

tataḥ manojavitvaṁ vikaraṇabhāvaḥ pradhānajayaḥ ca

tataḥ – subsequently; manojavitvaṁ = manah – mind + javitvaṁ – swiftness, rapidity; vikaraṇabhāvaḥ = vi – parting away from, dispersing + karana – creating, making + bhāvaḥ – mento-emotional energy, feeling; pradhānah – subtle matter; jayaḥ – conquest; ca – and.

Subsequently, there is conquest over the influence of subtle matter and over the parting away or dispersion of the mento-emotional energy, with the required swiftness of mind.

Analysis:

These aspects are on the mystic plane. This is attained after long practice of *dhāraṇā*. At first a yogi practices *dhāraṇā*, feeling that he mastered the *pratyāhār* sensual restraint. Thereafter he discovers that he only mastered particular phases of such restraint. Under direction of higher yogis, he revises the restraint practice. Then he again returns to *dhāraṇā*. This occurs frequently, until at last his perception of the subtle realities develops fully. What was subtle becomes gross; what was gross fades away completely. He purifies himself even further and grasps subtler reality.

Application:

Subsequently, he, having the required swiftness of mind, progresses into conquest over the influence of subtle matter and over the parting away or dispersion of the mental and emotional forces.

Verse 50

सत्त्वपुरुषान्यताख्यातिमात्रस्य सर्वभावाधिष्ठातृत्वं सर्वज्ञातृत्वं च॥ ५०॥

sattva puruṣa anyatā khyātimātrasya
sarvabhāva adhiṣṭhātṛtvaṁ sarvajñātṛtvaṁ ca

sattva – clarifying perception of material nature; puruṣa – the spiritual personality; anyatā – other than distinct from; khyātimātrasya = khyāti – the discriminating faculty of the intellect + mātrasya – only; sarva – all; bhāva –

states of feelings and perceptions; adhiṣṭhātṛtvaṁ – authority, complete disaffection; sarvajñātṛtvaṁ = sarva – all + jñātṛtvaṁ – knowledge, intuition; ca – and.

Only when there is distinct discrimination between the clarifying perception of material nature and the spiritual personality, does the yogi attain complete disaffection and all-applicative intuition.

Analysis:

Khyāti means the well-developed truth-yielding discrimination of the intellect. This is attained after long practice. Once developed, the yogi clearly sees the distinction between his spiritual person and the clarifying influences of material nature, influences from which he took assistance all along.

In advanced yoga, or *kriyā* yoga, one maintains the distinction between oneself and the perceiving instruments of the subtle body, even though initially one must take help from the instruments. *Adhiṣṭhātṛtvaṁ* means complete or full disaffection from the subtle influence of material nature, even from the clarifying powers which are so helpful.

Application:

Only when there is distinct discrimination between true perception of material nature and the spiritual personality, does the yogi attain complete disaffection from the same nature and all-applicative intuition in whatever he encounters.

Verse 51

तद्वैराग्यादपि दोषबीजक्षये कैवल्यम्॥५१॥

tadvairāgyāt api doṣabījakṣaye kaivalyam

tadvairāgyāt = tad (tat) – that + vairāgyāt – from a lack of interest; api – also, even; doṣabījakṣaye = doṣa – fault, defect + bīja – seed, origin, source + kṣaye – on elimination; kaivalyam – the absolute isolation of the self from what is lower than itself, isolation of the self from the lower psyche of itself.

By a lack of interest, even to that (discrimination between the clarifying mundane energy and the self) when the cause of that defect is eliminated, the absolute isolation of the self from its lower psyche, is achieved.

Analysis:

Kaivalyam, which is a popular word in yoga and meditation circles, is often mistranslated and misinterpreted. Its meaning is not that the yogi would become one with God. *Patañjali*, the master of yoga, never says that in these verses. *Kaivalya* is the isolation of the self from its lower psyche, such that the subtle mundane instruments of the psyche are separated from the self or *ātma*. The ātma becomes freed from reliance on those useful but domineering subtle tools.

Previously *Śrī Patañjali* described kaivalyam in this way:

tad abhāvāt saṁyogā abhāvaḥ
hānaṁ taddṛśeḥ kaivalyam

"The elimination of the conjunction which results from the elimination of that spiritual ignorance is the withdrawal that is the total separation of the perceiver from the mundane psychology." *(Yoga Sūtra 2.25)*

It is amazing how so many translators, following the oneness craze completely distorted *Patañjali* by giving misleading and out-of-context meanings for the term *kaivalyam*. Vaman Shivram Apte in his practical Sanskrit-English dictionary gives the following plain meanings for this term; perfect isolation, aloneness, exclusiveness, individuality, detachment of the soul from matter, identification with the Supreme Spirit, final emancipation or beatitude.

Application:

By a lack of interest, even to that skill, when the cause of that defect is eliminated, the absolute isolation of the self from the lower psyche, is achieved.

Verse 52

स्थान्युपनिमन्त्रणे सङ्गस्मयाकरणं पुनरनिष्टप्रसङ्गात्॥५२॥

sthānyupanimantraṇe saṅgasmayākaraṇaṁ
punaraniṣṭa prasaṅgāt

sthāni – person from the place a yogi would then attain if his material body died; upanimantraṇe – on being invited; saṅga – association; smaya – fascination, wonderment; akaraṇaṁ – non-responsiveness; punaḥ – again; aniṣṭa – unwanted features of existence; prasaṅgāt – due to association, due to endearing friendliness.

On being invited by a person from the place one would attain if the body died, a yogi should be non-responsive, not desiring their association and not being fascinated, otherwise that would cause unwanted features of existence to arise again.

Analysis:

A perfect example of a person who implemented this advice, long before *Patañjali* took his material body to write the *Yoga Sūtras*, is *Mudgala*, who in the *Mahābhārata* rejected proposals for transference to the *Swarga* angelic world. *Mudgala* had reached a stage of progression where he was eligible to live in a special palace of the lord of the angelic world. He was visited by *Matali*, the lord's charioteer, but when questioned by *Mudgala*, *Matali* admitted that there were defects in the angelic world, even for great yogins who would go there. They would again *(punaḥ)* have to revert back to this world after a period of enjoying paradisiacal pleasures. Thus *Mudgala* said that he did not want to go to such a place but would continue the austerities to go somewhere which was devoid of all unwanted features of existence *(aniṣṭa)*.

For others, who are not as strong and determined, it is easier said than done. They may not avoid the temptation of the angelic world. By developing endearing friendliness *(prasaṅgāt),* they will succumb to angelic association and the fascinations of such a world. Just as governments of the developed countries skim off the intelligent people from the lesser-developed lands, so the angelic people attract the higher minds of the earthly planets.

Application:

On being invited by a person from the gross or subtle mundane place one would attain, if the body died, a yogi should be non-responsive, not desiring their association and not being fascinated; otherwise that would cause unwanted features of existence to arise again. He would again take birth in this world or appear in a dimension near to this one, from which he would be transferred here again.

Verse 53

क्षणतत्क्रमयोः संयमाद्विवेकजं ज्ञानम्॥५३॥

kṣaṇa tatkramayoḥ saṁyamāt vivekajaṁ jñānam

kṣaṇa – moment; tat – that; kramayoḥ – on the sequence; saṁyamāt – due to the continuous effortless linkage of the attention; vivekajaṁ – the distinction caused by subtle discrimination; jñānam – knowledge.

By the continuous effortless linkage of the attention to the moment and to the sequence of the moments, the yogi has knowledge caused by the subtle discrimination.

Analysis:

Every word in these texts must be understood within the context and not according to our stage of development or agenda of spiritual mission. To understand *Patañjali* and to benefit the most from his *sūtras*, stay with his meanings and then try to progress and advance onwards in that context.

When a yogi can observe subtle mystic moments and see how they flow on one to another, he develops a very subtle insight which gives definite knowledge of things. *Viveka* means very subtle insight. *Jam* means what is caused or produced from the higher knowledge of that yogi.

Application:

By supernatural linkage of his attention to the moment in time and to the sequence of moments, the yogi has detailed supernatural information about the life durations of many species.

Verse 54

जातिलक्षणदेशैरन्यतानवच्छेदात्तुल्ययोस्ततः प्रतिपत्तिः ॥५४॥

jāti lakṣaṇa deśaiḥ anyatā anavacchedāt tulyayoḥ tataḥ pratipattiḥ

jāti – type, genus, general category; lakṣaṇa – individual characteristics; deśaiḥ – by what location; anyatā – otherwise, in a different manner; anavacchedāt – due to or resulting from lack of definition; tulyayoḥ – of two similar types; tataḥ – hence, subsequently; pratipattiḥ – perception.

Subsequently, the yogi has perception of two similar realities which otherwise could not be sorted due to a lack of definition in terms of their general category, individual characteristics and locations.

Analysis:

Persistence in higher yoga brings on more definition. Things which before, seemed to be one or seem to be merged, appear clearly by their category, individual characteristics and locations. This begins by the yogi understanding the intellect organ, the sense of identity, the life force and the other components of the psyche. A yogi develops mystic clarity.

Application:

Subsequently, the yogi clearly distinguishes between two similar realities which otherwise, could not be sorted due to lack of definition in terms of their general category, individual characteristics and location.

Verse 55

तारकं सर्वविषयं सर्वथाविषयमक्रमं चेति विवेकजं ज्ञानम्॥५५॥

tārakaṁ sarvaviṣayaṁ sarvathāviṣayaṁ akramaṁ ca iti vivekajaṁ jñānam

tārakaṁ – crossing over transcending; sarva – all; viṣayaṁ – subtle and gross mundane objects; sarvathā – in all ways; viṣayaṁ – subtle and gross mundane object; akramaṁ – without sequential perceptions; ca – and; iti – thus, subsequently; vivekajaṁ – the distinction caused by subtle discrimination; jñānam – knowledge.

The distinction caused by subtle discrimination is the crossing over or transcending of all subtle and gross mundane objects in all ways they are presented, without the yogi taking recourse to any other sequential perceptions of mind reliance.

Analysis:

Śrī Patañjali highlights the culmination of yoga, so that as yogis we can know where we are on the course of transcending the mundane reality which keeps us so occupied as we try to transcend it.

Application:

Thus the yogin need no longer take recourse to the normal methods of perception and analysis. For him the distinction caused by subtle discrimination is the transcending of all subtle and gross mundane objects in all ways they are presented.

Verse 56

सत्त्वपुरुषयोः शुद्धिसाम्ये कैवल्यमिति॥५६॥

sattva puruṣayoḥ śuddhi sāmye kaivalyam iti

sattva – intelligence energy of material nature; puruṣayoḥ – of the spirit; śuddhi – purity; sāmye – on being equal; kaivalyam – total separation from the mundane psychology; iti – thus.

When there is equal purity between the intelligence energy of material nature and the spirit, then there is total separation from the mundane psychology.

Analysis:

Readers should reference verses 2:25 and 3:36 to understand *Patañjali's* use of the terms *sattva, puruṣayoḥ* and *kaivalyam*. The key term in this verse is *sattva*. What is *sattva*? The aspiring yogi must use *sattva* to become self-realized. *Sattva* is the intelligent energy of material nature. This renders all questions as to why he must depend on material nature, irrelevant. It is not why he has to depend, but rather how he can protect himself or cause himself to be situated in alliance with the material nature in its primal purity *(śuddhi-sāmye).* What will happen to him thereafter? Is there something higher? Where will he go after that? What will be his status? Is there a world to which he will transit? Will that world have the same purified *sattva*-quality (intelligence energy of material nature)? Is there any place or world where he could encounter only energy like the spirit *(purusah)?*

These are the questions to be considered by the yogin.

Application:

When, by mastership of kriyā *yoga, there is equal purity between the intelligence energy of material nature and the spirit, then there is total separation from the error-prone, spiritually-misleading mundane psychology.*

Chapter 4
Kaivalya Pāda:
Segregation Accomplishment

Verse 1

जन्मौषधिमन्त्रतपःसमाधिजाः सिद्धयः ॥ १ ॥

janma auṣadhi mantra tapaḥ samādhijāḥ siddhayaḥ

janma – birth, particular species; auṣadhi – drugs; mantra – special sound; tapaḥ – physical bodily austerities in Haṭha Yoga; samādhi – continuous effortless linkage of the attention to a higher concentration force, object or person; jāḥ – what is produced from; siddhayaḥ – mystic skills.

The mystic skills are produced by taking birth in particular species, by taking drugs, by reciting special sounds, by physical bodily austerities or by the continuous effortless linkage of the attention to a higher concentration force, object or person.

Analysis:

The mystic skills are inherent in the subtle body of each creature but actual manifestation depends on particular circumstances. Taking birth in a species either as an animal, human being or angel, can cause one to express unusual powers. Taking narcotic drugs or stimulants may also cause shifts in pranic force in the subtle body. This would activate paranormal powers. Repeating special sounds or having these recited on one's behalf might affect the pranic arrangement in one's subtle body, resulting in paranormal powers. The practice of *haṭha* yoga would definitely cause the development of psychic powers. Finally, *samādhi*, listed last by *Śrī Patañjali,* is definitely yielding of paranormal perceptions.

Application:

The mystic skills are demonstrated on the material plane through the various abilities of the varying species of life one may assume. Each species facilitates a particular ability of the subtle body. One may be empowered with a mystic skill by taking drugs which alter the chemistry of a particular form. Skills may be exhibited after pronouncing certain special sounds which affect the constitution of a body. Physical austerities may change a body to make it do what is normally impossible for the particular species. And supernatural linkage of one's mystic attention may affect changes which are unusual for one's body.

Verse 2

जात्यन्तरपरिणामः प्रकृत्यापूरात्॥ २॥

jātyantara pariṇāmaḥ prakṛtyāpūrāt

jātyantara = jāti – category + antara – other, another; pariṇāmaḥ – transformation; prakṛiti – subtle material nature; āpūrāt – due to filling up or saturation.

The transformation from one category to another is by the saturation of the subtle material nature.

Analysis:

Recent authorities like Timothy Leary and Aldous Huxley, preferred the use of drugs for the development of higher perception, but *Śrī Gorakṣnāth* wanted us to use the *haṭha* yoga austerities. *Śrī Bābāji Mahasaya* recommended the *samādhi* continuous effortless linkage of the attention to a higher concentration force, object or person. Nowadays, spiritual masters from India usually hawk the special mantra sounds as the means of perfection, while some psychics say that a person should be gifted from birth with mystic abilities.

When a living entity develops a higher quality and when that expression becomes saturated in his nature, he is automatically transferred into a higher species of life, either as an elevated human being, an angelic personality or a divine being.

Śrī Bābāji Mahasaya gave me a notation for verse one:

> *"Each of the methods for developing or manifesting the mystic skills is listed in order of the particular efforts made by the yogi. The first is* janma *or birth opportunity. That is based on efforts in the past lives. Thus in the current life, no effort is required. Some might take the* janma *or appearance in higher realms like in* siddhaloka*. There, taking a* siddha *yoga body, one experiences the result of his previous austerities. Others take an earthly form again. By the force of past penance, they experience mystic skills even in another gross body."*

Auṣadhi means herbs, drugs or chemical means of adjusting the gross and subtle body. This method existed in the Vedic period. This is why one might read about the *soma* plant. This does not require much endeavor, only the acquirement of the particular plant species. By ingesting that plant in its concentrated form, pranic energy in one's subtle body is affected and certain abilities of the subtle body are manifested.

Herbs were used by shamans, the religious leaders of primitive people. The herbal method is a risky one, since the dosage may be wrong. It might be too high or too low, too concentrated or too diluted. It might kill or disable the body.

Mantra, special sound, is the general method preferred by most human beings. This operates the confidence energy of the person, but he may or may not succeed in experiencing something about the subtle body. This is an easy method requiring only the working of the vocal chords or silent mental sounding. This method remained popular for thousands of years due to human tendency for relying on hope and calling on superior authority for assistance.

Tapaḥ means the *haṭha* yoga austerities which purify both the gross and subtle bodies. This includes *kuṇḍalinī* yoga for displacing bad subtle energy. This is the classic method for attaining purity of the intelligence energy of material nature mentioned in verse 56 of the last chapter:

sattva puruṣayoḥ śuddhi sāmye kaivalyam iti

> When there is equal purity between the intelligence energy of material nature and the spirit, then there is total separation from the mundane psychology. *(Yoga Sūtra 3.56)*

If the subtle energy is not purified, the progress will be erratic causing the yogi to fall to a lower level sooner or later. The *haṭha* yoga austerities are the definite way for such purity. Krishna confirms this in the chapter 6 verse 12 of *Bhagavad Gītā*.

The last method which is the best is ***samādhi***, the continuous effortless linkage of the attention to a higher reality. This is preferred. However this is merely an advancement of the *tapah* or *haṭha* yoga austerity method. It does not stand alone. It is unlikely that one can attain *samādhi* without doing the *haṭha* yoga austerities proficiently.

In summary, *janma* means efforts in a past life. *Auṣadhi* means eating, drinking, smelling or otherwise ingesting chemicals which affect the subtle body. *Mantra* means using one's faith or confidence energy. *Tapaḥ* means physical austerities which eradicate impurities in the subtle form. *Samādhi* means using one's psychic force to reach higher realities.

Application:

The transformation from one life form to another or from one dimension to another, from one existential status to another, occurs by saturation of the subtle body with the energy from that other species, dimension or status that is to be adopted.

Verse 3

निमित्तमप्रयोजकं प्रकृतीनां वरणभेदस्तु ततः क्षेत्रिकवत्॥ ३॥

nimittaṁ aprayojakaṁ prakṛtīnāṁ
varaṇabhedaḥ tu tataḥ kṣetrikavat

nimittaṁ – cause, motive, apparent cause; aprayojakaṁ – not used, not employed, not causing; prakṛtīnāṁ – of the subtle material energy; varaṇa – impediments, obstacles; bhedaḥ – splitting, removing, disintegrating; tu – but, except; tataḥ – hence; kṣetrikavat – like a farmer.

The motivating force of the subtle material energy is not used except for the disintegration of impediments, hence it is compared to a farmer.

Analysis:

Even though a yogin is assisted by material nature, which exhibits powerful motivating forces from time to time, still his spiritual progress is not really caused by nature. Instead nature removes its own forces which act as impediments to the efforts of the yogi. Even though a farmer does many things to facilitate the growing of seeds, his actions are not the root causes of plant growth. The development from seeds to plant has more to do with the potential within the seed than it does with the farmer's activities. Similarly material nature does not cause a yogi's development, even though nature as supervised by time does facilitate the progression.

Application:

The motivating force of the subtle material energy, whereby it appears to inspire the yogi to endeavor for liberation, is not used except for the disintegration of the impediments placed before the yogi by the reliance on time, hence it is compared to a farmer who is not the real cause of growth of cultivated plants.

Verse 4

निर्माणचित्तान्यस्मितामात्रात्॥ ४॥

nirmāṇacittāni asmitāmātrāt

nirmāṇa – producing, creating, measuring, fabricating; cittāni – regions within the mento-emotional energy; asmitā – sense of identity which is developed in relation to material nature; mātrāt – from that only.

The formation of regions within the mento-emotional energy, arises only from the sense of identity which is developed in relation to material nature.

Analysis:

Even though the spirit's attention is singular, still because of the mento-emotional energy, there appears to be various regions within the mind and feelings of a personality. A yogi, by *kriyā* yoga, traces the mental regions and emotional moods to the sense of identity which is experienced whenever the attention goes in the direction of the gross or subtle material nature. Eventually one develops disgust *(nirvedaḥ),* and becomes serious about spiritual progression. He no longer wants to be entertained by the various imaginations within the mind.

Application:

A yogi is shown how the various parts of the mind and emotions come into existence because of the involuntary application of the sense of identity to the subtle material nature. That one component of psychology causes all the other subtle objects in the psyche to be ordered or disordered accordingly.

Verse 5

प्रवृत्तिभेदे प्रयोजकं चित्तमेकमनेकेषाम्॥ ५॥

pravṛtti bhede prayojakaṁ cittam ekam anekeṣām

pravṛtti – frantic activity, dispersal of energy; bhede – in the difference; prayojakaṁ – very, much used or employed; cittam – the mento-emotional energy; ekam – one; anekeṣām – of what is numberless.

The one mento-emotional energy is that which is very much used in numberless different dispersals of energy.

Analysis:

Keeping this in mind, a yogi takes steps to stop the innumerable impulsive operations of the mind.

Application:

The one mento-emotional energy is that which is very much used in numberless different dispersals of energy, which occur as ideas and images, arising from memory and sense perception. It is molded or shaped primarily through ideation and emotion.

Verse 6

तत्र ध्यानजमनाशयम्॥ ६॥

tatra dhyānajam anāśayam

tatra – there, in that case; dhyānajam – produced by the effortless linkage of the attention to a higher reality; anāśayam – without harmful emotions.

In that case, only subtle activities which are produced from the effortless linkage of the attention to a higher reality are without harmful emotions.

Analysis:

Āśayam is the seat of feelings, the place in the mento-emotional energy from which endearing but harmful emotions emerge. This location is difficult to track since it is a mystic province. Until a yogi gets clarity of consciousness, he cannot transcend feelings. He is continually fooled by emotions. When he masters the effortless linkage of the mind to higher realities, then he gains objectivity and can sort the endearing but harmful feelings, even the super-subtle impressions in the memory.

Application:

In that case, only subtle activities which are produced from linkage to higher realities are without harmful emotions; the others are rooted in the subtle material nature, which always affords reversals. The meditator shuffles between the two supports of material nature and transcendental reality. Eventually material nature is abandoned. The transcendence takes precedence as the place of shelter.

Verse 7

कर्माशुक्लाकृष्णं योगिनस्त्रिविधमितरेषाम्॥७॥

karma aśukla akṛṣnaṁ yoginaḥ trividham itareṣām

karma – cultural activity; aśukla – not white, not rewarding; akṛṣnaṁ – not black, not penalizing; yoginaḥ – of the yogis; trividham – three-fold; irtareṣām – for others.

The cultural activity of the yogis is neither rewarding nor penalizing, but others have three types of such action.

Analysis:

An advanced yogi, who mastered the *dhyāna* effortless linkage of the mind to a higher reality, may perform cultural activities just as others do, but for him, these do not result in rewarding, penalizing or fruitless results.

What then does the yogi gain from cultural activities? He gains absolutely nothing, because his detachment allows the reactions to fall back into material nature without a claimant.

Application:

Due to effective detachment and the ability to push the emerging ideas and images back into the pad of the mind or the territory of the emotions, the cultural activity of the advanced yogins is neither rewarding nor penalizing, but others have three types of such action. The relationship between material nature and the spirit is such that moody variations induce reflexive fluctuations in the consciousness when there is attachment. There is, however, involuntary attachment. In that case the induction is transmitted forcibly even though no choice was made by the individual concerned.

Verse 8

ततस्तद्विपाकानुगुणानामेवाभिव्यक्तिर्वासनानाम्॥८॥

tataḥ tadvipāka anuguṇānām
eva abhivyaktiḥ vāsanānām

tataḥ – subsequently; tad – that, those; vipāka – development, fruition; anuguṇānām – of the corresponding features; eva – only, alone; abhivyaktiḥ – manifestation; vāsanānām – of tendencies within the mento-emotional energy.

Subsequently from those cultural activities there is development according to corresponding features only, bringing about the manifestation of the tendencies within the mento-emotional energy.

Analysis:

Everything in the material creation works according to innate tendency, manifesting according to time and place. Sometimes it takes millions of years before something can manifest or be given any type of satisfaction.

In terms of the time of the earth, modern civilization is recent. Still we see that the majority of people feel comfortable within the modern world. This is due to latent desires that are being fulfilled under the present circumstances.

Because a yogi has mystic insight, he understands how numberless different dispersals of energy arise in the mento-emotional force by its proximity to the spirit's sense of identity. Thus he withdraws that sense and deactivates the mundane consciousness, freeing himself from being a slave to desires which arise in the seat of feelings. Others, however, must comply with the urges.

Application:

Subsequently for those cultural activities of common people, there is development according to corresponding features only, bringing about the manifestation of the tendencies within the mento-emotional energy, which causes pleasant and unpleasant emotions to be experienced. The promise of pleasure always beckons, but displeasure inevitably tags along behind and imposes itself when one least expects. Still, in the hope of invoking pleasure's application, a person continues despite the frustrations.

Verse 9

जातिदेशकालव्यवहितानामप्यानन्तर्यं स्मृतिसंस्कारयोरेकरूपत्वात्॥ ९॥

jāti deśa kāla vyavahitānām api ānantaryaṁ smṛti saṁskārayoḥ ekarūpatvāt

jāti – status; deśa – location; kāla – time; vyavahitānām – of what is placed apart or separated; api – even, also; ānantaryaṁ – timeful sequence; smṛti – memory; saṁskārayoḥ – of the impressions formed of cultural activities; ekarūpatvāt – due to one form.

Even though circumstances are separated by status, location and time, still the impressions which form cultural activities and the resulting memories, are of one form and operate on a timely sequence.

Analysis:

This answers why past lives affect the present one, even though the individual may not recall the past. A different status, place and time, though separated from a cultural activity of the past, is in fact timeful and in sequence according to how it was entered into the memory within the mento-emotional energy. Something that subjectively makes sense may seem inappropriate to the conscious mind which takes into account only what it can grasp about the present. Irrespective of present circumstances, the memory and the urges from past lives operate in timeful sequence.

Application:

Even though circumstances are separated by status, location and time, still the impressions which form cultural activities and the resulting memories, are of one form and operate on a full time sequence. Thus all who are involved in worldly life meet with unfavorable circumstances and are fatigued by favorable occasions, that endorse the vices which utilize their sensual energies.

Verse 10

तासामनादित्वं चाशिषो नित्यत्वात्॥ १०॥

tāsām anāditvaṁ ca āśiṣaḥ nityatvāt

tāsām – those; anāditvaṁ – what is without beginning, primeval; ca – and; āśiṣaḥ – hope and desire energies; nityatvāt – what is eternal.

Those memories and impressions are primeval, without a beginning. Energies of hope and desire are eternal as well.

Analysis:

When a yogi sees that the hope and desire energies are eternal, he makes a decision to let them be and to detach himself from the urges. He must, by all means, separate himself from the mento-emotional force or remain a victim of it. The memories and the circumstance-forming impressions will remain for all eternity. A yogin has no choice but to extract his existence from this realm.

Application:

Those memories and impressions are primeval without a beginning. Hope and desire energies are eternal as well. Thus the proposal which makes sense, recommends a removal of the individual spirit from this unalterable environment.

Verse 11

हेतुफलाश्रयालम्बनैः सङ्गृहीतत्वादेषामभावे तदभावः॥ ११॥

hetu phala āśraya ālambanaiḥ saṅgṛhītatvāt eṣām abhāve tad abhāvaḥ

hetu – cause; phala – effect; āśraya – storage place, causal plane, supportive base; ālambanaiḥ – by what supports or lifts; saṅgṛhītatvāt – what holds together; eṣām – of those, these; abhāve – in what is not there; tad – them; abhāvaḥ – not existing.

They exist by what holds them together in terms of cause and effect, supportive base and lifting influence. Otherwise if their causes are not there, they have no existence.

Analysis:

For a yogi, his involvement is the supportive element, which makes the subtle material nature exist for him and engage his consciousness. Thus if he detaches himself from the supportive element of involvement, material nature no longer affects him.

Application:

The memories, the impressions, the hope and desire energies, exist by what holds them together in terms of what produced them and what they generate, as well as the supportive basis and the lifting influences which reinforce their production. Otherwise, if their causes were not in existence, they would not register. Thus without supernatural perception and action one cannot become freed from the influence. Hence the practice of kriyā *yoga is essential.*

Verse 12

अतीतानागतं स्वरूपतोऽस्त्यध्वभेदाद्धर्माणाम्॥ १२॥

atīta anāgataṁ svarūpataḥ
asti adhvabhedāt dharmāṇām

atīta – the past; anāgataṁ – the future; svarūpataḥ – true form; asti – there is, it exists; adhvabhedāt – due to different courses or events; dharmāṇām – of the characteristics.

There is a true form of the past and future, which is denoted by the different courses of their characteristics.

Analysis:

Patañjali confirms that the past and future are real existences, having contents which cause the present. The future already exists. It limits the expansion of the present. The past already exists. It forces the present into the future. Both past and future may be compared to the two jaws of a vice which constantly squeeze a new present into existence.

Time is not an illusion. Because of definite characteristics, there is a certain course which time takes from the past into the present and into the yet-emerging future. The inherent characteristics *(dharmāṇām)* from the past mold the future. The changes which come about in the present are stockpiled by time as the basis for slight or major differences which are to come.

Application:

There is a true form of the past and future, which is denoted by the different courses of their particular characteristics. One is subjected to the future unless one escapes from time's dominance.

Verse 13

ते व्यक्तसूक्ष्मा गुणात्मानः ॥ १३ ॥

te vyakta sūkṣmāḥ guṇātmānaḥ

te – they; vyakta – gross; sūkṣmāḥ – subtle; guṇātmānaḥ = guṇā – subtle material nature + ātmānaḥ – of itself.

They are gross or subtle, all depending on their inherent nature.

Analysis:

The three phases of time, past, present and future are perpetually in relationship with one another. They are reliant on inherent energies which comprise the subtle and gross material nature. A limited being cannot permanently affect these, even though he may take part in their operations according to how he is positioned in time and place.

Application:

The manifestations, which are to a greater degree preset, are gross or subtle, all depending on inherent nature.

Verse 14

परिणामैकत्वाद्वस्तुतत्त्वम् ॥ १४ ॥

pariṇāma ekatvāt vastutattvam

pariṇāma – transformation, change; ekatvāt – singleness, uniqueness; vastu – object; tattvam – essence, actual composition.

The actual composition of an object is based on the uniqueness of the transformation.

Analysis:

Each object, no matter how similar, has certain unique qualities which are based on the particular transformations which caused its production. The varieties in material nature are researched by a yogi. Underlying all this, he finds the manifesting force of time along with the inherent qualities of material nature, mixed in various ways.

Application:

The actual composition of an object is based on the uniqueness of the primeval transformation which produced it, but this can only be viewed supernaturally.

Verse 15

वस्तुसाम्ये चित्तभेदात्तयोर्विभक्तः पन्थाः ॥ १५ ॥

vastusāmye cittabhedāt tayoḥ vibhaktaḥ panthāḥ

vastu – object; sāmye – in the same; citta – mento-emotional energy; bhedāt – from the difference; tayoḥ – of these two; vibhaktaḥ – separated, divided; panthāḥ – ways of viewing, prejudices.

Because of a difference in the mento-emotional energy of two persons, separate prejudices manifest in their viewing of the very same object.

Analysis:

Separate prejudices lie dormant in the mento-emotional energy of each living entity. When viewing the same object with the same composition, persons react differently. These prejudices are sponsored in material nature by time which, with the power of the past, regulates the present and future.

Application:

Because of a difference in the prejudices of the mento-emotional energy of the two persons, separate opinions manifest in their viewing of the very same object. This is inevitable. Yogis should therefore agree to disagree, realizing that they have no choice since they perceive from various perspectives.

Verse 16

न चैकचित्ततन्त्रं वस्तु तदप्रमाणकं तदा किं स्यात्॥ १६ ॥

na ca ekacitta tantraṁ ced vastu
tat apramāṇakaṁ tadā kiṁ syāt

na – not, nor; ca – and; eka – one; citta – mento-emotional perception; tantraṁ – dependent; ced = cet – if, otherwise; vastu – object; tat – that; apramāṇakaṁ – not being observed; tadā – then; kiṁ – what; syāt – would occur.

An object is not dependent on one person's mento-emotional perception. Otherwise, what would happen if it were not being perceived by that person?

Analysis:

Śrī Patañjali refutes the idea that the world is dependent on a limited mind or on a group of such minds. Otherwise if that mind or those limited minds were to lose perception of an object, the item would no longer exist.

Application:

An object is not dependent on one person's view of it; otherwise what would happen if it were not being perceived by that viewer? Would it cease to exist? We find that this is not the case. What would be missing is the observer's influence, but the object would still exist free of that force, unless it were factual that the person created and maintained the object. Generally speaking that is not the case.

Verse 17

तदुपरागापेक्षित्वाच्चित्तस्य वस्तु ज्ञाताज्ञातम्॥ १७॥

taduparāga apekṣitvāt cittasya vastu jñāta ajñātam

tad = tat – that; uparāga – color, mood; apekṣitvāt – from the expectation; cittasya – of the mento-emotional energy; vastu – object; jñāta – known; ajñātam – unknown.

An object is known or unknown, all depending on the mood and expectation of the particular mento-emotional energy of the person in reference to it.

Analysis:

The application or non-application of consciousness is what brings objects into purview.

Application:

An object is known or unknown, all depending on the mood and expectation of the particular mental and emotional energy of the viewer in reference to it. Thus each person must endeavor separately and individually for liberation.

Verse 18

सदा ज्ञाताश्चित्तवृत्तयस्तत्प्रभोः पुरुषस्यापरिणामित्वात्॥ १८॥

sadā jñātāḥ cittavṛttayaḥ tatprabhoḥ puruṣasya apariṇāmitvāt

sadā – always; jñātāḥ – known; citta – mento-emotional energy; vṛttayaḥ – the operations; tat – that; prabhoḥ – of the governor; puruṣasya – of the spirit; apariṇāmitvāt – due to changelessness.

The operations of the mento-emotional energy are always known to that governor because of the changelessness of that spirit.

Analysis:

Here, *Patañjali* explained why the spirit appears to be affected by the operations of the mento-emotional energy of the psyche. The changelessness of the spirit serves as a background for movements within consciousness.

Application:

The operations of the mind and emotions are always conducted by empowerment taken from the governing spirit. This is because the spirit is a perpetual energy source. However, the spirit is usually bewildered and is entertained by the usage of its powers.

Verse 19

न तत्स्वाभासं दृश्यत्वात्॥ १९॥

na tat svābhāsaṁ dṛśyatvāt

na – not; tat – that; svābhāsaṁ – self-illuminative; dṛśyatvāt – for it is due to being something to be perceived.

That mento-emotional energy is not self-illuminative for it is rather only capable of being perceived.

Analysis:

The mento-emotional energy has for its nature the capability of being perceived but is not self-illuminative and cannot assess itself. This has to be studied objectively in meditation by the particular yogin.

Application:

The separation of the mind and emotions are not generated by the mind or the emotions. For these are only capable of being perceived by a real viewer. It is like a viewing instrument which cannot see for itself even though it is useful to the vision of a human being.

Verse 20

एकसमये चोभयानवधारणम्॥ २०॥

ekasamaye ca ubhaya anavadhāraṇam

ekasamaye – at the same time; ca – and; ubhaya – both; anavadhāraṇam – of what cannot focus.

It cannot execute the focus of both at the same time.

Analysis:

This means that the mento-emotional energy cannot both focus on itself and the seer at the same time. This can be verified in deep meditation.

Application:

It cannot by itself execute the focus of itself or something else. It is incapable of objectivity.

Verse 21

चित्तान्तरदृश्ये बुद्धिबुद्धेरतिप्रसङ्गः स्मृतिसङ्करश्च॥ २१॥

cittāntaradṛśye buddhibuddheḥ atiprasaṅgaḥ smṛtisaṅkaraḥ ca

cittāntara – dṛśye = citta – mento-emotional energy + antara – another person + dṛśye – in the perception of; buddhi-buddheḥ = buddhi – the intellect organ + buddheḥ – of the intellect organ; atiprasaṅgaḥ – absurd argument, unwarranted stretching of a rule or argument; smṛti – memory; saṅkaraḥ – confusion; ca – and.

In the perception of mento-emotional energy by another such energy, there would be an intellect perceiving another intellect independently. That would cause absurdity and confusion of memory.

Analysis:

Patañjali stated that it is absurd to think that without a spirit one's mind could perceive another mind. That is absurd. Unless there is a spirit linked to a mind, there would be no objective perception of mental energy.

Application:

If it were possible for the mind or emotions to view themselves, then one mind would perceive another mind independently without involvement with a spirit, or one emotional reserve would objectively interact with another in the same way. That is absurd.

Verse 22

चितेरप्रतिसङ्क्रमायास्तदाकारापत्तौ स्वबुद्धिसंवेदनम्॥ २२॥

citeḥ apratisaṁkramāyāḥ tadākārāpattau svabuddhisaṁvedanam

citeḥ – of the spirit; apratisaṁkramāyāḥ – not moving from one position to another; tad = tat = that; ākāra – form, aspect; āpattau – turning into, changing, assuming; sva – itself, oneself; buddhi – intellect organ; saṁvedanam – perception.

The perception of its own intellect occurs when it assumes that form in which there is no movement from one operation to another.

Analysis:

Until the mind is still and the mento-emotional energy ceases to fluctuate, one cannot perceive one's intellect objectively. Otherwise, one feels as though the self and the intellect are part of a homogeneous consciousness.

Application:

The perceptions of a spirit's intellect occur when the intellect operates to create an image but as soon as the image begins to dissolve, it seems as if the intellect itself vanishes.

Verse 23

द्रष्टृदृश्योपरक्तं चित्तं सर्वार्थम्॥ २३॥

draṣṭṛ dṛśya uparaktaṁ cittaṁ sarvārtham

draṣṭṛ - the perceiver; dṛśya – the perceived; uparaktaṁ – prejudiced; cittaṁ – mento-emotional energy; sarvārtham - what is all-evaluating.

The mento-emotional energy which is prejudiced by the perceiver and the perceived, is all-evaluating.

Analysis:

When the mento-emotional force absorbs energy from the spirit, as well as from an object, it fuses both sides in an all-evaluating manner. Thus the spirit becomes absorbed by its default operations of analysis, conclusion and action.

Application:

When the mental and emotional forces are quieted, they do not display a prejudiced reaction. Under these conditions, their biases remain dormant. But as soon as there is an activation of the urges, the predispositions are displayed. These are attitudes and responses which were created previously by interactions of the perceiver, his sense energy and what was perceived.

Verse 24

तदसङ्ख्येयवासनाभिश्चित्रमपि परार्थं संहत्यकारित्वात् ॥ २४ ॥

tat asaṅkhyeya vāsanābhiḥ citram
api parārthaṁ saṁhatyakāritvāt

tat – that; asaṅkhyeya – innumerable; vāsanābhiḥ – subtle impressions; citram – diversified; api – even, although; parārthaṁ – for another's sake; saṁhatya – because of it; kāritvāt – activity, force, factor.

Although the mento-emotional energy is diversified by innumerable subtle impressions, it acts for the sake of another power because of its proximity to that other factor.

Analysis:

Everything done by the mento-emotional energy, even those subtle actions which seem to imperil the spirit, is done for the sake of the spirit itself, even when the spirit may not deliberately motivate the psyche.

The proximity *(saṁhatya)* of the spirit is itself the cause of the innumerable moods and urges.

Application:

Although the mind and emotions seem to combine to exhibit habits and unique behaviors, still those exhibitions only entertain the perceiver. It is that seer whose radiant energy causes the activation. The mind and emotions absorb its energy to entertain it.

Verse 25

विशेषदर्शिन आत्मभावभावनाविनिवृत्तिः ॥ २५ ॥

viśeṣadarśinaḥ ātmabhāva bhāvanānivṛttiḥ

viśeṣa – distinction, specific perception; darśina – of the one who sees; ātma – the spirit; bhāva – feeling; bhāvanā – absorption in feelings; nivṛttiḥ – total stopping of the operations of the mento-emotional energy.

There is total stopping of the operations of mento-emotional energy for the person who perceives the distinction between feelings and the spirit itself.

Analysis:

This is repeated again and again in different verses. A yogin has to sort between the spirit and the mento-emotional energy. He has to overcome the proximity of the two, discern the linkages of the feelings to the spirit, and then isolate the spirit by stopping the mento-emotional operations.

Application:

When a person can distinguish between itself and its auxiliary shadow-self, its detachment or ability to distance itself from the sensuality, empowers the person to push away the creative urges which arise in the psyche.

Verse 26

तदा हि विवेकनिम्नङ्कैवल्यप्राग्भारञ्चित्तम्॥ २६॥

tadā hi vivekanimnaṁ kaivalya prāgbhāraṁ cittam

tadā – then; hi – indeed; viveka – discrimination; nimnaṁ – leaning towards, inclined to; kaivalya – total separation from the mundane psychology; prāg – towards; bhāraṁ – gravitating; cittam – mento-emotional force.

Then, indeed, the mento-emotional force is inclined towards discrimination and gravitates towards the total separation from the mundane psychology.

Analysis:

The yogi has to achieve this. It does not come by wishful thinking. Only through higher yoga can this be accomplished.

Application:

Then a strange but glorious observation is made. One notices that the troublesome and once hard-to-control mind and emotions begin acting cooperatively, as if to actually please the self and function as desired. It exhibits a habit of discrimination, losing its impulsive tendency. It gravitates towards total separation from the self, something which it resisted before.

Verse 27

तच्छिद्रेषु प्रत्ययान्तराणि संस्कारेभ्यः॥ २७॥

tat cchidreṣu pratyayāntarāṇi saṁskārebhyaḥ

tat – that; chidreṣu – in the relaxation of the focus; pratyayaḥ – conviction or belief as mind content, inlaid impression in the mento-emotional energy; antarāṇi – in between, interval; saṁskārebhaḥ – from the subtle impressions.

Besides that, in the relaxation of focus, other mind contents arise in the intervals. These are based on subtle impressions.

Analysis:

One should work through these emerging impulses without becoming disappointed or frustrated. One should not abandon the higher yoga practice. One faces challenges with every step but one must forge ahead. One must work for emancipation from the helpless alliance with the mento-emotional force. The main energy is the mind's content, which is deeply inlaid in the mento-emotional force as urge-producing impressions from the past. Some of these surface as memory and others surface as pictures or sound formation, and are then expanded into meaningful or meaningless images and sounds which can distract by keeping one occupied in the picture-sound show of the mind. A yogi continually fights this to gain self-conquest.

Application:

However, whenever the self relaxes vigilance, that now-cooperative psychology again repeats the old behaviors, which are based on previous subtle impressions.

Verse 28

हानमेषां क्लेशवदुक्तम् ॥ २८ ॥

hānam eṣāṁ kleśavat uktam

hānam – killing off, complete removal; eṣāṁ – of these; kleśavad = kleśavat – like the mento-emotional afflictions; uktam – authoritatively said.

As authoritatively stated, the complete removal of these is like the elimination of the mento-emotional afflictions.

Analysis:

It is a personal struggle. God is present but each yogi has to master this personally. As a neophyte becomes preoccupied removing all causes for the mental and emotional troubles, so the advanced yogi has to remove the mind content which poses a botheration and which the mind clings to automatically when it is relaxed from the proper focus.

Great yogis went before us. They can help us with this inner struggle. They encourage us to practice. They have shown the way by their personal lives on earth, and in some cases, by their current austerities in higher dimensions. Besides that, each yogi has to endure this inner conflict alone.

Application:

When the yogi applies an effective method to remove the old impressions, his resulting condition is exactly like that experienced when the mental and emotional afflictions are no longer actuated.

Verse 29

प्रसङ्ख्यानेऽप्यकुसीदस्य सर्वथा विवेकख्यातेर्धर्ममेघः समाधिः ॥ २९ ॥

prasaṁkhyāne api akusīdasya sarvathā vivekakhyāteḥ dharmameghaḥ samādhiḥ

prasaṁkhyāna – in the abstract meditation; api – even so; akusīdasya – of one who has no interest or sees no gain in material nature; sarvathā – in all ways; vivekakhyāteḥ – with super discrimination; dharmameghaḥ = dharma – nature's way of acting for beneficial results + meghaḥ – mento-emotional clouds of energy; samādhi – continuous effortless linkage of the attention to higher reality.

For one who sees no gains in material nature, even while perceiving it in abstract meditation, one has the super discrimination. One attains the continuous effortless linkage of the attention to higher reality which is described as knowing the mento-emotional clouds of energy which compel a person to perform according to nature's way of acting for beneficial results.

Analysis:

Dharmameghaḥ is usually translated as cloud *(meghaḥ)* of virtue *(dharma).* However we took hints from I. K. Taimni, where he stated that *dharma-meghaḥ samādhi*, means the final *samādhi* in which the yogi shakes himself free from the world of *dharmas* which obscure reality like a cloud.

He is, perhaps, the first commentator who thoroughly understood this particular verse of *Śrī Patañjali.* The key to this verse lies in the term *akusīdasya*. *Kusīda* means moneylender or any money lent at a rate exceeding 5%. When *"a"* is added as a prefix, it means not having any desire to gain or profit.

Śrīla Yogeshwarananda asked us to develop *paravairāgya*, or complete disinterest in this world. *Śrī Patañjali* specifically states that one has to lose interest in even the very subtle aspect of material nature, aspects which we encounter in deep meditation on other levels of reality. This is indicated by the term *prasaṁkhyāne* which means that one may see something of value in deep meditation, in which case one cannot develop the *paravairāgya* and one will not lose interest in the *dharmas* or ways of righteous living which are legated by material nature for different beings on different gross and subtle levels.

If we want to benefit in any way *(sarvathā)* from material nature and on any level, we will be attracted proportionally, and we will fall under the cloud *(megha)* of values *(dharmas)* which dictate how we should act to gain in the particular realm of our interest. This will keep us in the material world.

All yogis are forewarned by *Śrīla* Yogeshwaranada, who warned this writer in the same way, that the main obstacle is the desire for fame as a spiritual master. From that comes the idea that one should develop a territory where one can have his own kingdom with loyal disciples. Material nature will then show one a layout of values which one must adapt for success as a territorial spiritual master or god. This will cause a fall from grace.

Even though *Śrīla* Yogeshwarananda left behind many books, as well as ashrams and spiritual missions, still when I see him come down from the causal level where he is completing more austerities and research, I never see him with disciples. He is not interested in any of the rules, regulations or *dharmas* which are established for spiritual masters who want to be worshipped as exalted saviors or gurus.

Everything in the material world, in the subtle, super-subtle or gross parts of it, is dangerous. We should know this. Many people came to me to be disciples and suggested they become elevated so that they can help others. All of them are distracted and have questionable motives.

Application:

The super discrimination, the highest degree of disinterest, is achieved by one who sees no gain in material nature, even in very abstract but potent conditions. Such a person attains an insight whereby he perceives the mento-emotional clouds of energy which dictate the laws of responsibility. Subsequently, he can sidestep such obligations.

Verse 30

ततः क्लेशकर्मनिवृत्तिः ॥३०॥

tataḥ kleśa karma nivṛttiḥ

tataḥ – subsequently; kleśa – afflictions; karma – cultural activities; nivṛttiḥ – stoppage of the operation of the mento-emotional energy.

Subsequently there is stoppage of the operation of the mento-emotional energy in terms of generation of cultural activities and their resulting afflictions.

Analysis:

The meaning of *dharma-meghaḥ* in the preceding verse is now explained by the subsequent result of the stoppage of generation of cultural activities which are dictated by various types of *dharma* righteous lifestyle for particular results in the gross or subtle mundane world. None of these karmas or cultural activities is completely free from afflictions. Thus when the yogi reaches the causal level and sees the various clouds of energy *(meghaḥ)* in which the *dharmas* or laws for righteous life, are created and maintained, he gets relief in the higher yoga practice. He smiles for he will never again fall into the trap of making spiritual missions to help or to save others. Such things are a complete farce, and are very disgusting to one who has seen the reality as it is.

An example of a yogin who left aside such things is *Swāmī Satyānanda* of Bihar. He completed all duties given to him by his spiritual master, the great *Swāmī* Shivananda, but did not continue to be a guru in this world. He carefully and efficiently left that aside to proceed honestly with advancement. Such a person is neither selfish nor conceited. If anything, he is realistic.

Application:

Unless instructed by a divine being, a yogi stops the participation of his auxiliary shadow-self, which has the mind and emotions as its chief components. These are restrained from generating further cultural activities, thereby ending potential afflictions.

Verse 31

तदा सर्वावरणमलापेतस्य ज्ञानस्यानन्त्याज्ज्ञेयमल्पम्॥ ३१ ॥

tadā sarva āvaraṇa malāpetasya
jñānasya ānantyāt jñeyam alpam

tadā – then; sarva – all; āvaraṇa – mental darkness; mala – impurities; āpetasya – of what is removed; jñānasaya – of knowledge; ānantyāt – due to being unlimited; jñeyam – what is known; alpam – small trivial.

Then, because of the removal of all mental darkness and psychological impurities, that which can be known through the mento-emotional energy, seems trivial in comparison to the unlimited knowledge available when separated from it.

Analysis:

For this world, the mento-emotional energy is the linking agent. It is the means of prying into various things. It shows us how to be interested in and invest in this world for benefit. Once we become free from that energy, and we experience the self by itself, we no longer consider this world as being precious.

Application:

Resultantly, the yogin considers his former insights and feelings to be trivial, when compared to his newly-earned visions.

Verse 32

ततः कृतार्थानां परिणामक्रमसमाप्तिर्गुणानाम्॥ ३२॥

tataḥ kṛtārthānāṁ pariṇāmakrama samāptir guṇānām

tataḥ – thus; kṛtārthānāṁ – having done their purpose; pariṇāma – changes, alteration; krama – a step, succession, progression, process of development; samāptir = samāptiḥ – end conclusions; guṇānām – of the influence of the subtle material nature.

Thus, the subtle material nature, having fulfilled its purpose, its progressive alterations end.

Analysis:

This is only for the yogin who achieved isolation from his mento-emotional energies and their impulsive operations. For him, the natural power transfer from his spirit to the mento-emotional force ceases. For others, it continues just as before.

Application:

Thus the subtle material nature having served a useful purpose, its progressive alterations which sometimes perplexed and sometimes entertained the spirit, come to an end.

Verse 33

क्षणप्रतियोगी परिणामापरान्तनिर्ग्राह्यः क्रमः॥ ३३॥

kṣaṇa pratiyogī pariṇāma
aparānta nirgrāhyaḥ kramaḥ

kṣaṇa – moment; pratiyogī – corresponding, being a counter-part; pariṇāma – change, alteration; aparānta – the end; nirgrāhyaḥ – clearly perceived; kramaḥ – process.

The process, of which moments are a counterpart, and which causes the alterations, comes to an end and is clearly perceived.

Analysis:

The advanced yogi alone achieves this. This is an individual accomplishment, where the yogi sees the moments that, in sequence, comprise time which is itself the changing mundane energy *(guṇānām)*. The yogi clearly perceives this from afar. What hypnotizes other and keeps them under its control subjectively and objectively, is looked upon by the yogin, just as God would normally see it.

sa eṣaḥ pūrveṣām api guruḥ kālena anavacchedāt

> He, this particular person, being unconditioned by time is the guru even of the ancient teachers, the authorities from before. *(Yoga Sūtra 1.26)*

Some of what is natural for God becomes natural for the yogin who made that much endeavor and who completed the course of higher yoga described by *Śrī Patañjali Muni.*

Application:

The once free and own-way (aniruddha) *auxiliary self stops its mental, sensual and emotional dominance, and ceases those rhythmic displays which the self was once forced to enjoy or endure.*

Verse 34

पुरुषार्थशून्यानां गुणानां प्रतिप्रसवः कैवल्यं स्वरूपप्रतिष्ठा वा चितिशक्तिरिति॥ ३४॥

puruṣārtha śūnyānāṁ guṇānāṁ
pratiprasavaḥ kaivalyaṁ
svarūpapratiṣṭhā vā citiśaktiḥ iti

puruṣārtha – the aims of a human being; śūnyānāṁ – devoid of; guṇānāṁ – of the influences of material nature; pratiprasavaḥ – reabsorption, retrogression, neutralization; kaivalyam – separation of the spirit from psychology; svarūpa – own form; pratiṣṭhā – established; vā – thus, at last; citiśaktiḥ – the power of pure consciousness; iti – that is all.

Separation of the spirit from the mento-emotional energy (kaivalyam) occurs when there is neutrality in respect to the influence of material nature, when the yogi's psyche becomes devoid of the general aims of a human being. Thus at last, the spirit is established in its own form as the force empowering the mento-emotional energy.

Analysis:

This ends the description of higher yoga practice, given to us by *Śrī Patañjali*, an authority for all times. Undoubtedly, *Patañjali* covered the entire spectrum in the mystic practice of yoga. All glories unto him.

Application:

When one sheds off the human type of character which was a combination of mentality, sensuality and emotion, one gains neutrality in reference to the subtle material nature. That separation from the auxiliary self is established. Thus one discovers the segregated real self which empowers the auxiliary shadow character.

END

Glossary of Sanskrit Terms

A

abhāva – absence of awareness
abhāvaḥ – disappearance, elimination, n ot existing
abhāvāt – resulting from the elimination
abhāve – in what is not there
abhibhava – disappearance
abhijātasya – of what is produced, all around or transparent
ābhimata – what is dearly desired
abhiniveśaḥ – strong focus on mundane existence which is due to instinctive fear of death
abhivyaktiḥ – manifestation
ābhyantara – internal
abhyāsa – effective yoga practice
ādarśa – sight
ādayaḥ – and related matters
adhigamaḥ – accomplishment
adhimātraḥ – substantial
adhimātratvāt – from intense
adhiṣṭhātṛtvaṁ – authority, complete disaffection
adhvabhedāt – due to different courses or events
adhyāsāt – resulting from the super-imposition
adhyātma – relationship between the supreme soul and the limited one
ādi – and the related mystic skills
ādīni – and the same for other aspects
ādiṣi – and similar aspects
ādiṣu – and by related qualities
adṛṣṭa – not perceived, not realized
āgamāḥ – correct reference
ahiṁsā – non-violence
ajñāna – spiritual ignorance
ajñātam – unknown
akalpitā – not manufactured, not artificial, not formed
ākāra – form, aspect
akaraṇaṁ – non-responsiveness
ākāśa – atmosphere
ākāśayoḥ – of the sky, atmosphere
akliṣṭāḥ – non-troublesome
akramaṁ – without sequential perceptions
akṛṣnaṁ – not black, not penalizing
ākṣepī – transcending
akusīdasya – of one who has no interest or sees no gain in material nature
alabdhabhūmikatva – not being able to maintain the progress made
ālambanā – support, prop, means of conversion
ālambanaiḥ – by what supports or lifts
ālambanaṁ – taking recourse
ālasya – lack of energy
aliṅga – without characteristics
aliṅgāni – that which has no indication
āloka – supernatural insight
ālokaḥ – illuminating
alpam – small trivial
anabhighātaḥ – non-obstruction, no shrinking, no attacking, no botheration
anāditvaṁ – what is without beginning, primeval
anāgata – future
anāgataṁ – the future, what has not manifested
ānanda – introspective happiness
ananta – endless, infinite
ānantaryaṁ – timely sequence
ānantyāt – due to being unlimited
anāśayam – without harmful emotions
anaṣṭaṁ – not finished, still existing, effective
anātmasu – in what is not the spirit
anavacchedāt – due to or resulting from lack of definition, unconditioned
anavacchinnāḥ – not restricted by, not adjusted by
anavadhāraṇam – of what cannot focus
anavasthitatvāni – unsteadiness in the progression
anekeṣām– of what is numberless
aṅga – limbs, part
aṅgamejayatva – nervousness of the body
aṅgāni – parts of a thing
aṇima – minuteness

aniṣṭa – unwanted features of existence
anitya – not eternal, temporary
añj – to smear with, to mix with
añjanatā – assuming the nature of or characterization of
āntaḥ – ending, extending to
antar – internal, psychological, concerning the thinking and feeling organs
aṅgaṁ – part
antara – another person, other
antarāṇi – in between, interval
antarāya – obstacle
antardhānam – invisibility, non-perceptibility
anu – following along, patterning after
anubhūta – the experience
anugamāt – by accompaniment, occurring with
anuguṇānām – of the corresponding features
anukāraḥ – imitation, patterning, assuming
anumāna – correct analysis
anumāna – what is surmised or seasoned out
anumoditāḥ – endorsed, approved
anupātī – reach full retrogression, followed by
ānuśāsanam – explanation
anuśayi – connected to, devotedly attached to
ānuśravika – what is conjectured on the basis of scripture, valid
anuṣṭhānāt – from consistent practice
anuttamaḥ – supreme, the very best
anvaya – following, connection, distribution, association
anya – others
anyatā – other than distinct from
anyatā – otherwise, in a different manner
anyatvaṁ – otherness, difference
anyatve – in difference
aparāmṛṣṭaḥ – unaffected
aparānta – of the other end, of death entry into the hereafter, the end
aparigraha – non-possessiveness
apariṇāmitvāt – due to changelessness
āpattau – turning into, changing, assuming
apavarga – liberation
apekṣitvāt – from the expectation
āpetasya – of what is removed
api – also, even, although, but
apramāṇakaṁ – not being observed
apratisaṁkramāyāḥ – not moving from one position to another
aprayojakaṁ – not used, not employed, not causing
apuṇya – demerits, vice
āpūrāt – due to filling up or saturation
ariṣṭebhyo – from portents
artha – purpose, objective, meaning
ārtham – for the sake of, value or purpose
arthaś – for the value of purpose
arthavāt – because of an object
arthavatava – purpose, value
arthavatva – value, worth
asaṁkīrṇayoḥ – of what is distinct or separate
asaṁpramoṣaḥ – retention
asaṁprayoge – in not contacting, on not contacting
asaṁsargaḥ – non-association, lack of desire to associate
āsana – body postures
āsanan – bodily posture
asaṅgaḥ – non-contact
asaṅkhyeya – innumerable
āsannaḥ – whatever is very near, what will occur soon
āśayaḥ – storage, reservoir
āśayaiḥ – by subconscious motivations
āsevitaḥ – sustained practice, aggressive interest
āśiṣaḥ – hope and desire energies
asmitā – identification, misplaced identity
asmitā – sense of identity which is developed in relation to material nature
asmitārūpa – I-ness, self-consciousness
āśraya – storage place, causal plane, supportive base
āśryatvam – what serves as a support for something else
aṣṭau – eight
asteya – non-stealing
asti – there is, it exists
aśuci – not clean, not pure

aśuddhi – impurity
aśukla – not white, not rewarding
āsvāda – taste
asya – of his, him
atadrūpa – not this form
atha – now
atiprasaṅgaḥ – absurd argument, unwarranted stretching of a rule
atīta – the past
ātma – spirit
ātmakaṁ – self, nature
ātmānaḥ – of itself
atyanta – excessively, extremely, very
auṣadhi – drugs
āvaraṇam – covering, mental darkness
avasthā – condition
avasthānam – is situated
āveśaḥ – entrance, penetration
avidyā – spiritual ignorance
aviplavā – unbroken, continuous
avirati – proneness to sensuality
aviṣayī – not an object of anything, imperceptible
aviśeṣa – what is regular
aviśeṣaḥ – not distinct, inability to distinguish
avyapadeśya – what is not to be defined, what is latent
āyuḥ – duration of life

B

bādhane – in annoyance or disturbance
bahiḥ – outside, external
bahiraṅga – external part
bāhya – external
bala – mystic force, strength
balāni – powers
baleṣu – by strength
bandha – bondage
bandhaḥ – confinement, restriction
bhāraṁ – gravitating
bhāva – states of feelings and perceptions, inherent nature, psychology
bhāvaḥ – mento-emotional energy, feeling
bhāvanā – absorption in feelings, producing
bhāvanam – manifesting, imagining, conceiving, considering
bhāvanātaḥ – abstract meditation
bhedaḥ – splitting, removing, disintegrating
bhedāt – from the difference
bhede – in the difference
bhoga – experience
bhogāḥ – type of experience
bhrāntidarśana – mistaken views
bhūmiḥ – ground, foundation, basis, territory, range
bhūmiṣu – in stages
bhūta – the various states of matter, mundane elements, creature
bhūtatvāt – the actual object
bhuvana – the solar system
bīja – seed, origin, source
bījam – origin
brahmacarya – sexual non-expressiveness which results in the perception of spirituality
buddheḥ – of the intellect organ
buddhi – the intellect organ

C

ca – and
cakre – on the energy gyrating center
cakṣuḥ – vision
candre – on the moon or moon-god
caturthaḥ – the fourth
ced (cet) – if, otherwise
cetana – sense consciousness
chidreṣu – in the relaxation of the focus
citeḥ – of the spirit
citiśaktiḥ – the power of pure consciousness
citram – diversified
citta – mento-emotional energy
cittam – mento-emotional force
cittāni – regions within the mento-emotional energy
cittasya – of the mento-emotional energy
cittavikṣepaḥ – scattered mental and emotional energy

D

darśana – sight, vision, what is seen
darśanam – the view of
darśina – of the one who sees
daurmanasya – of mental depression
deśa – location, place
deśaiḥ – by what location

dhāraṇā – linking of the attention to a concentration force or person
dharma – attributes, functions, quality, law, sustaining force
dharma – nature's way of acting for beneficial results
dharmāṇām - of the characteristics
dharmī – most basic condition
dhruve – on the Pole Star
dhyāna – effortless linkage of the attention to higher concentration forces
dhyānajam – produced by the effortless linkage of the attention to a higher reality
dhyānam – effortless linking of the attention to a higher concentration force or person
dhyānāt – from effortless linkage of the mind to a higher concentration force
dīrgha – long
dīrgha – prolonged
divyaṁ – divine, supernatural
doṣa – fault, defect
draṣṭā – the perceiver
draṣṭṛ – the observer
dṛḍha – firm
drg (drk) – supernatural vision
dṛśeḥ – of the perceiver
dṛśi – perception, consciousness
dṛṣṭa – what is seen or perceived directly
dṛśya – the perceived
dṛśyam – what is perceived
dṛśyasya – of what is seen
dṛśyatvāt – for it is due to being something to be perceived
dṛśyayoḥ – of what is perceived
dṛśye – in the perception of
duḥka – distress
duḥkhaiḥ – with distress
duḥkham – distress
dvandvāḥ – the dualities of happiness and distress, heat and cold
dveṣa – impulsive emotional disaffection

E

eka – one
ekāgra – ability to link the attention to one concentration force or person
ekāgratā – of what is in front of one aspect before the attention
ekāgratayoḥ – of the one aspect before the attention
ekam – one
ekarūpatvāt – due to one form
ekasamaye – at the same time
ekātmatā – having one nature, identical
ekatra – in one place, all taken together as one practice
ekatānatā – one continuous threadlike flow of attention
ekatvāt – singleness, uniqueness
eṣaḥ – this particular person
eṣām – of those, these
etaya – by this
etena – by this
eva – only, alone, indeed

G

gamanam – going through, passing through
gati – course of heavenly planets and stars, the flow
grahaṇa – flow perception, sensual grasping
grahītṛ – perceiver
grāhya – appropriating, grasping, sensual perceptiveness
grāhyeṣu – in what is perceived
guṇa – influences of material nature
guṇānām – of the influence of the subtle material nature
guruḥ – the spiritual teacher

H

hana – avoidance
hānam – killing off, complete removal, withdrawal, escape
hasti – elephant
hetuḥ – cause, reason
hetutvāt – that which causes
heya – that which is to be avoided
heyāḥ – what is fit to be abandoned or left aside
heyaṁ – that which is to be avoided

hi – indeed
hiṁsa – violence
hlāda – happiness
hṛdaye – on the samyam, on the causal body

I

indriya – sense organs, sensual energy
indriyajayaḥ – the mastery of the sensual energy by psychological control
indriyāṇām – of the senses
indriyeṣu – by the sensual energy
irtareṣām – for others
iṣṭadevatā - cherished divine being
Īśvara – Supreme Lord
itaratra – at other times
itareṣām – for others
itaretara – one for the other
iti – that is all, thus, subsequently
iva – as if, as it were, seems to be, like

J

jāḥ – what is produced from
jala – water
janma – birth, particular species
japaḥ – murmuring
jāti – species, status of life, category
jaya – conquest
jāyante – is produced
jayāt – from the conquest of, from the mastery
jñāna – knowledge
jñānadīptiḥ – radiant organ of perception
jñānam – information, knowledge
jñānasaya – of knowledge
jñāta – known
jñeyam – what is known
jugupsā – aversion, disgust
jvalanam – shining, burning, blazing, with fiery glow
jyotisi – on the shinning light
jyotiṣmatī – spiritually luminous

K

kaivalya – total separation from the mundane psychology
kaivalyam – separation of the spirit from psychology
kāla – time
kālena – by time
kaṇṭaka – thorns
kaṇṭha – throat
karaṇa – cause, causing, creating, making
kārita – cause to be done
kāritvāt – activity, force
karma – cultural activities, action
karuṇā – compassion
kathaṁtā – how, the reason for
kāya – body, subtle body
khyāteḥ – insight
khyāteḥ–of a thorough awareness
khyāti– the discriminating faculty of the intellect
khyātiḥ – what is known or identified, insight
kiṁ – what
kleśa – mento-emotional afflictions, troubles
kleśavad – like the mento-emotional afflictions
kliṣṭā – agonizing
krama – a step, succession, progression, process of development
kramaḥ – process
kramayoḥ – on the sequence
kriyā – action
kriyāyogaḥ – dynamic yoga practice
krodha – anger
kṛt – fulfilled, done
kṛta – done
kṛtārthānāṁ – having done their purpose
kṣaṇa – moment
kṣaya – decrease
kṣayaḥ – dissipation, removal
kṣayāt – from the elimination
kṣaye – on elimination
kṣetram – field, existential environment
kṣetrikavat – like a farmer
kṣīṇa – great reduction
kṣīyate – is dissipated
kṣut – hunger
kūpe – on the gullet
kūrma – tortoise, a particular subtle nerve

L

lābhaḥ – what is gained, obtained
laghu – light
lakṣaṇa – individual characteristics, shape
lāvaṇya – charm
liṅgamātra – a mark, that which is indicated

lobha – greed

M

madhya – mediocre
mahā – great
mahatva – largeness, cosmic proportions
mahāvratam – great commitment
maitrī – friendliness
mala – impurities
manasaḥ – of the mind
maṇeḥ – of a gem
manojavitvaṁ – swiftness of mind, rapidity
mantra – special sound
mātra – only, merely
mātraḥ – measure or extent
mātrasya – only
mātrāt – from that only
meghaḥ – mento-emotional clouds of energy
mithyājñānam – false information
moha – delusion
mṛdu – minor, slight
muditā – joyfulness, cheerfulness
mūlaḥ – root, cause
mūle – in the cause
mūrdha – the head

N

na – not, nor
nābhi – navel
nāḍyāṁ – on the nadi or subtle nerve
nairantarya – uninterrupted, continuous
naṣṭam – destroyed, non-existent, non-effective
nibandhanī – bond, fusion
nidrā – sleep
nimittaṁ – cause, motive, apparent cause
nimnaṁ – leaning towards, inclined to
niratiśayaṁ – unsurpassed
nirbhāsā – shining
nirbhāsaṁ – illuminating
nirbījaḥ – not motivated by the mento-emotional energy
nirbījasya – not motivated by the mento-emotional energy
nirgrāhyaḥ – clearly perceived
nirmāṇa – producing, creating, measuring, fabricating
nirodha – restraint, cessation, suppression, non-operation
nirodhāt – resulting from that non-operation
nirodhe – on the non-operation
nirupakramaṁ – dormant, destined
nirvicāra – non-investigative linkage
nirvitarka – fusion or linkage without deliberation or analysis
nitya – eternal
nityatvāt – what is eternal
nivṛttiḥ – cessation, suppression
niyama – recommended behaviors
nyāsāt – from placing or applying

P

pañcatayyaḥ – fivefold
paṅka – mud
panthāḥ – ways of viewing, prejudices
para – another, of others
parair – with others
paraṁ – highest (non-interest)
paramā – highest, greatest
parārthaṁ – for another's sake
parārthatvāt – what is apart from another thing
paridṛṣṭah – measured, regulated
pariṇāma – transformation, change, alteration
pariśuddhau – on complete purification
paritāpa – distress
parvāṇi – phases, stages, parts
paryavasānam – termination
paśyaḥ – what is perceived
phala – effect
phalāḥ – results
pipāsā – thirst
prabhoḥ – of the governor
pracāra – channel flow
pracchardana – exhalation
pradhānah – subtle matter
prādurbhāvaḥ – coming into existence, manifesting
prāg – towards
prajñā – insight
prajñābhyām – from the two methods of insight
prakāśa – clear perception, light
prakṛiti – subtle material nature
prakṛtilayānām – of those who are diffused into subtle material nature

prakṛtīnāṁ – of the subtle material energy
pramāda – inattentiveness
pramāṇa – correct perception
pramāṇāni – true perception, correct perception
prāṇasya – of the vital energy
praṇavaḥ – the sacred syllable āuṁ (Oṁ)
prāṇāyāma – breath enrichment of the subtle body
praṇidhānāni – profound religious meditation
praṇidhānāt – derived from profound religious meditation
prānta – boundary or edge
prāntabhūmiḥ – stage
prasādaḥ – clarity and serenity
prasādanam – serenity
prasaṁkhyāna – in the abstract meditation
prasaṅgāt – due to association, due to endearing friendliness
praśānta – spiritual peace
prasava – expressing, going outwards
prasupta – dormant
praśvāsayoḥ – of the exhalation
prati – opposing, reverting back, toward
pratibandhī – the preventer, that which effectively suppresses something
prātibha – the shining organ of divination
prātibhāt – resulting from samyama on the shinning organ of divination
pratipakṣa – what is opposite or contrary
pratipattiḥ – perception
pratiprasavaḥ – re-absorption, retrogression, neutralization
pratiṣedha – removal
pratiṣṭhā – established
pratiṣṭham – positioned, based
pratiṣṭhāyāṁ – on being firmly established
pratiyogī – corresponding, being a counter-part
pratyāhar – sensual energy withdrawal
pratyāhāraḥ – withdrawal of sensual energy and its focus on the mind
pratyak – backwards, inwards, in the opposite direction
pratyakṣa – direct but correct perception
pratyayah – conviction or belief as mental content, instinctive interest
pratyayaḥ – mental content, objective awareness within the psyche
pratyayānām – pertaining to the mind content, convictions, idea
pratyayasya – of the mind content
pravibhāga – differentiation, sorting, classification, mental clarity
pravṛtti – destined activity, the force of cultural activity
pravṛtti – frantic activity, dispersal of energy
pravṛttiḥ – the operation
prayatna – effort
prayaya – objective awareness, opinions and motives of mind content
prayojakaṁ – very, much used or employed
punaḥ – again
puṇya – merits, virtue
puruṣa – of the spiritual person, individual spirit
puruṣārtha – the aims of a human being
puruṣasya – of the spirit
pūrva – before, previous
pūrvakaḥ – caused by, proceeded by, previously practiced
pūrveṣām – of those before, the ancient teachers

R

rāga – a tendency of emotional attachment, craving
rasa – essence
ratna – gems, precious things
ṛtaṁbharā – reality-perceptive, truth discerning
rūḍho – developed, produced
rūpa – form
ruta – sound, cry, yell, language

S

śabda – sound
śabdādi – sound and the related sensual pursuits
śabdajñāna – written or spoken information
sabījaḥ – with motivation from the mento-emotional energy
sadā – always

sādhāraṇatvāt – common, normal, universal
sah – he, that
sahabhuvaḥ – occurring with the symptoms
śaithilyāt – due to relaxation, collapse
sākṣātkaraṇāt – from causing to be visibly present, direct, intuitive
śakti – power, potency, energy
śaktyoḥ – of the two potencies
sālambanaṁ – leaning on, resting on, support
samādhi – continuous effortless linkage of the attention to a higher concentration force or person
samāna – digestive energy
samāpatteḥ – of meeting, of linking
samāpattibhyām – meeting, encounter
samāpattiḥ – linkage fusion
samāptir – end conclusions
samaya – condition
saṁbandha – relationship
saṁbodhaḥ – full or correct perception
saṁhananatvāni – definiteness, hardness
saṁhatya – because of it
saṁjñā – consciousness, demeanor, mind-set
saṁkāra – impression
saṁkhyābhiḥ – with numbering, accounting
saṁpat – wealth, prosperity, perfection
saṁprajñātaḥ – the observational linkage of the attention to a higher concentration force
saṁprayogaḥ – intimate contact
saṁśaya – doubt
saṁskāra – impression in the mento-emotional energy
saṁskārāt – from the impressions derived
saṁskārayoḥ – of the impressions formed of cultural activities
saṁskārebhaḥ – from the subtle impressions
saṁvedanam – perception
saṁvedanāt – from knowing
saṁvegānām – regarding those who practice forcibly
saṁvit – thorough insight
saṁyamād – from the complete restraint of the mento-emotional energy
saṁyamah – complete restraint
saṁyamāt – from the complete restraint of the mento-emotional energy
sāmye – on being equal, in the same
saṁyoga – conjunction
saṁyogo – the indiscriminate association
saṅga – association
saṅgṛhītatvāt – what holds together
saṅkaraḥ – confusion, intermixture
saṅkīrṇā – blending together, mixed
sannidhau – presence, vicinity
śānta – tranquilized, settled, subsided, collapsed
saṅtoṣa – contentment
saṅtoṣāt – from contentment
saptadhā – seven fold
śarīra – body
sārūpyam – with the same format, conformity
sarva – all
sārvabhaumāḥ – relating to all standard stages, being standard
sarvajña – all knowing
sarvajñātṛtvaṁ – all knowledge, intuition
sarvam – everything, all reality
sarvārtham - what is all evaluating
sarvārthatā – varying objective
sarvathā – in all ways
sati – being accomplished, there is existing
satkāra – reverence, care attention
sattva – clarifying perception of material nature
sattva – intelligence energy of material nature
satya – realism
śauca – purification
śaucāt – from purification
saumanasya – concerning benevolence
savicāra – investigative linkage of one's attention to a higher concetration force
savitarkā – thoughtfulness, reasoning, deliberation
śeṣaḥ – what is remaining
siddha – the perfected being
siddhayaḥ – mystic perfectional skills
siddhiḥ – perfection, skill

śīlaṁ – form, disposition
smaya – fascination, wonderment
smṛtayaḥ – memory
smṛti – memory
sopakramaṁ – set about, undertaken, already operative
śraddhā – confidence
śrāvaṇa – hearing
śrotra – hearing sense
śrotram – hearing sense
śruta – what is heard
stambha – restrained, suppressed, restrictive
stambhe – on the suspension
sthairyam – steadiness
sthairye – in the consistent
sthāni – the place a yogi would attain if his material body dies
sthira – steady
sthitau – regarding steadiness or persistence
sthiti – stability, steadiness
stūla – gross form
styāna – idleness
śuci – pure
śuddaḥ – purity
śuddhi – purification
sukha – happiness
sukham – comfortable
sūkṣma – subtle
sūkṣmaḥ – subtle energies, hardly noticeable
śunya – devoid of
śūnyam – empty, void, lacking
śūnyānāṁ – devoid of
sūrye – on the sun-god or the sun planet
sva – own nature, own psyche, itself, oneself
svābhāsaṁ – self-illuminative
svādhyāya – study of the psyche
svādhyāyāt – from study of the psyche
svāmi – the master, the individual self
svapna – dream
svarasavāhī – it's own flow of energy of self preservation
svārtha – one's own, self interest
svarūpa – own form
svarūpataḥ – true form
svarūpe – in his own form
śvāsa – inhalation
śvāsapraśvāsāḥ – labored breathing
syāt –would occur

T

tā – they
tad – that
tadā – then
tadarthabhābanam – that value with deep feelings
tadeva – that only, alone
tānatā – thread of fiber
tantraṁ – dependent
tanū – thinking reducing
tāpa – strenuous endeavor
tapaḥ – austerity
tārā – stars
tārakaṁ – crossing over, transcending
tāsām – those
tasmin – on this
tasya – of it, of this, of him, of his
tat – that
tataḥ – hence, subsequently
tatha – just as, so it is
tatra – there, in that location
tatstha – basis foundation
tattva – standard method in pursuit of reality
tattvam – essence, actual composition
tayoḥ – of these two
te – these, they
tīvra – very intense
traya – threefold
trayam – three
trividham – three-fold
tu – but, except
tūla – cotton fluff
tulya – similar
tulyayoḥ – of two similar types
tyāgaḥ – abandonment

U

ubhaya – both
udāna – air which rises from the throat and enters the head
udārāṇām – expanded
udayau – and increase
udita – emergent
uditau – and agitated, emerging
uktam – authoritively said, described
upalabdhi – obtaining experience
upanimantraṇe – on being invited

uparāga – color, mood
uparaktaṁ – prejudiced
upasargāḥ – impediments
upasthānam – approaching, waiting upon
upāyaḥ – means, method
upekṣaṇam – indifference, neutrality, non-responsiveness
utkrāntiḥ – rising above
utpannā – produced, brought about
uttareṣāṁ – of the other afflictions

V

vā – thus, at last, or
vācakaḥ – what is denoted or named
vāhī – flow current, instinct for self-preservation
vāhita – flow
vaira – hostility
vairāgyābhyāṁ – non-interest, a total lack of concern, non-interference
vairāgyam – non-interest
vairāgyāt – from a lack of interest
vaiśāradye – on gaining competence
vaitṛṣṇyam – freedom from desire
vajra – diamond-like, infallible
varaṇa – impediments, obstacles
vārtāḥ – smell
vāsanābhiḥ – subtle impressions
vāsanānām – of tendencies within the mento-emotional energy
vaśīkāra – through control
vaśīkāraḥ – mastery of the psyche
vastu – object
vastuśūnyaḥ – devoid of reality, without reality
vaśyatā – subdued, subjugation, control
vedana – touching
vedanīyaḥ – what is experienced or realized
vi – parting away from, dispersing
vibhaktaḥ – separated, divided
vicāra – deliberation, reflection
vicchedaḥ – the separation
vicchina – alternating, periodic
videhā – bodiless state
vidhāraṇābhyāṁ – by inhalation
viduṣaḥ – the wise man
vikalpa – imagination
vikalpaiḥ – with option, alternative, doubt, uncertainty
vikṣepa – distraction
viniyogaḥ – application, employment, practice
vipāka – development, fruition
vipākaḥ – what is resulting
viparyaya – incorrect perception
viprakṛṣṭa – remote
virāma – losing track of, dropping
virodhāt – resulting from confrontation or clashing aspects
vīrya – vigor, stamina
viṣayā – object
viṣayaṁ – an object or person
viṣayaṁ – subtle and gross mundane objects
viṣayāṇāṁ – relating to attractive objects
viṣayatvaṁ – what is concerning the nature of gross objects
viṣayavatī – like normal sensuality, something different but similar to a normal object
viśeṣa – distinction, specific perception
viśeṣaḥ – rating
viśokāh – sorrowless
vīta – without
vitarka – doubt, argument, analysis
vitṛṣṇasya – of one who does not crave
viveka – discrimination
vivekajaṁ – the distinction caused by subtle discrimination
vivekakhyāteḥ – with super discrimination
vivekinaḥ – the discriminating person
vṛttayaḥ – vibrational modes of the mento-emotional energies
vṛtteḥ – concerning the mento-emotional operations
vṛtti – vibrational mode of the mento-emotional energy
vṛttiḥ – activity, movement, operation
vyādhi – disease
vyākhyātā – explained
vyākhyātāḥ – is described
vyakta – gross
vyavahita – concealed
vyavahitānām – of what is placed apart or separated
vyūha – arrangement, layout, system
vyutthāna – expression
vyutthāne – in expressing, going outwards, rising up

Y

yama – moral restraints
yatha – as, according
yatnaḥ – endeavor
yoga – yoga process
yogaḥ – the skill of yoga
yogānuśāsanam – yoga and its practice
yoginaḥ – of the yogis
yogyatā – being conducive for abstract meditation
yogyatvāni – being fit for yoga or abstract meditation

Index to Verses: Selected Sanskrit Words

A

abhiniveśaḥ 2.9
abhyāsaḥ 1.32
adhyātmaprasādaḥ 1.47
ahiṁsā 2.30, 35
āloka 3.27
ānantyāt 4.31
anāśayam 4.6
anavadhāraṇam 4.20
aṇimādi 3.46
antaraṅgaṁ 3.7
antardhānam 3.21, 22
anuguṇānām 4.8
aparigrahāḥ 2.30
āsana 2.29, 46
asmitā 2.6, 3.48
asmitāmātrāt 4.4
asteya 2.30
ātmabhāva 4.25
ātmadarśana 2.41
auṣadhi 4.1
āvaraṇam 2.52; 4.31
avidyā 2.4, 5, 24
āvivekakhyāteḥ 2.28

B

bahiraṅgaṁ 3.8
bhāvanānivṛttiḥ 4.25
'bhiniveśaḥ 2.9
bhogāḥ 2.13
bhogāpavargārthaṁ 2.18
brahmacarya 2.30, 38
buddhibuddheḥ 4.21

C

candre 3.28
citeḥ 4.22
citiśaktiritiṁ 4.34
cittabhedāt 4.15
cittam 4.5, 23, 26
cittāntaradṛśye 4.21
cittasaṃvit 3.35
cittavikṣepaḥ 1.30
cittavṛtti 1.2

D

deśa 3.1; 4.9
dhāraṇā 2.29; 3.1
dhāraṇā 3.1
dhāraṇāsu 2.53
dharmameghaḥ 4.29
dharmī 3.14
dhruve 3.29
dhyāna 2.29; 3.2
dhyānaheyāḥ 2.11
dhyānajam 4.6
dhyānāt 1.39
draṣṭā 2.20
draṣṭṛ 4.23
draṣṭuḥ 1.3
dṛg 2.6
dṛśya 4.23
dṛśyatvāt 4.19
dvandvāḥ 2.48
dveṣaḥ 2.8

E

ekacitta 4.16
ekāgra 2.41
ekāgratāpariṇāmaḥ 3.12
ekasamaye 4.20

F,G

guṇānām 4.32, 34
guṇaparvāṇi 2.19
guṇātmānaḥ 4.13
guṇavṛtti 2.15
guruḥ 1.26

H

hānam 4.28
hṛdaye 3.35

I

indriyajaya 2.41
iṣṭadevatā 2.44, 45
Īśvara 1.23, 24
Īśvarapraṇidhānāni 2.32, 45

J

janma 4.1
japaḥ 1.28
jāti 4.9

jātyantara 4.2
jñānadīptiḥ 2.28
jyotiṣmatī 1.36

K

kaivalyam 2.25; 3.34, 51, 56; 4.26
kāla 4.9
kaṇṭhakūpe 3.31
karma 3.15, 23; 4.7, 30
karmāśayaḥ 2.12
kāya 2.43; 3.21, 43
kāyasaṁpat 3.47
khyātimātrasya 3.50
kleśa 2.2; 4.30
kleśavat 4.28
kriyā 2.18
kriyāyogaḥ 2.1
krodha 2.34
kṣaṇa 3.53
kṣetram 2.4
kūrmanāḍyāṃ 3.32

L, M

lobha 2.34
mahāvidehā 3.44
mahāvratam 2.31
manasaḥ 2.53
mantra 4.1
moha 2.34
mūrdhajyoti 3.33

N, O

nābhicakre 3.30
nimittaṁ 4.3
nirbījaḥ 1.51; 3.8
nirmāṇacittān 4.4
nirodhaḥ 1.2, 51; 3.9
nirvicāra 1.44, 47
nirvitarka 1.43
nivṛttiḥ 3.31; 4.30
niyama 2.29, 32
nyāsāt 3.27

P

panthāḥ 4.15
paraśarīrāveśaḥ 3.39
pariṇāmāḥ 3.13,15; 4.2, 14
pradhānajayaḥ 3.49
prāgbhāraṁ 4.26
prajñā 1.48; 2.27
prajñālokaḥ 3.5
prakāśa 2.18, 52; 3.21, 44
prakṛtyāpūrāt 4.2
prāṇasya 1.34
praṇavaḥ 1.27
prāṇāyāma 2.29, 49
praṇidhānāt 1.23
prasaṁkhyāne 4.29
prasaṅgāt 3.52
praśāntavāhita 3.10
prātibhāt 3.34, 37
pratipattiḥ 3.54
pratiprasavaḥ 4.34
pratyāhāra 2.29, 54
pratyakcetana 1.29
pravṛitti 3.27; 4.5
pravṛtti 4.5
Puruṣārthaśūnyānāṁ 4.34
puruṣaviśeṣaḥ 1.24

R

rāgaḥ 2.7
ṛtaṁbharā 1.48

S

sabījaḥ 1.46
sākṣātkaraṇāt 3.18
samādhiḥ
1.46, 51; 2.2, 29; 3.3, 38; 4.29
samādhipariṇāmaḥ 3.10
samādhisiddhiḥ 2.45
samāpattIḥ 1.42; 2.47
samāptir 4.32
saṁbodhaḥ 2.39
saṁprayogaḥ 2.44, 45
saṁskāraḥ 1.50; 2.15; 3.9, 10; 4.27
saṁyamaḥ
3.4, 16, 17, 27, 42, 43, 45, 48, 53
saṁyogaḥ 2.17, 23, 25
saṅtoṣa 2.32, 42
sattva puruṣa 3.50, 56
sattvaśuddhi 2.41
satya 2.30
satyapratiṣṭhāyāṁ 2.36
śauca 2.32, 40
savicāra 1.44
siddhadarśanam 3.33
siddhiḥ 2.43; 3.38; 4.1
śrotram 3.42
śuddhi 3.56
sūkṣmāḥ 2.10, 50; 3.27; 4.13
sūrye 3.27

sva svāmiśaktyoḥ 2.23
svābhāsaṁ 4.19
svādhyāya 2.1, 32, 44, 45
svapna 1.38
svarūpa 1.3; 2.23; 3.45, 48
svarūpapratiṣṭhā 4.34
svarūpaśūnyam 3.3
svarūpataḥ 4.12

T, U

tantraṁ 4.16
tapaḥ 2.1, 32; 4.1
tapasaḥ 2.43
upasargāḥ 3.3

V

vairatyāgaḥ 2.35
vāsanānām 4.8
vastusāmye 4.15
vastutattvam 4.14
vibhaktaḥ 4.15
viniyogaḥ 3.6
virodhāt 2.15
viśeṣadarśinaḥ 4.25
vitarkaḥ 2.34
vivekajaṁ 3.55
vivekakhyātiḥ 2.26; 4.29
vivekanimnaṁ 4.26
vivekinaḥ 2.15
vṛttiḥ 1.2, 4; 3.44
vyakta 4.13
vyutthāna 3.9

W, X, Y,.Z

yama 2.29, 30
yogā 2.28
yogaḥ 1.1
yoginaḥ 4.7
yogyatā 2.53
yogyatvāni 2.41

Index to Verses: Selected English Words

A

absurdity, 4.21
afflictions,
  defined, 2.2
  elimination, 4.28
  reduction, 2.2
  stages, 2.4
air, 3.40
analysis, 1.7, 17
anger, 2.34
atmosphere, 3.43
attachment, 2.3
aum, 1.27, 28
austerity, 2.1; 4.1
  recommended, 2.32
  results, 2.43

B

beautiful form, 3.47
behavior, see recommended behavior
benevolence, 2.41
birth,
  perception of, 2.39
  realized/non-realized, 2.12
  skills attained by, 4.1
  species, 2.12
bodiless state, 3.44
body,
  layout, 3.30
  possession of another's, 3.39
  sky, 3.43
bondage, 3.39
breath enrichment, 2.29
breath regulation, 2.49-51
breathing, labored type, 1.31

C

causal body, 3.35
cause and effect, 4.11
celibacy, 2.30
  -also see sexual non-expressiveness
charm, 3.47
cheerfulness, 1.33
circumstances, 4.9
clairvoyance, 3.19
clashing aspects, 2.15
clouds of energy, 4.29
compassion, 1.33
competence, 1.47
condition,
  basic type, 3.14
  moral restraint, 2.31
confidence 1.20
conjunction, 2.23-25
contentment, 2.32, 42
conviction, 2.20
correct perception 1.6, 7
cotton fluff, 3.43
craving, 2.7
cultural activities,
  emotional distress, 2.12
  impressions, 2.12
  meditative restraint, 3.23
  stoppage, 4.30
  timeful, 4.9
  yogis', 4.7

D

death,
  instinctive fear, 2.3, 9
  invitation, 3.52
delusion, 2.34
demerit, 2.14
depression, 1.31
desire, 4.10
diamond-like definition, 3.47
disaffection, 2.3; 3.50
discrimination, 1.43
disease, 1.30
disgust, 2.40
dispersals of energy, 4.5
distress,
  cause of, 2.14
  distracted mind, 1.31
  non-manifested type, 2.16
divination skills, 3.38
divine being,
  -see cherished divine being
doubt, 1.30; 2.33, 34
drugs, 4.1
dualities cease, 2.48

E

elephant, 3.25
emotions, non-harmful ones, 4.6
endeavor, strenuous, 2.15
energy, lack of, 1.30
exhalation, 1.34
experience,
  defined, 3.36
  nature's purpose, 2.18

F

farmer, 4.3
fear of death, 2.9
feelings, distinct from spirit, 4.25
focus on mundane existence, 2.3
friendliness, 1.33; 3.24
future, 3.16; 4.12

G

ghost, 3.52
governor, 4.18
greed, 2.34
gross forms, 3.45
gullet, 3.31
guru, supreme lord, 1.26

H

happiness,
  best type, 2.42
  cause of, 2.14
  craving produced, 2.7
hearing sense, 3.37, 42
hereafter,
  invitation, 3.52
  known, 3.23
hope, 4.10
hostility, abandoned, 2.35
hunger, 3.31

I

identifying powers, 3.48
identity, misplaced, 2.3
idleness, 1.30
ignorance,
  afflictions, 2.3
  as environment, 2.4
  avoidance of, 2.26
  conjunction, 2.24
  doubts, 2.34
  exhibited, 2.5
imagination, 1.6, 9
impediments, 4.3
impressions,
  insight, 1.50
  storage, 2.12
impurity,
  elimination, 2.43
  removed, 4.31
inattentiveness, 1.30
individual self, see self
individual spirit realized, 3.36
infinite, meeting, 2.47
inhalation, 1.34
inherent nature, 4.13
insight,
  continuous, 2.26
  developed, 3.5
  impression, 1.50
  into cultural activities, 3.26
  limited type, 1.49
  of previous lives, 3.18
  shining light, 3.33, 34
  stages, 2.27
  steady type, 2.28
  subtle nature, 1.45
  reality perceptive, 1.48
intellect,
  limited, 4.21,
  perception of, 4.22
interval, 3.11, 12; 4.27
introspective happiness, 1.17
introspective memory, 1.20
intuition, 3.50
invisibility, 3.21
inwardness, 1.29
isolation of self, 3.51

K, J

knowledge, origin, 1.25
kriya yoga, 2.1
kurmanadi subtle nerve, 3.32

L

language, 3.17
liberation, purpose, 2.18
light, subtle, 3.33, 34
linkage of attention,
  breath regulation, 2.53
  competence, 1.47
  continuous effortless 1.20, 2.1
  continuous, 3.3

linkage of attention, cont'd,
decreasing objectives, 3.1
deliberate, 1.42
effortless, 1.39, 3.2
effortless/continuous, 1.46
investigative/non-investigative, 1.44
location, 3.1
mystic skills caused, 4.1
non-analytical, 1.42
non-motivated, 1.51
observational type, 1.17
obstacles, 3.38
without characteristics, 1.45
yoga process, 2.29
location in mento-emotional energy 3.1

M

material nature,
alterations end, 4.32
distinction, 3.50
phases, 2.19
purpose fulfilled, 4.32
matter, 3.12
mento-emotional energy,
channels, 3.39
conformity, 1.4
insight into, 3.35
known by spirit, 4.18
limited, 4.19
memory purified, 1.43
motivational, 1.46
non-interest, 1.15,16
non-operation, 1.2
objectives decreased, 3.11
parting away/dispersion, 3.49
perceptible, 4.19
prejudiced, 4.23
proximity, 4.24
regions of dispersal, 4.4, 5
restraint, 3.17
restraint of , 3.10
scattered 1.30
serenity, 1.33
stopping operations, 4.25
meditation,
-see also linkage of attention
abstract, 1.33-39
complete restraint, 3.4, 6
fusion and steadiness, 1.35
on dearly desired force, 1.39
on material nature, 4.29
meditation, cont'd,
on someone, 1.37
on supreme lord, 1.23; 2.32; 2.45
proficiency, 2.41
profound religious, 2.1
sorrowless/spiritually luminous, 1.35
subtle impressions, 3.10
suppression, 1.51
timeful, 4.9, 10
vibrational mode, 1.6, 11
mental darkness, 2.52, 3.44, 4.31
mento-emotional operations,
-see vibrational modes
merit, 2.14
mind,
-also see mento-emotional energy
content , 3.12
distracted type, 1.31
swiftness, 3.49
minuteness, 3.46
moment, 3.53; 4.33
moon, 3.28
moral restraints,
great commitment, 2.31
listed, 2.29
non-adjustable 2.31
motivation,
impulsive type, 2.15
subtle type, 2.10
mud, 3.40
mundane existence, focus on, 2.9
mundane objects, 3.55
mystic force, 3.47
mystic skills, 4.1

N

nature, 3.45
-also see material nature
navel energy gyrating center, 3.30
nervousness, 1.31
neutrality, 4.34
non-possessiveness, 2.30, 39
non-responsiveness, 1.33
non-stealing, 2.30, 39
non-violence, 2.30, 35

O

object,
composition, 4.14
transcendent type, 1.35
observer, 2.17

obstacles to progress. 1.29, 32
om, 1.27, 28
omniscience, 3.34

P

past and future, 3.16
past, 4.12
peace, 3.10
perceiver, 1.3; 2.20
  -also see observer
perception,
  correct/incorrect, 1.6
  radiant organ, 2.28
  types, 2.18
perfected beings, 3.33
perfection, 2.43
person,
  -also see self
  discriminating type, 2.15
  without craving, 1.37
personality distinction, 3.50
planets, 3.29
polestar, 3.28, 29
portents, 3.23
posture, 2.29, 46, 47
pranayama, 2.51
prejudice, 4.15
progress, 1.30
psyche,
  -also see study of psyche
  fiery glow, 3.41
  fusion, 1.41
  isolated, 3.51
  mastery of, 1.40
  psychological organs, 3.7
  steadiness, 3.32
  study, 2.1, 44
purification, 2.32, 40, 41
purity, 3.56

Q, R

realism, 2.30, 36
reality of an object, 4.16
reality,
  known, 3.34
  pursuit of, 1.32
  similar types, 3.54
recommended behavior, 2.29, 32
reference, 1.7
reflection, 1.17
reincarnation, 3.18, 52; 4.2
relationship control, 1.40
retrogression, 3.14

S

samana digestive force, 3.41
saturation of subtle material nature, 4.2
seeing, 3.37
self consciousness, 1.17
self distinction, 4.25
self preservation, 2.9
self psyche, 2.22
self realization, 3.36
sense control, 2.54
sense of identity, 4.4
sensual energy conquest, 2.41
sensual energy withdrawal, 2.29, 54
sensual grasping, 3.48
sensuality, 1.30
separation of perceiver,
  2.25; 3.56; 4.26, 31, 34
sexual non-expressiveness,
  2.30, 38
sharp objects, 3.40
shining organ of divination, 3.34, 37
sleep, dream-dreamless, 1.6, 10, 38
smelling, 3.37
solar system, 3.27
soul, types, 1.47
sound, 3.17, 22; 4.1
space, 3.42
spirit, 2.41
  -also see self
spiritual ignorance, see ignorance
spiritual perception, 2.30
stamina, 1.20
stars, 3.28, 29
state, 1.18, 19
states of matter, 3.45
status/moral restraint, 2.31
strength, 3.25
study of psyche, 2.44
subtle activities, 4.6
subtle body perfection, 3.46
subtle material energy, 4.3
sun planet, 3.27
sun-god, 3.27
Supreme Lord/Supreme Soul,
  1.23, 24-27; 2.1, 32, 45

T

tasting, 3.37
telepathy, 3.19
tendencies, 4.8
thirst, 3.31
throat, 3.40
time, moral restraint, 2.31
touching, 3.37
transformation, 3.15, 16; 4.2
transition, 4.2

U, V

uniqueness, 4.14
vibrational modes,
  abandoned, 2.11
  distress causing, 2.15
  fivefold, 1.5
  non-operational, 1.2, 12, 51
  reduction, 1.41
  stoppage, 4.30
views, mistaken type, 1.30
vigor, 2.38
vision, 2.6
vital energy, 1.34

W

water, 3.40
weightlessness, 3.43
withdrawal,
  -see sensual energy withdrawal
word, 1.42

Y

yoga practice,
  defined, 1.2
  eight parts, 2.29
  introduced, 1.1
  persistence for, 1.13, 14
  rates 1.21, 22
  results, 2.28
  standard method, 1.32

Index to Analysis and Application

A

ābhimata, 65
abhīnīveśah, 90, 96
abhorrence, 92, 116
Absolute Truth, 131
abstract meditation, 152
abstractions, 156
absurdity, 240
act or react, 111
action, 241
activity, 116
adhiṣṭhātṛtvam, 220
Ādiśeṣa, 9, 154
adṛṣṭa, 104
advancement, 38
affinity, 34
afflictions,
  listed, 88
  reduction, 87
  stoppage, 246
algebraic computations, 110
agenda, 223
agnihotra, 38
ahiṁsā, 140
air mastery, 211
akṣa, 25
akṣaradhāma, 12
akusīdasya, 245
alabdhabhūmikatva, 50
ālasya, 50
Aldous Huxley, 227
all-applicative intuition, 220
allergic to Supreme Being, 53
alteration, 248
anal region, 212
analysis,
  correct type, 25
  impulsive, 241
  observational, 35
  samādhi, 36
  value, 36
analytical linkage, 78
analytical orb, 72, 97
analytical orb diagram, 135, 138
anavasthitatvāni, 50
ancient teachers, 45
aṅg, 160
angelic world, 222
anger, 146
animals,
  memory, 104
  power, 212
aniruddha, 249
aniṣṭa, 222
antar, 168
aṇu, 65
anvaya, 218
apāna, 202, 211
aparigrahāh, 141
appetite, 202
application of consciousness, 238
appropriation, 69
Apte, 163
Arjuna, 23 ,170
art, 185
āsana, 34
āśayam, 231
asmitā, 88
aspect in perception, 82
assistance, 53
association, 151, 215
associative thinking, 29
asteya, 141
astronomer, 25, 193
atheism, 154
atheistic masters, 45
atma, 221
atmosphere, 214
attachment, 88
attentive I-self, 72
attitudes, 242
āuṁ, 46-47
aura, 187
auṣadhi, 227-228
austerity, 85, 143-144, 153, 226
author, 22, 30
authorized worship, 44
autonomy, 18
auxiliary self, 249
avidyā, 132
avirati, 50
avoidance, 181

B

B.K.S.Iyengar, 154
Baba, Bengali, 38
Bābāji, Śrī, 204, 227
back of head pull, 16
bacteria, 191
bandhah, 162
bane of yoga, 96
basic condition, 180
batsman, 111
battle within, 172
beautiful form, 217
behaviors, 139-140, 143
belief, 111
benchmarks, 212
benevolence, 152, 190
Bengali Baba, 38
Bhagavad Gītā, 23, 50, 193
Bhāgavatam, 23
bhakti, 65, 85, 143
Bharata, 192
bhastrika, 202
bhaumā, 142
bhogah, 207
bhrāntidarśana, 50
bhūtendriya, 179
Bihar, 247
birth,
  cause, 150, 226-227
  memory details, 104
  millions, 33
blank mind, 27, 51, 134
blend, 69
bodiless state, 38, 214
body entry, 209
body link, 214
body of light, 205
body types, 191
booby trap, 89
boomerang effect, 37
botherations, 155
bottleneck, 184
brace, 38
brahma, 12
Brahma, 44
brahmacarya, 141-142
brahmarandra, 204, 208
breath conditions, 157
breath infusion, 53, 55, 139-140, 157, 159
breath regulation, 156
British Government, 187
brow chakra, 81
Buddha, 53
buddhi organ, 40
buddhi yoga, 50
bus, 189

C

Caitanya, Mahāprabhu, 85
cannibal, 148
car gears, 28
Castagna, Paul, 22
category, 223
causal body, 41, 205-206
causal plane,
  adjustment, 210
  retreat, 29
cause-effect, 234
celibacy, 149, 152
celibacy yoga, 141
ceremonial success, 38
change, 181
changelessness, 239
chanting oṁ, 47,49
characteristics, 223
charm, 217
cheap labor, 149
cheerfulness, 56
chemical means, 227-228
chemistry, 226
cherished divine being, 153
circumstance-forming impressions, 234
circumstances, 233
cit ākāśa, 12, 20, 59
citta, defined, 11, 160
cittavikṣepah, 51
claimant, 231
clairaudience, 213
clairvoyance, 150, 186
clashing aspects, 111
clouds of energy, 245
collapsed, 180
commitments, 145
compassion, 56
complete restraint, 165
components of psyche, 223
composition, 237
compulsion, 147, 161
compulsive habits, 92
computations, 110
consumption, 115

contemplative practice, 34
conclusion, 241
condition, 142
conditioning,
distressful, 111
infinite, 129
conduit, 30
confidence, 39, 228
conflicts, 88, 93
confusion of memory, 240
conjunction, 129-131
connecting instinct, 218
conquest, 215
conquest of sense energy, 152, 218-219
consciousness,
application, 238
location, 28
movements, 64
conservation, 47
content, 181
contentment, 143-144, 152
context, 223
continuous effortless linkage, 164, 226
continuous linkage, 139-140
convention, 12
conviction, 117
core-self,
autonomy, 18
coloration, 127
detachment, 30
distinct, 134
experience, 24
insecure, 19
lack of control, 54
retraction, 17
segregated, 137-138
correct perception,
details, 25
function, 20-21
corridor, 28
cosmic intellect, 36
cosmic parameters, 184
cosmic sense of identity, 36
cosmic survival instinct, 94
cotton fluff, 214
craving, 33, 92
creative urges, 19
critical nature, 141
cultural activities,
attractive, 191
contrary, 233
destined, 189
distress potential, 112
stoppage, 246
yogi retarded by, 50
yogis' 231
curiosity, 217
cycles, billions, 129
cynical attitude, 92

D

dark mind-space, 159
daytime, 192
death, 167
de-energization, 53
degradation of yogi, 50
delusion, 146
demerits, basis, 111
denial of Supreme Person, 54
depression, 55
deśa, 162
desire,
dominance, 232
eternal, 234
freedom from, 34
lack of, 151
destiny corrupts, 211
detachment, 30
Devī, 211
devotee, transited, 43-44
devotion, 65, 143
dhāraṇā, 21-22, 47, 159
dharma, 22, 140, 180, 245
dharma-meghah, 245
dharmāṇām, 235
dhyāna, 49, 163, 165
diagram,
psychic organs, 23, 72
retraction, 14-15
diamond, 217
diet control, 212
difference in transformation, 181
diffused beings, 38
dimension,
jumped, 51
spiritual type, 156
switching, 64
dīpena, 81
dirt, 116

disaffection, 88, 92, 220
disciple,
assisted, 49
perilous, 36
discrimination,
disconnection from, 28
ultimate, 220
discriminative insight, 132-133, 145
disease, 48
disgust, 130, 151, 168
disharmony, 93
disintegration of impediments, 229
dispersals, 230, 232
displace energies, 51
dissolution, 13
distinction, 90, 224, 242
distracted mind, 55
distress,
addiction, 92
attachment to, 92-93
avoidance, 113
result, 110
symptom, 55
divination, 204, 208-209
divine beings, 38
doubt, 49, 52, 145-146
drawn back, 186
dreamless sleep, 65
dṛg/dṛk śakti, 91
dṛśi, 117
dṛṣṭa, 104
drugs, 226-228
dualities, 155
Durgā, 211

E

earth, 111
effortless linkage, 39, 49, 65, 84, 139-140
eight-part yoga, 130
ekatānatā, 163
electrostatic charge, 117
elephant, 190-191
emancipation, 244
embryos, 202
emergent, 180
emotion, 231
emotional force defined, 160
emotion-shape, 230
end of alteration, 248
endearment, 65, 150
endeavor, 111
energy displacement, 219
energy distribution, 203
energy-gyrating center, 194
engine, 9
engine of intellect, 46
entrance into a body, 209-210
environment, 89
environmental pressure, 127-128
equal purity, 224
equipoise, 93
eruptions, 95
essential self, 17, 88
evolution, 110
evolutionary adaptations, 182
excitement, 152, 217
experience,
cause, 115, 206-207
details, 115, 127
parcels, 20
variations, 116
exploitation, 149
expression,
idea, 170
mento-emotional, 20
types, 24
eye of consciousness, 24

F

facial area retraction, 15
factor, 186
faith, 63, 228
false perception, 20-21
fame, 150
farmer, 229
fascination rebirth, 221
fate's terms, 54
fear of death, 88
featureless state, 79
features of energy, 20
files, 70
film theater, 181
fish-eater, 147
fitness for meditation, 152
flash memory, 72, 97
flesh-eater, 148
focus on mundane existence, 88
following, 186
foothold, 37
form of time, 235-236
forms, foothold lost, 37
foundation, 169

friendliness, 56, 190
fruits of light, 193
fulfillments, 33
fundamental religious ideas, 111
fungus, 191
fused condition, 117
fused into transcendence, 35
fusion broken, 91
fusion of mind, 59
fusion with higher reality, 62
future, 183, 235-236

G

galaxy, 194
Gangotri, 81
gasoline, 9
Gautama Buddha, 53
gears of memory, 46
gears, 28
gem, 116
Gherwal, 187
gifted person, 227
God, 249
God as yogi? 216
Goddess Durgā, 211
gods of these worlds, 39
gomsha, 49
Goṇikā,154
good-for-nothing, 188
Gorakṣnāth, Śrī, 204,210, 227
governor, 239
great commitment, 142
greed, 146
growth, 92
gullet, 202-203
guru contact, 204
guru devotion, 85
guru worship, 246

H

happiness,
 attachment, 92
 introspective, 35
 result, 110
harassment, 172
harmlessness, 140
haṭha yoga, 201-202, 226-228
hearing sense, 213
hearing, 208
heart chakra, 23
herbs, 227-228
hereafter, 189-190
Hiraṇyagarbha, 24
hope-eternal, 234
hostility, 147
hṛ, 160
hunger, 202-203
Huxley, 227

I

I.K.Taimni, 94
idea, 170
idea formation, 27
ideation, 230
identity,
 cosmic type, 36
 crisis, 114
 indelible, 130
 misplaced, 88
 supported, 19
 worth, 36
idleness, 49, 51
ignorance, 88-90, 130 132
illuminating insight, 166
imagination,
 defined, 27
 function, 20-21
imagination orb/faculty,
 change, 170
 converted, 81
 curbed, 22
 magical, 114
 useful, 27
imaginative powers, 79
impression, remaining, 37
impediments, 229
impersonalism, 154
impressions,
 form of, 233
 interpreted, 141
 itchy, 104
 motivations, 110
 not understood, 104
 primeval, 234
impulsion, 146, 232
impurity, 133, 153
inability, 131
in-and-out, 174
inattentiveness, 49, 53
incorrect perception, 26
independence, 18
indicated phase, 116

individuality, 208
indriyāni, 160
induction, 232
I-ness, 35
influenced attentive I-self, 73
information,
  conduit, 30
  imaginative, 27
ingesting chemicals, 228
inherent nature, 38
initiation, 204
insecurity of core-self, 19
insight, 39, 41, 81, 132-133, 166
instinctive fear, 88
instinctive life force, 93
intellect,
  conditions, 96
  cosmic type, 36
  curbed, 22
  disconnection, 28
  memory, 29
  non-person, 240
  perception, 40
  psychic organ, 91
  purity, 186
  retired, 216
  self blackmailed by, 70
  senses control, 26
  senses-allies, 70
  shining light, 204
  spiritual perception, 133
  views of, 50, 241
intelligent energy, 206, 224
interference, 29
interim, 171
internalization, 47
interval, 170, 244
introspective happiness, 35-36
introspective memory, 39, 41
introspective yoga, 95
intuition, 186, 220
investigative linkage, 78
invisibility, 187
invisible reality, 52
invited, 221
involuntary application, 230
inwardness, 46
I-self, 72, 97, 105, 113
isolation, 131, 220
iṣṭadevatā, 153
Īśvarapraṇidhānāni, 85
Iyengar, 154

J

Jain, 141
jam, 223
janma, 227-228
Jesus Christ, 44, 193, 211
jewel compared, 66-67
jñāna dīptih, 133
jñāna dīpah, 24, 133, 204
jñāna dīpena, 81
jñāna cakṣus, 24, 81, 133
jumping dimensions, 51

K

Kailash, 204
kaivalyam, 131, 220-221, 224, 249
karma āśayah, 96
karma yoga, 51
kāya, 217
khyāti, 220
killing, 141
known, 238
Krishna, Lord, 23, 27, 38, 44, 52, 85, 128, 186, 192, 205
kriyā yoga,
  Bhagavad Gītā, 86
  conjunction removed, 131
  definite, 86
  described, 85
  essential, 235
  master, 169
  necessary, 132
  purpose, 87
kṣaṇa, 170
kṣayāt, 153
Kūmara, 211
kuṇḍalinī,
  ageless, 53
  chakra, 50
  frontal passage, 198
  power central, 113
  śakti, 211
  spinal passage, 195
  yoga, 93, 141, 202
kurma nāḍi, 203
Kurukṣetra, 170
kusīda, 245

L

labor, 149
labored breathing, 55
lack of energy, 50
lack of interest, 34, 220
lacking urges, 169
language, 185
latent, 180
laws of nature, 111
laws of responsibility, 246
layout of body, 198
laziness, 49
Leary, 227
levitation, 214
liabilities, 29
liberation,
  cause, 115
  improbable, 201
  individual, 128
  mass, 128
  selective, 49
life durations, 223
life force,
  cosmic, 94
  curbed, 93
  duties, 203
  path ways, 158
life without material nature, 116
lifting influence, 234
link, 164
link the attention, 21-22, 152, 159, 162
link to moment, 222
linkage of attention, 35, 130-140
linkage,
  non-analytical, 70
  Supreme Soul/limited soul, 81
  types, 78
living entity limited, 89, 117
Lobsang Rampa, 210
location, 142, 162-163, 165, 233
loneliness, 19
lotus posture, 154, 203
love, 65

M

Mahābhārata, 222
mahāvidehā, 214
Mahāvīra, 141
mahāvrata, 143
Māṇḍūkopaniṣad, 38
maṇipuraka, 201
mantra, 228
Manu reign, 38
manual, 27
map, 27
mass liberation, 128
master-of-the-species, 140
mastery of psyche, 65
Matali, 222
material nature/energy,
  cause? 229
  effectiveness, 128
  end, 248
  featureless state, 79
  person attracted, 34
  phases, 116
  upper-hand, 110
mātra, 117
matratva, 65
Matsyendranāth, 210
maturation, 92
mental content, 38
meditation,
  blankness, 170
  on Supreme Lord, 143-144, 154
  optic retraction, 14
  profound, 85
  silent, 57
meghah, 245
memory,
  components, 105, 113
  counterproductive, 64
  details, 29, 96
  diagrams, 97-
  eradicated, 37
  function, 20-21
  intellect appropriates, 29
  interaction 75
  machinations, 114
  neutralizing, 29
  primeval, 234
  purified, 70
  purity of results, 71
  reliance on, 29
  stored, 72-77
  supplemental, 173
  troublesome, 104
mental darkness, 158, 214
mental process revealed, 69
mental symbolization, 27

mento-emotional energy/force,
citta, 11
cooperative, 243
described, 239-240
dual, 19
empowered, 249
fivefold, 19
mimics, 43-44
motivational, 79
non-objective, 240
parasitic, 242
prejudices, 241
reduction, 87
regions, 229
responsibility-attracted, 164
restrained, 169, 214, 242
merged, 131, 208
merits, 111
mind content, 181, 244
mind reader, 186
mind reliance, 224
mind, suspicious of, 32
mind/non-person, 240
mind-space, 159
minuteness, 216
miracles, 214
misplaced identity, 88, 91
missions, 247
mistaken views, 53
mistaken vows, 50
moment, 222
momentary blankness, 170
moment's counterpart, 248
moneylender, 245
monopoly,
mood cause, 242
moon, 193
moral principles, urge against, 145
moral restraints, 139-140, 142
most basic condition, 180
motivation,
abandoned, 95
distressful, 111
force, 229
regressed, 94
movements of consciousness, 64
mud, 211
Mudgala, 222
mūlādhār, 212
mūrdhajyotiṣi, 204
mystic actions, 168
mystic force, 217
mystic province, 231
mystic skills, 209, 226

N

naad oṁ sound, 23, 52, 174-175
nāḍīs, 157, 216
Nārada, 85
narcotics drugs, 226, 228
nature, 115-116
navel, 194
navel chakra entry, 198, 201-202
negative excitation, 38
nervousness, 55
neutral stage fusion, 35
neutrality, 93, 114, 249
night-time, 192
nirbhasam, 164
nirodhakṣaṇa, 170
nirvāṇa, 208
nirvedah, 130, 230
nirvicāra samādhi, 81
niyama, 139
non-attachment, 30
non-expressiveness, 140
non-interest, 33-34
non-interference, 30
non-investigative linkage, 80
non-obstruction, 216
non-operation, 30
non-possessiveness, 140-142, 150
non-responsiveness, 56-57
non-stealing, 140-142, 149
non-violence, 140, 142, 147
not there, 164
notion, 170

O

object, 237-238
objectivity, 28, 130
objects, spiritual, 62
observational linkage, 35
observer, segregated, 114
obstacles
listed, 48
removal, 56
odds, 112
old behaviors, 244
Oṁ, 23, 46-47
one aspect, 173

oneness, 131
operations, content, 181
opponent, 173
optic perception, 14
organ of divination, 204
organ of perception, 133-134
organs, psychological, 168
outcome environments, 111

P

padmāsana, 154, 203
parallel worlds, 162
paranormal, 226
paraśarīrāveśaḥ, 210
paravairāgya, 245
pari, 70
past, 183, 235-236
Patañjali,
  inspired author, 30
  criticized, 143
  dismissed, 12
  icon, 9
patience, yoga practice, 133
Paul Castagna, Sir, 22
perceive details, 127, 241
perceiver, 19, 241-242
perception,
  analytical orb, 138
  assistive type, 83
  clear type, 115
  correct type, 25
  details, 115
  incorrect type, 26
  influence rated, 238
  spiritual type, 83, 132
  traditional limited, 82
  types, 20
perfected beings, 203
perfection of body, 153
perfection of subtle body, 216
perfectional powers, 183
perpetual energy source, 239
persistence, 32
person differences, 237
Person God relationship, 144
person, transcendental type, 64
Personality of Godhead, 79
personality, 34, 36
perspectives, 237
phases, 116
photo art, 185
pictorials, 185
Polestar, 194
pollutions, 151
popularity, 150
portents, 189-190
possessiveness, 142
posture, 139-140, 154
power of the past, 237
practice,
  described, 32
  reverence of, 33
prakāśa, 115, 159
prakṛti, 34, 180
prakṛtilāya, 40
pramāda, 49
prāṇāyāma,
  avoidance, 34
  learnt, 156
  necessary, 53
  required, 59
  sense purity, 26
praṅdhānāni, 143
praṇidhāna, 43-44
prāntabhūmih, 142
prasaṅgāt, 222
praśānta, 173
prati, 160
prātibha, 204
pratiprasava, 94
pratiṣṭa, 148
pratyāhār, 26, 47, 94, 160
pratyak, 47
pratyakṣa, 25
pratyayah, 38, 163
pravṛtti, 62
precious things, 149
predispositions, 190, 242
prejudices, 237
presumptions about practice, 42
previous lives known, 185
primitive being, 29
profile, 127
profit, 149
profound insight, 39,41
profound religious meditation,
  43-44, 143-144, 154
progress,
  bothersome, 36
  integrated, 35
  maintenance, 50, 53

promises of salvation, 33
providence, 54, 143
province, 231
proximity, 232, 242
psyche control, details, 25
psychic aspects, 167
psychic people, 40
psychological impurities, 247
psychological make-up, 38
psychological objects, 47
psychological opponent, 173
psychological organs, 168
psychological storage compartment, 96
psychological violence, 142
purity, 70, 224
purification of psyche, 152
purification, 141, 143-144, 151
purity subtle body, 216
purity-of-the-psyche yoga, 153
puruṣa, 34
puruṣayoh, 224

Q,R

queen, 210
quiescence, 16-17
radiant organ of perception, 133-134
radio waves, 188
rāja yoga, 34, 94, 202
Rampa, 210
random focus, 37
raw material, 130
real nature, 215
realism, 140-142, 148
realities sorted, 223
reality, 148
reality-perceptive insight, 82
rebirth,
 avoidance, 210
 cause, 150
 fate formation, 110
 invitation, 221
 memory related, 104
 review, 150
recognition essential, 131
recommended behavior, 143
record, 169
rebirth, 110
reference, 25
reflection, 35-36
reflexive fluctuation, 232
regions, 229
regression, 151
regular phase, 116
relationship with God, 144
relationships, 66
relaxation of effort, 155
reliable source, 27
religious meditation, 85, 143-144
remaining impressions, 37
reproduction, 92
reproductive switch, 113
resentment, 213
responses, 242
responsibilities, 80, 164
restraint, 169
retraction diagrams, 14-15
retraction of energy, 13
retraction, core-self, 17
retrograde, 180
reverse gear, 28-29
review, 169
righteous life style, 140
Rishi Singh Gherwal, 187
ṛtaṁbharā buddhi, 81
rūḍhah, 94

S

salvation promises, 33
samādhi,
 causes listed, 226-227
 described, 41
 duration, 35
 effortless, 164
 flawed type, 36
 practice, 40
 progression, 205
 symptoms, 172
samāna, 212
samāpattih, 69
saṁprajñātah, 35-36
saṁprayoga, 187
saṁśaya, 49
saṁskār, 141
saṁyama, 165, 167, 205
saṁyogā, 129, 131
sand, 116
Śaṅkarācārya, 210-211
Sanskrit dictionary, 163
sārvabhaumā, 142
sattva, 207, 224
sattva guṇa body, 217
sattva-śuddhi, 152

saturation, 227-228
satya, 141
Satyānanda, 247
saviors, 246
scattered energy, 51, 54
seat of feelings, 231
seed impression, 29
seedless, 169
seeing, 208
seer, 242
segregated real self, 250
self,
influenced, 33, 130
intellect disconnected, 28
isolation, 220
lacking, 89
limited, 129
raw material, 130
subjectivity, 130
Supreme Spirit link, 81
self-awareness, 36
self-assessments, 36
self-conquest, 244
self-consciousness, 35, 37
self-focus, 17
self-implicated, 127
self-knowledge, 206
self-less results, 148
self-profile, 127
self-realization, 90, 208
sense consciousness, 46
sense energy reversal, 47
sense of identity,
cause, 232
control, 88
cosmic type, 36
distinct, 134
enclosure, 136, 138
material nature related, 229
origin, 80
perceived, 223
permanent, 130
sense withdrawal, 160
senses,
control intellect, 26
intellect allied, 70
resistant, 161
sensual attraction, 33
sensual compulsion, 161
sensual energy,
defined, 160
outpouring, 37
study, 218
withdrawal, 139-140
sensual grasping, 218
sensual influence, 127
sensual magic, 216
sensual orbs, 72
sensual orbs diagrams, 97-
sensual perception, 26
sensuality, 50, 53, 66
separation, 131, 224, 243, 249
sequence, 166, 233
sequential changes, 181
sequential perceptions, 224
serenity, 57
serpentine bed, 154
sex reservoir, 197-
sexual association, 151
sexual intercourse, 203
sexual non-expression, 142, 149
shadow-self, 243, 247
shamans, 228
sharp objects, 211
shining light, 203
shining organ, 204, 208
Shiva, 38, 44, 139, 186, 191, 204-205, 211
Shivananda, 247
Shivram Apte, 163
siddha, 85
siddhaloka, 181, 227
siddhas seen, 204
siddhi, 183
signposts, 32
silent meditation, 57
Skanda Kūmara, 139, 211
skills, obstacles, 209
sky link, 214
sky of consciousness, 12, 20, 24
slave to desires, 232
sleep,
curbed, 24
described, 28
details, 24
dreamless, 65
function, 20-21
location, 28
smelling, 208, 228
social relationships, 66

solar system, 192, 194
Soma, 227
sorrow-less states, 63
soul, 117
sound, 184-185, 188, 226-228
spatial existence, 39
species, 92, 110
specific phase, 116
spinal passage, 195-
spirit,
acts after, 110
changeless, 239
compliance, 38
matter attracted, 89
non-preliminary, 110
perpetual, 239
purity, 224
removal, 234
segregation required, 90
self established, 249
visionary power, 91
spiritual beings, 166
spiritual energy, 84
spiritual ignorance, 88-90, 130, 132
spiritual master, rebirth avoidance, 210
spiritual missions, 247
spiritual objects, 62
spiritual organs, 168
spiritual peace, 173
spiritual perception, 132
spiritual personality, 34
spiritual psyche, 82
spiritual radiation, 36
spiritual realms, 63
spiritual relationship, 63
spy, 188
Śrīmad Bhāgavatam, 23
stability, 116
stairway, 36
stamina, 39
stars, 193
states, sorrow-less, 63
status, 142, 233
steadiness, 59, 203
stealing tendency, 149
stimulants, 226, 228
stoppage of operations, 246
storage compartment, 96
stored memory, 72-77
strength, 190-191
student yogi, 181
study of psyche, 85, 153
styāna, 49
subconscious impressions, 141
subconscious motivations, 44
subconscious wait, 111
subjective research, 78
subtle body,
blaze, 213
floatation, 214
objectified, 93
worse, 151
subtle discrimination, 215, 222, 224
subtle matter conquest, 219
subtle objects, 159
subtle sound, 174
subtle tubes, 216
śuddha, 70
śuddhi-sāmye, 225
suicide, 53
Śūka, 85
sun god, 192
śūnyam, 164
super-consciousness, 64
supernatural perception, 94, 163
supernatural place, 29
supernatural power, 191
supernatural visionary power, 20, 91
supported identity, 19
supporting base, 234
supports, 234
suppression of idea, 170
Supreme Lord, knowledge, 44
Supreme Being,
allergy to, 53
authority, 191
blame lifted, 130
omniscient, 183

Supreme Lord/Person,
denial of, 54, 86
described, 43-44
meditation upon, 143-144, 154
Suratha, 38
surrender to higher reality, 78
survival instinct, 94
suśumnā nāḍi, 212
sutras, concluded, 30
sva-bhāva, 88

svādhyāya, 85
svarūpa, 17, 164, 218
Swarga, 222
swiftness of mind, 219
syllabus, 9

T

T. Lobsang Rampa, 210
tagged responsibilities, 80
Taimni, I.K., 94, 163, 245
tapah, 85, 228
tasting, 208
teacher/teachers,
  ancient, 45
  reverence, 33
teaching, 36
telepathy, 30
telescope, 25
tendencies, 232
territorial god, 246
theater, 181
theistic masters, 45
third eye cleansed, 81
thirst, 202
threadlike flow, 163
three as one, 165
throat chakra, 202
time transcendence, 45
time, 142, 233, 235-236
timely sequence, 233
Timothy Leary, 227
tīrthankaras, 141
tiṣṭa, 148
touching, 208
train, 189
transcendental transfer, 41
transfer, spiritual type, 41
transformation, 181, 227-228, 237
transit, 40, 165
transition, 35
transmigration, 150
transmitter, 188
treads, 36
trees of light, 193
trees, memory, 104
truth, hazards, 142
truthfulness, 141
tug, 49
turbulence, mento-emotional, 56

U

udāna, 211-212
Uddhava, 23, 52, 85
umbilical cord, 198
union, 131
unique, 237
Universal Form, 139
universe, 13, 189
unknown, 238
unwanted features, 221
ūrdhvaretā, 150
urge,
  cause, 242
  mastery, 66

V

vaikuṇṭha, 13
vairāgya, 30
Vaishnavas, 85
Vaivasvata Manu, 38
Vaman Shivram Apte, 221
vāśīkarāh, 65
vatī, 62
vibration, recognition of, 21
vibrational energy, 12
vibrational modes,
  five, 19
  non-operation, 11
vice-habit,
  restraint, 146
  subtle form prone, 151
  victimization, 233
vice-tool, 235
videhas, 38
vigilance, 141
vigor, 149-150
violence, contrary, 146
viruses, 191
viṣaya, 62
vision of spirit, 152
Viṣṇu, 154
vistas, 216
vitarkā, 69
viveka, 223
vivekakhyātih, 132, 141, 145
void, 51, 53, 164, 168, 172
vrittis, details, 24
vyādhi, 48
Vyāsadeva, 85

W

water, 211
withdrawal of senses, 160
withdrawal ultimate, 131
word, 69-70
world of responsibilities, 164
worship of God, 44
writer integration, 36

X,Y,Z

yamah, 139, 165
yatnah, 32
yoga guru, 204
yoga practice,
  forceful type, 41
  instinct, 218
  lengthy, 218
  motivational, 42
  pre-qualification, 159
  rates, 42
yoga siddha body, 204
yoga,
  6 parts, 139, 165
  accomplishment, 13
  bane of, 96
  confidence, 40
  divine allowance, 191
  expounded, 9
  lonesome, 11
  parts, 139-140
  siddhas seen, 204
  skill, 11
Yogeśvarānanda, 13, 22, 81, 184, 246
yogi,
  advanced practice, 83
  atomic control, 65
  attitude required, 151
  birth known, 150
  clairvoyance, 186
  conquest, 215
  cosmic control? 65
  degradation, 50, 202
  destiny, 184
  exploitation, 149
  following, 186
  god status, 79
  God, 216
  immoral acts, 146
  ineffective, 148
  influenced, 188
  limited, 96, 183
  memory battle, 71
  mind reader, 186
  nature avoided, 115
  no gain, 231
  non-interference, 186
  past/future, 183
  perception assists, 83, 205
  permission required, 184
  regressions, 151
  reorientation, 156
  short-circuited, 143
  siddha body, 204
  stalls, 209
  struggle incremental, 34
  supportive element, 235
yogyatā, 159

About the Author

Michael Beloved (Yogi *Madhvāchārya)* took his current body in 1951 in Guyana. In 1965, while living in Trinidad, he instinctively began doing yoga postures and tried to make sense of the supernatural side of life.

Later in 1970, in the Philippines, he approached a Martial Arts Master named Mr. Arthur Beverford. He explained to the teacher that he was seeking a yoga instructor. Mr. Beverford identified himself as an advanced disciple of *Śrī* Rishi Singh Gherwal, an astanga yoga master.

Beverford taught the traditional Astanga Yoga with stress on postures, attentive breathing and brow chakra centering meditation. In 1972, Michael entered the Denver Colorado Ashram of *kuṇḍalinī* yoga Master *Śrī* Harbhajan Singh. There he took instruction in bhastrika pranayama and its application to yoga postures. He was supervised mostly by Yogi Bhajan's disciple named Prem Kaur.

In 1979 Michael formally entered the disciplic succession of the Brahma-Madhava-Gaudiya Sampradaya through *Swāmī* Kirtanananda, who was a prominent sannyasi disciple of the Great Vaishnava Authority *Śrī Swāmī* Bhaktivedanta Prabhupada, the exponent of devotion to Sri Krishna.

However, Yoga has a mystic side to it, thus Michael took training and teaching empowerment from several spiritual masters of different aspects of spiritual development. This is consistent with *Śrī* Krishna's advice to Arjuna in the *Bhagavad Gītā*:

tad viddhi praṇipātena paripraśnena sevayā
upadekṣyanti te jñānaṁ jñāninas tattva darśinaḥ

This you ought to know. By submitting yourself as a student, by asking questions, by serving as requested, the perceptive, reality-conversant teachers will teach you the knowledge. (*Bhagavad Gītā* 4.34)

Most of the instructions Michael received were given in the astral world. On that side of existence, his most prominent teachers were *Śrī Swāmī* Shivananda of Rishikesh, Yogiraj *Swāmī* Vishnudevananda, *Śrī Bābāji Mahasaya* - the master of the masters of *Kriyā* Yoga, *Śrīla* Yogeshwarananda of Gangotri - the master of the masters of *Rāj* Yoga (spiritual clarity), and Siddha *Swāmī* Nityananda the Brahma Yoga authority.

If you have some interest in yoga, nurture and develop it. *Śrī* Krishna, the Supreme Being offers all encouragement to those who are attracted to yoga. This is what the God said:

tatra taṁ buddhi saṁyogaṁ labhate paurva dehikam
yatate ca tato bhūyaḥ saṁsiddhau kuru nandana

In that environment (in the new birth), he (the yogi) is inspired with the cumulative intellectual interest from a previous birth. And from that time, he strives again for yoga perfection, O dear son of the Kurus. (*Bhagavad Gītā* 6.43)

Meditation Series

Meditation Pictorial

Meditation Expertise

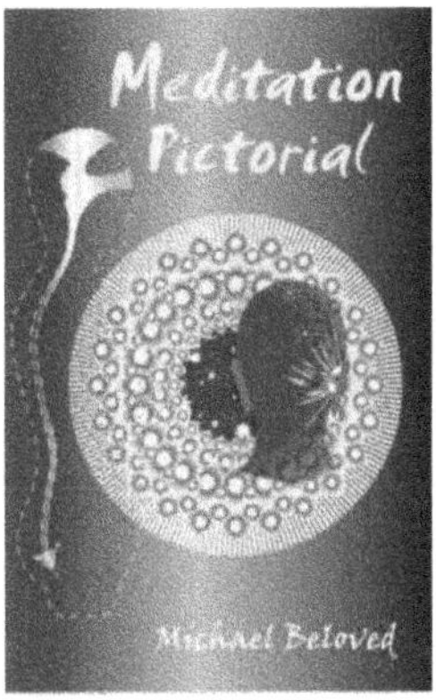

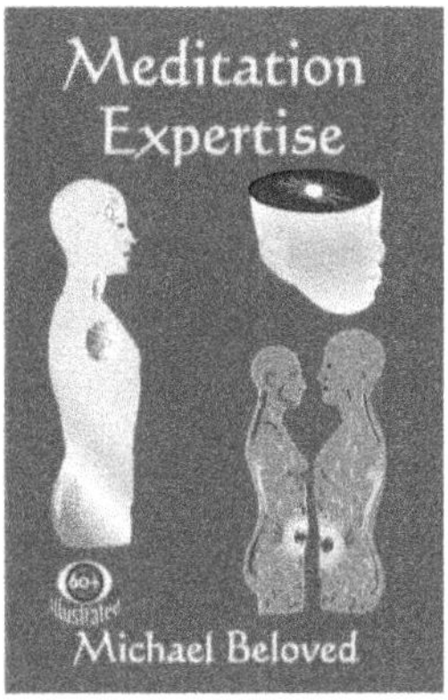

The speciality of these books is the mind diagrams which profusely illustrate what is written. This shows exactly what one has to do mentally to develop and then sustain a meditation practice.

In the **Meditation Pictorial**, one is shown how to develop psychic insight, a feature without which meditation is imagination and visualization, without any mystic experience per se.

In the **Meditation Expertise**, one is shown how to coral one's practice to bring it in line with the classic syllabus of yoga which Patanjali lays out as the ashtanga yoga 8-staged practice.

Both books are profusely illustrated with mind diagrams showing the components of psychic consciousness and the inner design of the subtle body.

Specialty Topics

sex you!

The mystery of sex and reincarnation is explained in detail, not in terms of religion or superstition but by psychic facts which any

individual can observe, if he or she can shift focus to the psychic plane. Books like the Bardo Thodol (Tibetan Book of the Dead) and the Egyptian Book of the Dead (Papyrus of Ani), along with Bhagavad Gita, the reincarnation teaching of Buddha and other vital books, took humanity through a spiritual technological leap through time into the hereafter. Perhaps none of these texts dealt with the incidences of sex and reincarnation head on, especially the link between you and the sexual act of your parents which produced your body. In this book you get the details in plain terms without mystery and religious impositions.

Spiritual Master

Practically every positive and negative aspect of having a guru is discussed in this book with recommendations of how to deal with gurus safely. A non-proficient guru can be useful despite his faults, but one must know how to side-step hassles and get to the business at hand, which is to get effective techniques from a spiritual master.

In some cases the spiritual master will be a complete fraud but one should not let that deter one from making spiritual progress in his association. "But why," one might ask, "should one stay with a fraudulent guru?" The answer is that if providence puts one in that position, one should honor providence but one should do so without getting hurt by the unqualified spiritual master. This and similar topics are discussed in this book.

English Series

Bhagavad Gita English

Anu Gita English

Markandeya Samasya English

Yoga Sutras English

Uddhava Gita English

These are in 21st Century English, very precise and exacting. Many Sanskrit words which were considered untranslatable into a Western language are rendered in precise, expressive and modern English, due to the English language becoming the world's universal means of concept conveyance.

Three of these books are instructions from Krishna. **In Bhagavad Gita English** and **Anu Gita English**, the instructions were for Arjuna. In the **Uddhava Gita English,** it was for Uddhava. Bhagavad Gita and Anu Gita are extracted from the Mahabharata. Uddhava Gita was extracted from the 11th Canto of the Srimad Bhagavatam (Bhagavata Purana). One of these books, the **Markandeya Samasya English** is about Krishna, as described by Yogi Markandeya, who survived the cosmic collapse and reached a divine child in whose transcendental body, the collapsed world was existing. Another of these books, the **Yoga Sutras English,** is the detailed syllabus about yoga practice.

My suggestion is that you read **Bhagavad Gita English,** the **Anu Gita English,** the **Markandeya Samasya English,** the **Yoga Sutras English** and lastly the **Uddhava Gita English**, which is much more complicated and detailed.

For each of these books we have at least one commentary, which is published separately. Thus your particular interest can be researched further in the commentaries.

The smallest of these commentaries and perhaps the simplest is the one for the Anu Gita. We published its commentary as the **Anu Gita Explained**. The Bhagavad Gita explanations were published in three distinct targeted commentaries. The first is **Bhagavad Gita Explained**, which sheds lights on how people in the time of Krishna and Arjuna regarded the information and applied it. Bhagavad Gita is an exposition of the application of yoga practice to cultural activities, which is known in the Sanskrit language as karma yoga.

Interestingly, Bhagavad Gita was spoken on a battlefield just before one of the greatest battles in the ancient world. A warrior, Arjuna, lost his wits and had no idea that he could apply his training in yoga to political dealings. Krishna, his charioteer, lectured on the spur of the moment to give Arjuna the skill of using yoga proficiency in cultural dealings including how to deal with corrupt officials on a battlefield.

The second commentary is the **Kriya Yoga Bhagavad Gita**. This clears the air about Krishna's information on the science of kriya yoga, showing that its techniques are clearly described free of charge to anyone who takes the time to read Bhagavad Gita. Kriya yoga concerns the battlefield which is the psyche of the living being. The internal war and the mental and emotional forces which are hostile to self realization are dealt with in the kriya yoga practice.

The third commentary is the **Brahma Yoga Bhagavad Gita**. This shows what Krishna had to say outright and what he hinted about which concerns the brahma yoga practice, a mystic process for those who mastered kriya yoga.

There is one commentary for the **Markandeya Samasya English**. The title of that publication is **Krishna Cosmic Body**.

There are two commentaries to the Yoga Sutras. One is the **Yoga Sutras of Patanjali** and the other is the **Meditation Expertise**. These give detailed explanations of the process of Yoga.

For the Uddhava Gita, we published the **Uddhava Gita Explained**. This is a large book and requires concentration and study for integration of the information. Of the books which deal with transcendental topics, my opinion is that the discourse between Krishna and Uddhava has the complete information about the realities in existence. This book is the one which removes massive existential ignorance.

Explained Series

Bhagavad Gita Explained

Uddhava Gita Explained

The speciality of these books is that they are free of missionary intentions, cult tactics and philosophical distortion. Instead of using these books to add credence to a philosophy, meditation process, belief or plea for followers, I spread the information out so that a reader can look through this literature and freely take or leave anything as desired.

When Krishna stressed himself as God, I stated that. When Krishna laid no claims for supremacy, I showed that. The reader is left to form an independent opinion about the validity of the information and the credibility of Krishna.

There is a difference in the discourse with Arjuna in the Bhagavad Gita and the one with Uddhava in the Uddhava Gita. In fact these two books may appear to contradict each other. In the Bhagavad Gita, Krishna pressured Arjuna to complete social duties. In the Uddhava Gita, Krishna insisted that Uddhava should abandon the same.

Commentaries

Yoga Sutras of Patanjali

Meditation Expertise

Krishna Cosmic Body

Bhagavad Gita Explained

Kriya Yoga Bhagavad Gita

Brahma Yoga Bhagavad Gita

Uddhava Gita Explained

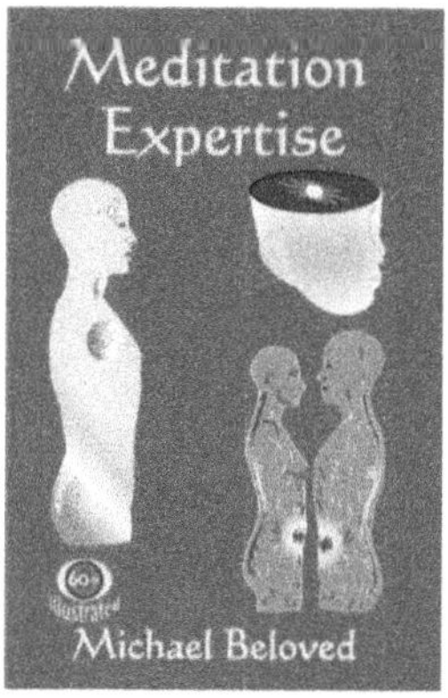

Yoga Sutras of Patanjali is the globally acclaimed text book of yoga. This has detailed expositions of yoga techniques. Many kriya techniques are vividly described in the commentary.

Meditation Expertise is an analysis and application of the Yoga Sutras. This book is loaded with illustrations and has detailed explanations of secretive advanced meditation techniques which are called kriyas in the Sanskrit language.

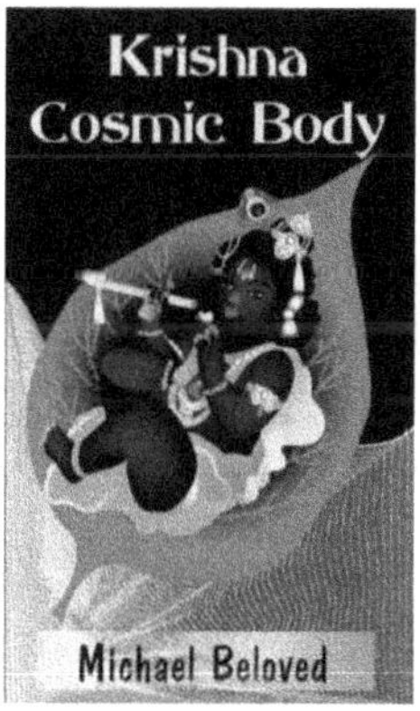

Krishna Cosmic Body is a narrative commentary on the Markandeya Samasya portion of the Aranyaka Parva of the Mahabharata. This is the detailed description of the dissolution of the world, as experienced by the great yogin Markandeya who transcended the cosmic deity, Brahma, and reached Brahma's source who is a divine infant Krishna.

Bhagavad Gita Explained shows what was said in the Gita without religious overtones and sectarian biases.

Kriya Yoga Bhagavad Gita shows the instructions for those who are doing kriya yoga.

Brahma Yoga Bhagavad Gita shows the instructions for those who are doing brahma yoga.

Uddhava Gita Explained shows the instructions to Uddhava which are more advanced than the ones given to Arjuna.

Bhagavad Gita is an instruction for applying the expertise of yoga in the cultural field. This is why the process taught to Arjuna is called karma yoga which means karma + yoga or cultural activities done with a yogic demeanor.

Uddhava Gita is an instruction for apply the expertise of yoga to attaining spiritual status. This is why it is explains jnana yoga and bhakti yoga in detail. Jnana yoga is using mystic skill for knowing the spiritual part of existence. Bhakti yoga is for developing affectionate relationships with divine beings.

Karma yoga is for negotiating the social concerns in the material world and therefore it is inferior to bhakti yoga which concerns negotiating the social concerns in the spiritual world.

This world has a social environment and the spiritual world has one too.

Right now Uddhava Gita is the most advanced informative spiritual book on the planet. There is nothing anywhere which is superior to it or which goes into so much detail as it. It verified that historically Krishna is the most advanced human being to ever have left literary instructions on this planet. Even Patanjali Yoga Sutras which I translated and gave an application for in my book, **Meditation Expertise**, does not go as far as the Uddhava Gita.

Some of the information of these two books is identical but while the Yoga Sutras are concerned with the personal spiritual emancipation (kaivalyam) of the individual spirits, the Uddhava Gita explains that and also explains the situations in the spiritual universes.

Bhagavad Gita is from the *Mahabharata* which is the history of the Pandavas. Arjuna, the student of the Gita, is one of the Pandavas brothers. He was in a social hassle and did not know how to apply yoga expertise to solve it. Krishna gave him a crash-course on the battlefield about that.

Uddhava Gita is from the *Srimad Bhagavatam (Bhagavata Purana),* which is a history of the incarnations of Krishna. Uddhava was a relative of Krishna. He was concerned about the situation of the deaths of many of his relatives but Krishna diverted Uddhava's attention to the practice of yoga for the purpose of successfully migrating to the spiritual environment.

Website:

http://michaelbeloved.com

Forum:

http://www.inselfyoga.com

Contact:

axisnexus@gmail.com

www.ingramcontent.com/pod-product-compliance
Lightning Source LLC
Chambersburg PA
CBHW072135090426
42739CB00013B/3195
* 9 7 8 0 9 8 1 9 3 3 2 5 2 *